Marx's Temporalities

Historical Materialism Book Series

The Historical Materialism Book Series is a major publishing initiative of the radical left. The capitalist crisis of the twenty-first century has been met by a resurgence of interest in critical Marxist theory. At the same time, the publishing institutions committed to Marxism have contracted markedly since the high point of the 1970s. The Historical Materialism Book Series is dedicated to addressing this situation by making available important works of Marxist theory. The aim of the series is to publish important theoretical contributions as the basis for vigorous intellectual debate and exchange on the left.

The peer-reviewed series publishes original monographs, translated texts, and reprints of classics across the bounds of academic disciplinary agendas and across the divisions of the left. The series is particularly concerned to encourage the internationalization of Marxist debate and aims to translate significant studies from beyond the English-speaking world.

For a full list of titles in the Historical Materialism Book Series available in paperback from Haymarket Books, visit:
www.haymarketbooks.org / category / hm-series

Marx's Temporalities

by
Massimiliano Tomba

Translated from the Italian by
Peter D. Thomas and Sara R. Farris

Haymarket Books
Chicago, IL

First published in 2013 by Brill Academic Publishers, The Netherlands
© 2013 Koninklijke Brill NV, Leiden, The Netherlands

Published in paperback in 2013 by
Haymarket Books
P.O. Box 180165
Chicago, IL 60618
773-583-7884
www.haymarketbooks.org

ISBN: 978-1-60846-339-8

Trade distribution:
In the US, Consortium Book Sales, www.cbsd.com
In Canada, Publishers Group Canada, www.pgcbooks.ca
In the UK, Turnaround Publisher Services, www.turnaround-psl.com
In Australia, Palgrave Macmillan, www.palgravemacmillan.com.au
In all other countries, Publishers Group Worldwide, www.pgw.com

Cover design by Ragina Johnson.

This book was published with the generous support of
Lannan Foundation and the Wallace Global Fund.

Printed in the United States.

10 9 8 7 6 5 4 3 2 1

Library of Congress Cataloging-in-Publication data is available.

Contents

Preface

Il faut être absolument moderne
(A. Rimbaud, *Une Saison en enfer*)

'Historical materialism' as a theory of history or a materialist conception of history does not exist. 'Historical materialism' is not a *passe-partout* for the comprehension of history, but a practical mode of intervention into history. The goal of this book is both to study Marx's concepts of time and history, and to rethink the idea of historical time beyond the universal conception of history that was expressed by many 'cold streams' of Marxism.[1] The book tries to reconnect to Marxism's 'warm streams', reactivating Bloch's idea of a 'multiversum' and Benjamin's considerations on the concept of time. Moving into the 'warm stream' allows for the production of a different representation of the temporalities of capitalist modernity, by means of an alternative, transcendental approach. This change of perspective not only constitutes the content of the book, but is also embodied in its style, the goal of which is to effect a shift away from the current view of capitalist phenomena. Since form and content depend on each other, the break with the unilinear conception of time must be expressed in the very form and spatial organisation of the text. The book's focus necessarily stands at its centre, constituting the second chapter on the 'new phenotype'. Capitalism transforms the environment, de-naturalising nature, destroying space through the acceleration of time, and altering the form of human experience and human being itself. This is the real starting point of the book, which proceeds in both directions: towards the first chapter, in order to sketch out the different 'types' confronting the crisis; and towards the third chapter, where the perspective is transformed into the paradigm of plural temporalities. The two appendices constitute 'laboratories'. They are approaches to a historiography of historical temporalities.

---

1. Bloch 1986, p. 209: Bloch distinguished between a 'cold stream' in Marxism, that is, analysis and the path taken, and a 'warm stream', that is, the 'liberating intention' as goal and passion. According to Bloch, cold and warm streams are intertwined, together ensuring that the path taken and the goal to be reached are never separated from one another.

This book is written with the conviction that an entirely new consideration of time and space is needed if we are to confront our contemporary world. The materials of this first book (a second monograph on *Time, Space and Anthropology* is currently in progress) are assembled according to the spirit of the 'warm stream' of Marxism and Marx himself.

It is remarkable that Marx himself does not use the term 'historical materialism', but, instead, uses the expressions 'practical materialist' and 'communist materialist': types able to produce new historiographical images by creating separation and choice in relation to the present. The 'practical materialist' does not presuppose a conception of history, be it idealist or materialist, but rather intervenes into an historical situation, delineating its force-fields and opening a new terrain of possibilities. This figure requires two preliminary moves: on the one hand, a critique of the singularisation of histories in the collective-singular *Geschichte* [history];[2] and, on the other hand, a historiography able to consider history in its incompleteness.[3] Thus, it is never an object of which we could give an objective representation. Insofar as it is incomplete, history is produced constructively by a historiography able to trigger off the explosive charge of the past in the present. This 'presentification' of the past is the opposite of its 'actualisation'. The latter tends to cancel out differences and historical ruptures, while the presentification of the past reopens, in the moment of a current struggle, the possibility of beginning another history, alternative to the course of capitalist modernisation. Rethinking different historical temporalities of the global present means rethinking and reopening other possible paths of modernisation that stand *before* us; that is, behind us and in front of us at the same time, pieces of the future that are encapsulated in the past. This task has become difficult or even almost impossible, since capitalism and the modern state have become metahistorical or even 'natural' 'facts'. It is possible to imagine their reform; it is even possible to imagine them destroying the planet once and for all; but it is not possible to imagine their overcoming. The naturalisation of historical concepts produces the self-representation of modernity as something that cannot be transcended. The question is: how was and is this kind of naturalisation of historical presuppositions possible?

The singularisation of the concept of history, which occurred in the German conceptual vocabulary between the end of the eighteenth and beginning of the nineteenth century, constituted not only the condition of possibility for the processualisation of history in the direction of the theories of history of the nineteenth century, but also produced the processualisation of political

---

2. Koselleck et al. 1975, pp. 647–91. I have analysed these aspects in relation to the post-Hegelian philosophies of history in Tomba 2002a.

3. Benjamin 2002, p. 471.

concepts. Concepts like democracy or equality thus became vectors of historical process, new concepts with new words: democratisation, levelling. These
semantic changes occurred in the historiographical reflection on the French
Revolution, as an attempt to domesticate it, inserting it into a long process of
centralisation of state-power that began with the *ancien régime*, was continued
during the Revolution, and culminated in the dictatorship of the two Napoleons. In representing this temporal arc, stretching between tragedy and farce,
Marx's *Eighteenth Brumaire* produced a background-image of political modernity: a long nineteenth century, still unfinished. The processualisation of history, elevating *Weltgeschichte* to *Weltgericht*,[4] also submitted history to process,
in a sort of auto-reflection. Unilinear historical progress allowed the measuring of the level of (Western) civilisation attained by populations with histories
different from those of Europe, thus justifying the domination of those who
were represented as lower down the scale. The East India Company clerk
John Stuart Mill did precisely this when confronted with 'backward' states of
society populated by 'nonage' races.[5] This still occurs today when different
political forms in various countries are related to medieval Europe.

This modern concept of history orders and temporalises an enlarged geographical field of experience by producing an axiology between that which is
developed and that which is residual. It produces a determinate imaginary
of politics and, therefore, a determinate figure of politics that we call 'progress'. This conception is not reducible merely to the 'magnificent progressive
destiny' of our civilisation, faith that Giacomo Leopardi already denounced
two centuries ago; rather, progress is a synonym of advancing along a vector
of a given orientation, whose tendency the theory of history claims to be able
to discern.[6] The modern concept of progress, which combines a continuously
growing knowledge of nature with an increasingly extensive domination of
it, in the nineteenth century became a political slogan simultaneously legitimating the reformist claims of social democracy and the colonialism of the
liberals.

In the third chapter, I consider the current concept of linear time and progress through the prism of Marx's concept of *phantasmagoria*. Within this perspective, I try to explain how the modern image of the indefinite and unlimited
character of progress, whose temporality is one of homogenous and empty
time, expresses the lack of proportion of the process of valorisation. According to Marx, capitalist progress emancipated humanity from the limits of

---

4. 'The history of the world is the world's court of judgment': Hegel 2001, § 340,
p. 266.
5. Mill 1989, p. 13.
6. On the transition from the philosophy of history to the theory of history, see
Tomba 1997.

nature and dissolved the old communitarian bonds; the autonomisation of capital did not, however, open up the possibility of liberation, but, rather, led humanity and nature to a state of extreme degradation. The use-value of commodities is not neutral, but, rather, expresses a specifically capitalist nature that is manifested in machines whose end is to increase the production of exchange-value and to eliminate the 'pores' in the working day. The capitalist use-value of machinery retroacts on technique, technology, science and modern rationality itself. The genesis of this capitalist modernity can, therefore, be studied only from the perspective of the possibility of its demise. As the categories of capitalist modernity present themselves as impossible to transcend, the main problem is to delimit their reality in a highly determinate historical moment. However, in the observation of the historical character of categories, the observer is, at the same time, that which is being observed.

We need to undertake a change of perspective in order to abandon not only the spatial and geographical provincialism of the Eurocentric perspective, but also the temporal provincialism that produces the self-representation of the Western world as the tip of the arrow of historical time. Marx overturned this perspective in his late anthropological studies: the study of so-called primitive societies led him to show, conversely, the historical, non-eternal character of the capitalist mode of production, of private property, and of individualism. He questioned the attempt by the Russian anthropologist Maxim Kovalevsky to analyse pre-Columbian societies by means of European categories of feudalism and of private property; he criticised the distortions introduced by Ludwig Lange when he interpreted the common property of ancient Rome in the light of individual property.[7] Furthermore, he sketched out a historiography that is able to comprehend politically the action of the past on the present and the action of the present on the past. I investigate these interactions in the two appendices.

In the *Eighteenth Brumaire of Louis Napoleon*, Marx remarks that 'the tradition of all dead generations weighs like a nightmare on the brains of the living',[8] but, at the same time, that the past tradition can also be revitalised in order to change the present. In an early letter to Ruge, Marx wrote:

---

7. Anderson 2002, p. 92. This book was already completed before the publication of his remarkable book (Anderson 2010), which also focuses on the topic of a mutilinear theory of history in Marx. I fully agree with Anderson, according to whom Marx's multilinear perspective on historical and social development is connected to his historical studies and his considerations on the international struggles, which brought out the anticolonialist side of Marx's thought by the late 1850s. In my work, I also seek to highlight the categorial level of this change in Marx's perspective through his reflections on the competition of capitals and the combination between different forms of exploitations.

8. Marx 1979a, p. 103.

It will then become plain that the world has long dreamed of something
of which it has only to be conscious in order to possess it in reality. It will
become plain that it is not a question of drawing a sharp mental line between
past and future, but of *completing* the thought of the past. Lastly, it will
become plain that mankind is not beginning a *new* work, but is consciously
bring about the completion of its old work.[9]

The nightmare immobilises; the dream shows in the present a task from the
past that still has to be completed. In 'awakening', humanity explains to
itself the meaning of its own actions;[10] it is the moment in which humanity
becomes conscious that it has a task for which 'our coming was expected on
earth'.[11] The new, retroacting in the past to the point of modifying the order
of the tradition, brings the dead back to life. It was in this sense that, at the
beginning of the great historiographical experiment called *Thomas Müntzer*,
Ernst Bloch wrote: 'Thus we certainly do not look back, even here. Rather, we
involve ourselves vigorously. And the others also come back, transformed,
the dead return, their acts want to be fulfilled once again with us'.[12] For the
historical materialist, the problem that Marx managed to pose can be of even
greater actuality for our present than it had for his contemporaries. Previous
attempts at liberation await their completion. This is the political problem of
'remembrance', as against the postmodern destruction of memory. As Daniel
Bensaïd emphasises, 'far removed from the "duty to remember" and other
commemorative pedagogies, commemoration, according to Benjamin, is a
struggle for the oppressed past in the name of defeated generations'.[13] Events
need to be thought simultaneously in a historical and in a non-historical way:
historical, because they belong to the past; non-historical, because they leap
out of the past as a possible future. This rethinking of history, announced
in the early years of the twentieth century, is now being undertaken in different fields of research: the critique of the iconography of progress and of
the linear conception of history in the paleontological studies of Stephen Jay
Gould;[14] the rethinking of anachronisms in the history of art by Georges Didi-
Huberman;[15] the questioning of the 'direction' of time and of the principle

---

9. Marx 1956a, p. 346.
10. Ibid.
11. Benjamin 2003, Thesis II, p. 390.
12. Bloch 1969, p. 9. See also Farnesi Camellone 2009.
13. Bensaïd 2002, p. 88.
14. Jay Gould 1992; 1990.
15. Didi-Huberman 2000.

of causality in quantum physics, as the possibility of changing the past by means of a present-day measurement.[16]

A sentence that Anaïs Nin ascribes to the *Talmud* states: 'We do not see things as they are, we see them as we are'. In order to produce a different view of modernity, we need to effect a change in our viewpoint and in ourselves. By means of the metaphor of the *'camera obscura'* and of the 'mirror', Marx tried, on numerous occasions, to provide an image of modernity as 'inversion'. This inversion regards the relation between value and use-value: production, no longer directed towards use-values, destroys the limits of community and becomes indifferent to the quality of the objects of use, which, beginning with the means of production, take on an intrinsically capitalist use-value. The relation between man and thing takes the place of the relation between man and man; value subsumes use-value. This overturning gives rise to the fetishistic image of the world and to a new anthropology: the modern individuals entrapped in the garden of Calypso. Human desires become animal desires: needs to be satisfied. The desire of the *novum* is crushed in the incessant, always self-same repetition of novelties. The crisis of experience that accompanies the subsumption of use-value in exchange-value is displayed in Benjamin's *Passagenwerk;* it generates Beaudelaire's search for excess, Benn's freezing of history, Ballard's explosions of violence. In this horizon, the idea itself of political change collapses, becoming unthinkable.

Here, the historical materialist has the task of producing an image of reality that is able to illuminate the possibility of change. However, if the representation of reality is always mediated by categorial frames and takes shape from the perspective of observation, it is a case of producing a shift in perspective, which does not move in the direction of a greater objectivity – any vision can claim the title of 'objectivity' – but towards a vision able to grasp what another perspective occludes. This shift effects a revelation, or an illumination. The postmodern image of the indifferent plurality of points of view is, indeed, nothing but the completed self-representation of the modern that veils this dissymmetry of perspectives.

From this book's perspective, the appearance of the *spatialisation of time* is nothing other than the inverted image of the harder *temporalisation of space*. The former juxtaposes spatially the different times in contemporaneity, reproducing the image of that which appears; the latter, instead, intervening with its own specific temporality, shows how temporalities are placed in hierarchies and come into conflict. Time is not transformed into space, but rather

---

16. Wheeler 1983, p. 203: 'To say "no elementary phenomenon is a phenomenon until it is an observed phenomenon" is to make no small change in our traditional view that something has "already happened" before we observe it'.

impresses on it a constant rescaling, a redefinition of the spatial scales and of the hierarchical scales of state-regulation that traverse different nation-states,[17] redefining their sovereign-functions without at all dissolving them. Geography does not take the place of history, but rather cannot neglect the temporal and historical dimension of capitalist accumulation.[18] In this scenario, there opens up the question of the possibility of another history. This was the hypothesis that Marx studied extremely seriously together with the Russian populists. I consider this topic in the Appendix following Chapter Three.

Much of twentieth-century Marxism remained imprisoned in the unilinear conception of historical time that allowed different social forms to be pigeonholed as advanced or backward. That was and is an index of the level of internalisation of capital in the Western conscience, an internalisation that was denounced, during the anti-colonial struggles, by the critique of the Eurocentric conception of Marx and the faith in progress that sometimes emerged in his comments on colonialism. The same critique emerges in the debate opened up by subaltern studies.[19] Those denunciations were valid and remain so, even when they are philologically disputable. Only one problem remains open. The postcolonial critique of the Eurocentric construction of modern historiography, of the social sciences, and so forth, remains an ideological critique of ideology. Fanon gave a correct indication of the way out of this impasse when he wrote that 'Europe is literally the creation of the third world'.[20]

As it universalises itself, the capitalist mode of production encounters different forms and modes of production, which it subsumes in hybrid-forms. While apparently allowing diverse social forms to subsist, capital changes them, subjects them to its own command, measuring their intensity and the productive power of their labour. The temporal gaps between different modes of production are synchronised by socially-necessary labour-time, such that the different modes have to be understood as contemporaneous. On this point, Bloch's 'multiversum' allows us to think history as 'a polyphony of a unity'; it allows us to think the division between historical temporalities where nobody can talk for another or claim for oneself to be located on the high point of the tendency. The gambit consists in thinking politically temporal diversities, as against the processual and abstract temporality of modernity. Marx correctly wrote that the concept of universal history is itself an historical product.

---

17. On this aspect, see Brenner 2004, pp. 57 et sq.
18. See, for example, the symposium on the 'Geographies of the *Grundrisse*' in *Antipode. A Radical Journal of Geography*, Vol. 40, No. 5, 2008; see also Glassman 2006; Sewell 2008, p. 528.
19. On this debate, see the essays collected in Bartolovich and Lazarus (eds.) 2002.
20. Fanon 2005, p. 58.

It presupposes a new and universal temporality that is, in global capitalism, that of socially-necessary labour-time. The problem is to think the temporalities that are asynchronic in relation to the process of synchronisation.

   Global society, whose proper name is the world-market, requires a historiographical paradigm that is adequate to the combination of a plurality of temporal strata in the violently unifying historical dimension of modernity. The postmodernist juxtaposition of a plurality of historical times, where forms of peasant-slavery exist alongside high-tech production in the superannuation of the dualism between centre and periphery, not only explains nothing, but is obfuscatory. The mosaic of temporalities and forms of exploitation, even when it speaks of inter-relation, poses the diverse times as being in a state of reciprocal indifference, when the real problem is their combination by means of the world-market's mechanisms of synchronisation.[21] As I argue in the third chapter, the nexus of socially-necessary labour and value is, today, the category most able to assist in the comprehension of the mechanisms through which the labour-time of an automated productive cycle necessitates – and is combined with – the rhythm of forced labour in agriculture in California.[22]

   Capital, due to its indifference to different cultural horizons and social or familial structures, is able to functionalise different temporalities to the rhythm of socially-necessary labour. It can graft capitalist exploitation onto the trunk of servile relations not regulated by European laws, or utilise pre-existing social hierarchies in order to secure command and control over labour. The clash and conflict between these different temporalities, often represented in terms of cultural conflict, feed the production of new differentiations that can be rendered either functional to capital, or diverted against it. Marx's final anthropological studies on communist and pre-individualistic forms respond to a double question of contemporary relevance:[23] relativising the founding institutions of capitalist modernity, above all private property, they show that there were and are possible histories different from that taken by Western Europe. At this point, the non-capitalist forms of 'precapitalism' function as indicators for possible postcapitalist forms. The issue is not a vague romantic longing after premodern forms of civilisation. Primitivists and postmodernists are victims of this same specular error: the former glimpse an exit from modernity in the return to a style of life that is supposed to be primitive and

---

21. The question is posed by contemporary historians who, investigating the modern character of slavery in the global market, necessarily have to work with a 'plurality of temporal strata', which, although 'discontinuous, asymmetrical, nonsynchronous', are 'unified through the multiple spatial-temporal dimension of the world economy': see Tomich 2003, pp. 94, 119.
22. Walker 2004, pp. 73–4.
23. For the notebooks on Lewis H. Morgan and Henry S. Maine, see Marx 1972.

natural; the latter try to find the traces of a superannuation of modernity in new technologies or in the most recent tendency of the capitalist organisation of labour. But the *novum* is not hidden in the latest novelty; it explodes in the clash between different times. In this clash, the most recent novelty, striking the past, makes the future encapsulated in it leap out, reconfiguring it as an alternative to most contemporary modernity of the novelty itself.

This book would not have been possible without the common discussions during the last five years of seminars on 'Marx, History and Time' at the University of Padua. I thank sincerely my students, colleagues and friends who have participated in our seminars.

Chapter One
The Practical Materialist

> *Qu'est-ce que les périls de la forêt et de la prairie*
> *auprès des chocs et des conflits quotidiens de la*
> *civilisation?*
> (Ch. Baudelaire, *Fusées*, XIV)

Historical experience: rupture and continuity

The generation that lived through its formative years during the years immediately preceding the Revolution of 1848 [*Vormärz*] experienced revolutionary ruptures that forced it to engage anew with the proto-caesura that was the French Revolution. The revolutionary process that had begun in 1789 seemed to refuse to reach its conclusion; in fact, its gradual unfolding saw it assume an increasingly conspicuous class-character. It would take at least a couple of generations for the revolutionary rupture to be properly 'metabolised' in terms of historical experience. This would involve attenuating its radicality by situating it within a long-term historical process that could be teleologically reconstructed starting from the present, while simultaneously opening up prospects for the future. What was crucial was not so much the actual fact of the Revolution, but rather, the way it was experienced by a generation that sought not only to understand it, but also to master its character as a caesura. The Revolution was situated within a long-term crisis that comprised the dissolution of the *ancien régime*, the revolutionary event itself,

Napoleonic centralisation, and also the outbreak of new revolutionary crises during the nineteenth century. The new generation opted for a panoramic view. The chain of historical events that began with the Revolution was conceptualised as a process that needed to be situated within a broad historical timeframe. In order to understand and normalise the revolutionary ruptures within the historical continuum, the generation that followed Hegel turned the philosophy of history into a theory, considering history from the perspective of a long-term process.[1] It was this extended and processual temporality that gave rise to the notion of an acceleration of time,[2] or of a series of events whose density increased the closer one moved to the present. The notion of an acceleration produced by a historical time that had become processual provoked a crisis of historical experience: a crisis of the capacity to give one's present a coherent meaning by reference to past experiences and exemplary stories, in order then to conceptualise future action on this basis.

As Lamartine noted in 1849, the problem faced by the new generation concerned the very possibility of writing history. *Excidat illa dies aevo!*, wrote Michelet in his *Journal*, in an effort to erase, by a final desperate gesture, the story of the June 1848 insurrection. In a similar vein, Georges Duval referred to the 'lugubrious days of September 1792'. In the 1826 preface to his *Essai*, Chateaubriand had already noted that the Ciceronian topos of *historia magistra* had become meaningless, and that every attempt at comparative history had been rendered impossible.[3] The generation of the *Vormärz* confronted the revolutionary rupture, which had begun in France in 1789 and grown more acute in July of 1830, when a cycle of workers' struggles called for the conceptualisation of a new historical experience. The crisis also had terminological repercussions: the term-concept *Stand* [estate] yielded to that of *Klasse* [class].[4] The anti-monarchist campaign initiated by the French republicans encountered the demands of the workers' movement; the Société des droits de l'homme meshed with the working-class radicalism of Lyon. Evidence that this constituted a qualitative leap can be found on the opposite front as well: the government repressed the revolt of April 1834 by bombarding the neighbourhoods of the 'rebels'. The development by which war became social war was captured, in an almost photographic manner, in the massacre on the Rue Transnonain. Between 1831 and 1834, the red flags raised on the barricades of

---

1. On this development, see Tomba 1997.
2. On the disaggregation of the space of historical experience and the process of acceleration, see Koselleck et al. 1975, pp. 50 ff., 146, 288.
3. On this point, see Hartog 2003.
4. Conze 1992.

Lyon and the subsequent repression marked the end of the dream of national homogeneity. The insurrection shattered the idea of the *Peuple*.

Historical temporalities

Various non-synchronous temporalities combine and interlink with one another. Different temporal pathways develop and unfold according to a multiversal logic,[5] rather than following the single rhythm of *Weltgeschichte*. The peasant-revolts that fuelled the French Revolution were directed not so much against the nobility and the state, as against modernisers: enclosers and merchant-capitalists.[6] If, as Hannah Arendt maintained,[7] the 'genie of social revolution' was kept in the bottle in North America, where slaves were excluded from the Revolution and the colonial élite joined forces with the impoverished whites protesting British rule, in France 'the genie finally made it out of the bottle and spread across the European continent and back across the Atlantic to Haiti and South America'.[8] The revolutionary events in France connected with the revolutionary temporality of the colonies: the slave-rebellions that began with the great revolt of August 1791 spread in 1793 and 1794, until, in February of 1794, 'the Convention in Paris decreed emancipation in all the French colonies, and the Committee of Public Safety assembled an expedition to the New World with instructions to undertake a revolutionary war of liberation of the slaves'.[9] Meanwhile, Toussaint L'Ouverture had begun providing refuge to rebel-slaves.[10] If 1791 had confirmed the power of an aristocracy of white, male proprietors, the countertemporalities of the Revolution were already calling that first outcome into question:[11] Olympe de Gouges penned a *Declaration of the Rights of Woman and the Female Citizen*, the insurrection of the slaves in the colonies ended the 'whiteness' of the revolutionaries,[12] and the popular movements imposed 'maximum'-prices by means of which to restore wage-earners' purchasing power, while also seeking to impose a 'maximum' on property – their answer to the unlimited right to property. The San Domingo insurrection had repercussions for the development of the French Revolution, promoting the invocation of revolutionary natural law and giving rise, in 1793, to the first non-colonialist constitution.

---

5. Bloch 1990.
6. Silver and Slater 1990, p. 166.
7. Arendt 1963.
8. Silver and Slater 1990, p. 167.
9. Silver and Slater 1990, p. 170.
10. See also James 1963.
11. My reading of countertemporalities is, in many ways, in agreement with that of Daniel Bensaïd. See Bensaïd 1995; 2004.
12. L'Ouverture 2008.

This was the unacceptable *dérapage*.[13] If anything was 'blown off course', then it was the liberal tradition, ever keen to defend individual liberty against state-authority in 'civilised' countries while legitimating the despotism of 'race' – which 'may be considered as in its nonage'[14] – in the colonies. If the colonial question and anticolonial Jacobinism[15] were elided throughout nineteenth and twentieth-century historiography, then this was due precisely to the liberal tradition. From the point of view of liberal-historicist historiography, François Furet was right to consider the Terror a *dérapage* or 'brief parenthesis' in the 'liberal trend that dominated France from 1570 to 1850'.[16] Furet's model is that of a historiography that exists as if in a vacuum, recognising no moments of tension, one in which the 'liberal trend' plays out by a kind of inertia. Events that disrupt the mechanical sequence of the historical calendar represent a *dérapage*. The victors can place such 'deviations' between parentheses or ignore them. It is in this spirit that anti-colonial struggles, Olympe de Gouges's *Declaration*, and the popular uprisings of 1791 are uprooted from their context, that of revolutionary natural right,[17] while the principles of *liberté, égalité, fraternité* are encapsulated in a tradition capable of coexisting with slavery and colonialism. Yet the 'genie' of social revolution overstepped the boundaries of the state and demonstrated its expansive nature.

During the nineteenth century, reactionary historiography sought to restore the historical continuum, not just by smoothing over the roughness of the caesurae, but also by synchronising the various historical times so as to reconnect them to the one and only temporality of the state. Donoso Cortés attempted to 'metabolise' the experience of nineteenth-century revolutions by inserting them into a long-term historical process, within which the French Revolution appears as one moment among others. Cortés's image of the French Revolution is that of an infernal threshold, a gate on which are inscribed the three dogmas of 'Calvary'.[18] Armed with the *geschichtsphilosophische* instruments of an increasingly long-term historical process, Cortés situated modernity's proto-caesura in the Protestant Reformation, which he defined as a 'great

---

13. In their book *La revolution française*, François Furet and Denis Richet speak of the revolutionary movement being 'blown off course' between 1791 and 1792 (Furet and Richet 1986, p. 9).
14. Mill 1989.
15. On how anticolonialism has been elided in the historiography of the French Revolution, see Benot 2004, pp. 205–17.
16. Furet and Richet 1986, p. 10.
17. Bloch 1987, p. 153 ff.; Gauthier 1989; 1992.
18. Donoso Cortés 2000, p. 49.

scandal that was political and social as well as religious'.[19] This philosophy of history allowed him to read all of modern history as a process of 'constant decadence', represented by deism, pantheism, and atheism in religion, and by liberalism, republicanism, and communism in politics.

The same diagnosis can already be found in the work of the 'progressive conservative' August von Cieszkowski,[20] who sought to correct Hegel's philosophy of history by making it rigorously abide by the threefold structure of the dialectic. In doing so, he founded the 'historiosophy' and a 'philosophy of praxis' that later influenced the young Hegelians. According to Cieszkowski, the modern era was inaugurated by Christianity and characterised by the most extreme individualism. Cieszkowski agreed with De Maistre that *'il n'y a plus de religion sur la terre – le genre humain ne peut rester dans cet état!* [there is no more religion on earth – humankind can not remain in this condition!]', commenting 'This is just the disease, the famine of our time!'[21] Historiosophy's task is that of developing a vision of the third epoch, that of synthesis, during which humanity will consciously produce its own history by means of its own actions. Cieszkowski developed a theory of history that was capable not only of conceptualising history as a process, but also of identifying its tendencies, thereby restoring the possibility of formulating predictions; moreover, he developed a perspective that was sufficiently long-term to allow for smoothing over the revolutionary rupture. Just like the religious and scientific revolutions, the French Revolution was reduced to a further stage in the destruction and transformation of antiquity: 'but these reformations are not yet the founding of a new age. They are only the destruction or transformation of the old'. The event that was the French Revolution 'definitely dissolved the Middle Ages, but it did not yet resolve the Modern Age'.[22] In the face of the turbulences and shocks of contemporary events, the reaction consisted in assuming a remote perspective: given sufficient distance, ruptures disappear and there remains only a straight line. Cieszkowski's historiosophy is symptomatic of an ambivalence proper to modern theories of history: all of these theories, whether conservative and reactionary or more revolutionary, build on a common set of core-notions.

The new notion of history – the conceptualisation of history in terms of processuality and acceleration – results from the assumption of a remote perspective on the revolutionary ruptures of 1789, 1792–3, 1830, 1834, 1848...Political concepts become temporal vectors; democracy, atomism, and equality become

---

19. Donoso Cortés 2000, p. 54.
20. See Tomba 2006a.
21. Cieszkowski 1919, p. 248.
22. Cieszkowski 1919, p. 32.

tendencies: democratisation, atomisation, and levelling. Thus temporalised, political concepts elide the possibility of political change, replacing it with the prefiguration of a future that is probable, desirable, or to be prevented.[23] Understood as part of a process, the historical present allows one to reconnect the dimension of the past with that of a future that is contained, *qua* potentiality, within the present itself. The categories associated with the notion of the historical process allow for a new synthesis of historical experience, thereby providing the subject and its political practice with a new sense of direction, within a history that has been domesticated thanks to the identification of its tendencies. The various currents that emerged from the dissolution of Hegelianism as early as the 1840s went on to show that prospects of revolution and bouts of reaction result from one and the same temporalisation of political categories.[24] Once the crisis of philosophical and political concepts is confronted, the nexus of crisis and critique is constantly reconfigured, be it with an eye to a possible exit from the crisis or within the vortex of the polemics of the time.

The reflections conducted during the *Vormärz* derived their specific character from the fact that the revolution had not yet rolled into German territory; there was a persistence of anachronistic elements that required thinkers to come to terms with the conflictual coexistence of different temporalities. Despite all efforts to liquidate these anachronisms, treating them as mere residues, they continually reasserted themselves within the constellation of the present.

In his mature writings, Marx reformulated this problem as a political issue. With reference to the German situation, he wrote in the 1867 'Preface' to *Capital*, that alongside 'modern evils', there exists a gamut of 'inherited evils', the product of outdated modes of production and the 'anachronistic [*zeitwidrig*]' social and political relations associated with them. These anachronistic temporal elements interact with the temporality of capital, thus producing an accumulation of evils. Consequently, Marx concluded, '[w]e suffer not only from the living, but from the dead. *Le mort saisit le vif!*' The suffering that anachronistic relations entail adds to present evils. Thus Marx posed the central question for any attempt to conceptualise the contemporaneity of non-contemporaneous elements. Anachronisms may become revolutionary possibilities,[25] but they can also be swept under the carpet of the reigning

---

23. Farnesi Camellone 2007, p. 147.
24. Tomba 2002a.
25. Vadée distinguishes three forms of possibility in Marx: abstract or theoretical possibility, concrete or historical possibility, and practical possibility or freedom: Vadée 1998, p. 32.

Weltgeschichte, from whence they return in the form of zombies hungry for the flesh of the living. The historical materialist regards history the way an archaeologist regards the various layers of soil at an archaeological site, or the way a geologist regards rock-strata. Centuries and millennia exist contemporaneously before his eyes. A slight finger-movement indicates a jump across several centuries. The past is as present as the most pressing issues of the contemporary age. These are the problems that pushed political thought towards a conception of history adequate to the crisis.

The katechonic figure

The present study does not examine the model of the historicist historiographer, for whom historical continuity reflects the image of progress. This model is, in fact, so closely linked to the modern conception of history that one finds it in many hybrid-figures of modern and contemporary historiography.

Within the post-Hegelian thought of the *Vormärz*,[26] the different models were not yet clearly distinguished from one another; they display radical and conservative, progressive and reactionary, democratic and aristocratic features at one and the same time. In their writings from the early 1840s, both Bauer and Stirner exposed the limits and contradictions of liberal pretensions to political emancipation. Stirner confronted the liberal horizon of 'emancipation' with the practice of 'self-liberation'.[27] In so doing, he sought to set the entire issue on a new footing: emancipation, he argues, remains within the horizon of a liberation that comes from outside or is conceded – that of an imposed liberty.[28] Yet a liberty that is merely conceded does not genuinely liberate: it turns us into the more or less grateful slaves of whoever makes himself our liberator: 'The man who is set free is nothing but a freedman, a *libertinus,* a dog dragging a piece of chain with him: he is an unfree man in the garment of freedom, like the ass in the lion's skin'.[29] Liberty is not something one asks for, as if it were a concession like any other, for 'only the freedom one *takes* for himself, therefore the egoist's freedom, rides with full sails'.[30] It is this relationship between liberty and power that Stirner seeks to emphasise and give an anti-statist thrust. He reconceptualises legal rights in a similar manner. Everyone disposes of the rights that he succeeds in conquering for himself on the concrete terrain of struggle: 'Peoples that let themselves be

---

26. See Tomba 2009a.
27. Stirner 1907, p. 220.
28. Ibid.
29. Ibid.
30. Ibid.

kept in nonage have no right to the condition of majority; if they ceased to be in nonage, then only would they have the right to be of age. This means nothing else than 'What you have the *power* to be you have the *right* to'.[31] The conceptual operation Stirner aims at is twofold. On the one hand, he wants to delink right from the state. On the other hand, he wants to reconceptualise liberty beyond any relationship of dependence.

Although Stirner intends to set himself apart from Bauer, their positions coincide on a great many points. Bauer's reflection is devoted to liberty's conditions of possibility;[32] *Kritik*, Bauer's central concept for both understanding and intervening in reality, does not grant liberty: liberty exists as such only for those who conquer it directly in historical struggle. Liberty cannot be granted, either by the state or by anyone else, precisely because it depends on the subjective element of the person who conquers it for himself. Just like Stirner, Bauer holds that being the object of another's liberty amounts to being unfree: we are always the subjects of our own liberty. *Kritik* draws attention to what stands in the way of liberty, but it is up to the individual protagonists on history's *Kampfplatz* to clear away the obstacles to their liberty, and no-one can do this for them. Bauer emphasises repeatedly that no-one can be forced to be free; it is in this sense that *Kritik* leaves 'to those who are not free the freedom not to be free'.[33]

Just as in Stirner, one finds in Bauer a scarcely concealed aristocratic notion of liberty, one that implies a condescending gaze on those who lack the courage to conquer for themselves the liberty they might achieve. Like the rights of man, liberty represents 'the prize of battle',[34] and everyone disposes of as much liberty as he succeeds in conquering for himself. This revolutionary aristocratism, shared by Bauer and Stirner, is related to a certain way of conceptualising the crisis as a historical process. On the one hand, the tendency towards the atomisation of the social sphere is described with reference to the dissolution of inherited relations of social stratification and authority; on the other hand, Stirner and Bauer fear that individuality might itself be eroded by the general levelling that the state and a purely abstract equality have produced.

---

31. Stirner 1907, p. 247.
32. See Tomba 2006b. See also Moggach 2003.
33. B. Bauer 1989, p. 270; see also B. Bauer 1843a, p. 12.
34. 'The rights of man are, therefore, not a gift of nature, a gift of past history, but the prize to be won in the battle against the accidentality of birth and the privileges that history has thus far allowed one generation to bequeath to the next. They are the result of education, and they are only for those who have conquered and earned them': B. Bauer 1843b, p. 19.

Reflection on the French Revolution is central to this line of thought. The crisis is related to the dissolution of those differences and dividing lines that derive from society's division into social estates; while these differences and dividing lines separated the individual from others, they also united all individuals within a multiplicity of relations.[35] From the general absence of differences, a general condition of in-difference, there emerge the masses, and, with them, a new form of 'universal subordination': the one that led, historically, to the 'dictatorial powers' of Napoleon.[36] This was how the crisis that began with the Revolution developed in the long term: 'The Revolution found its logical conclusion in absolutism', wrote Bauer in 1846.[37] The Revolution is viewed in such a way as to make its prehistory and its subsequent history appear as elements of a single process. There are striking affinities, here, with the geneaological work undertaken several years later by Tocqueville,[38] who succeeded, by virtue of the same singular, processual notion of history, in keeping the *ancien régime* and the Revolution bound up with one another as elements of a single historical phenomenon, and who spoke of a tendency towards an unheard of concentration of power[39] thus predicting unfettered centralisation and democratisation.

Stirner also views the revolutionary crisis as an expression of the transition from the *ancien régime* to democratic despotism: 'The Revolution effected the transformation of *limited monarchy* into *absolute monarchy*'.[40] 'The monarch in the person of the "royal master" had been a paltry monarch compared with this new monarch, the "sovereign nation"'.[41] It is this transformation that interests Stirner. The question becomes that of understanding its logic. The 'sovereign nation', which exists by means of its representatives, no longer encounters any obstacles; there is no counterpower to confront it. Its reach extends directly to the single individual, who is politically stripped bare before it. If pre-revolutionary absolute monarchy could still be defined as 'limited,' then post-revolutionary *Gewalt* gives rise to an absolute and unlimited monarchy. In the course of this transition, the *'principle of estates*, the principle of little monarchies inside the great, went down', and there emerged a 'much more complete and absolute monarchy'.[42] Once the nation is made the only

---

35. B. Bauer 1844a, p. 211.
36. B. Bauer 1972a, pp. 253, 255.
37. B. Bauer 1972a, p. 230.
38. Tocqueville 2011.
39. Chignola 2004, p. 539. The hypothesis that Tocqueville meant to avoid the collapse of civilisation is maintained by Coldagelli 2005, p. 248.
40. Stirner 1907, p. 132.
41. Ibid.
42. Stirner 1907, p. 135.

political subject – once the people has become 'the source...of all right, and the source of all – power', as Mirabeau says in a passage quoted by Stirner[43] – right and power coincide: 'He who has power has right'. Whoever acts in the name of the nation disposes of a new type of power, one that knows no limits: 'the *majority of the representatives* has become *master*'.[44] The power wielded by the democratic majority would have been unthinkable under the monarchic rule of former times. In thus reconstructing the history of the French Revolution, Stirner makes use of the materials studied and compiled by Bruno Bauer's brother Edgar.[45] According to Stirner, the liberation of individuals from the fetters of social estate effected by the French Revolution has turned into its very opposite and produced the nullity of the individual: 'Before the supreme *ruler*, the sole *commander*, we had all become equal, equal persons, i.e. nullities'.[46] The equality of rights and the social equality demanded by radicals and liberals have been realised to an extent of which they never dreamt, but they have been realised in accordance with the principle of the modern state: 'Among the States of to-day, one has carried out that maxim of equality more, another less'.[47] And this very maxim of equality has rendered the individual insignificant.

The same idea can be found in Bauer, and in particular in his critique of *Nivellement* – a critique that leads Bauer to consider the dark side of the dialectic of levelling.[48] Bauer begins his reflection in 1843 and 1844; its first formulation (Bauer's countless writings on the history of the French Revolution aside) is 'Was ist jetzt der Gegenstand der Kritik?', an article published in the eighth issue of the *Allgemeine Literatur-Zeitung* (July 1844). This was the issue that prompted Stirner to add an eight-page 'note' to the chapter on 'humanitarian liberalism' in his *The Ego and his Own*, the manuscript of which had already been prepared for the publication.[49] Stirner was perfectly aware, when he wrote his note, of the difficulties involved in tracing

---

43. Stirner 1907, p. 131.
44. Ibid.
45. Stirner is citing E. Bauer 1843, pp. 113, 133.
46. Stirner 1907 p. 154. On the annihilation of the individual, see Seliger 1995, pp. 53 ff.
47. Stirner 1907, p. 134.
48. The relationship between the transvaluation effected by the Revolution and the return to pure theory [*reine Theorie*] evident between 1843 and 1844 has also been stressed by Lambrecht 1989, p. 748.
49. Stirner writes: 'But criticism is restlessly pressing forward, and thereby makes it necessary for me to come back to it once more, now that my book is finished, and insert this concluding note.' With reference to the motive for this revision, he writes: I have before me the latest (eighth) number of the *"Allgemeine Literatur-Zeitung"* of Bruno Bauer': Stirner 1907, p. 190.

Bauer's criticism back to humanism or a hypostasis of the concept of human essence: '[T]he critic has even begun already to gibe gently here and there at the thought of Man, of humanity and humaneness, because he suspects that here a thought is approaching dogmatic fixity'.[50] Yet Stirner accused Bauer of applying this criticism only within the domain of thought, or of wanting to 'break up thoughts by thinking'.[51] Stirner claims to proceed by *'unthinking* force' and strives to situate himself beyond the distinction between 'the unthinking and [the] thoughful ego [*gedankenlosen und gedankenvollen Ich's*]'.[52] On the one hand, Stirner recognises that the Bauer of 1844 is closer to his own positions than he suspected; on the other hand, this very kinship prompts him to radicalise his own position.[53] He genuinely wants to be 'his own'. To situate oneself beyond the distinction between 'the unthinking and [the] thoughful ego' is to present one's own irreducible uniqueness as a philosophical problem – one that cannot be conceptualised within philosophical discourse, though it can be represented by means of a break with the traditional form of the philosophical treatise.

The same period saw Bauer critically re-examining his own concepts:

> The French Revolution was an experiment that fully belongs to the eighteenth century. It was intended to set up a new human order, but the ideas it evoked did not lead beyond the state of affairs the Revolution sought to overcome by violence. Thus, having done away with the fetters of feudalism in the life of the people, the Revolution was forced to cater to and even promote the pure egoism of nationality while simultaneously balancing this egoism by means of its necessary complement, recognition of a Supreme Being – that supreme confirmation of the universal essence of the state, which must hold together the individual egoist atoms.[54]

The privilege of nationality replaces the privileges of feudalism, reconstituting the principle of *exclusive* identity by means of which the individual atoms liberated from the fetters of social estate can, once more, be unified. In this transition from the plural to the singular, from privileges to privilege, nothing seems to be augmented except the intensity of the one remaining political power.

---

50. Stirner 1907, p. 194ff.
51. Stirner 1907, p. 196.
52. Stirner 1907, p. 199.
53. On Stirner and his relationship to Hegel and Hegelianism, see Ridder 2008.
54. B. Bauer 1844a, p. 209.

Gigantographies of the crisis

'Critique is the crisis [*Kritik ist die Krise*]',[55] wrote Bauer. The statement can be understood in a twofold sense. On the one hand, the crisis is destructively projected onto the concepts and categories of philosophy, rendering them incapable of reproducing, even in the realm of thought, the dissolving world of the past. On the other hand, and by virtue of this projection, *Kritik* ceases to be a mere expression of the crisis: it becomes its driving force, and begins to produce crises on its own account. This is why Bauer came to maintain that *Kritik* is a historical force, a statement Marx would comment on sarcastically. Bauer strove to understand the relationship between history and crisis by means of grand historiographical panoramas. They were intended to represent the epoch in a different way, and thereby to inaugurate a new epoch. Bauer meant for his pen to replicate the performative gesture of the evangelists, who gave rise to Christianity by means of their literary-artistic compositions.[56]

The dialectic of the crisis having transformed individual liberty into its opposite, the specific problem of the Revolution – that is, of the object of investigation proper to Bauer's *Kritik* – becomes that of grasping the relationship between the production of a mass of egoist atoms and the unheard-of concentration of power that keeps them united. Bauer writes the *Geschichte* of these events in the singular: it is a history of those possibilities that were victorious. This allowed him to remark that when Robespierre, 'the genuine executor of the Revolution', sacrificed to his 'Cult of the Supreme Being the atheist leaders of the party of communal councils',[57] such that the Reign of Terror became the means of creating a 'free people', everything was ready for the revolutionary period's Napoleonic outcome. Bauer's approach was teleological; it consisted of looking back on the route travelled from the perspective of its destination.

For Bauer and his collaborators from the *Norddeutsche Blätter*,[58] differences of social estate had not yet been properly abolished; they had merely been singularised and converted into a single, universal distinction between 'people'

---

55. B. Bauer 1972b, p. 204.
56. These were the stakes in the polemic between David Strauss and Bruno Bauer. See Tomba 2002b, p. 63 ff.
57. B. Bauer 1844a, p. 210.
58. This was a journal published by a group sympathetic to Bauer's positions. It has been reprinted in B. Bauer, E. Bauer et al. 1846. Many of the articles published in the journal are anonymous, and their authors have still not been definitely identified. Bruno and Edgar Bauer penned some of the contributions, and they were, in any case, among the inspirators of the journal, which was edited by Köppen, Fränkel, and Szeliga.

and 'government'.[59] Equality [eguaglianza] was crushed between these two forces, becoming a 'universal relation of subordination to the totality of the state, which dominates everyone in the same way'.[60] Instead of producing universal liberty, struggles with egalitarian ends [uguaglianza] were transformed by the state into formal equality, a condition in which everyone is subjected equally. Bauer stressed that this dialectic of levelling typified modernity, with the Janus face of both liberation and dictatorship. Thus the French Revolution comes to be seen as one momentary culmination of a long-term crisis, but not as the final one: 'Pure man [der reine Mensch] has become a mere object of governance, and the Revolution has ended in absolutism – an absolutism whose further development the Revolution has bequeathed to the nineteenth century as its legacy'.[61] The tearing down of the barriers of social estate and the consequent destruction of privileges have not given rise to 'free man', but only to 'pure man', who has no features to distinguish him but those of being a man; faced with a power whose concentration is no longer limited by anything, the individual becomes ever smaller and ever more insignificant, until it disappears – politically, at least.

For Stirner, the Revolution of 1848 represents the last hope of escaping the crisis and going beyond the modern principle of representation. He hopes to achieve this by inserting apparently pre-modern concepts, such as that of the 'imperative mandate', into modernity's constellation of political concepts. By his reactivation of pre-modern concepts, Stirner attempts to disrupt the despotic mechanism by which the mandate given the representative by his voters is considered irrevocable.[62] The imperative mandate is, indeed, quite unthinkable within the conceptual constellation proper to modern popular sovereignty, since the people, being sovereign, is the only political subject capable of acting politically. Stirner's invocation of the imperative mandate must, therefore, be understood as an attempt to bring out the differences between various political realities, avoiding the reductio to the principle of popular sovereignty and, with it, levelling. Stirner thinks of the vortex of the European revolutions of 1848 as offering a last chance to alter the course of a modernity gone awry, by reconceptualising a European federalism functioning as 'a form of politics superior to centralisation'.[63] These are the terms of Stirner's proposition: federalism is the possible exit from centralisation, just as

59. See 'Die Menschenrechte 1793. Erster Artikel', Norddeutsche Blätter, No. VII (January 1845), p. 3.
60. Ibid.
61. B. Bauer 1965, p. 238.
62. Stirner 1848a.
63. Stirner 1848b.

the Empire [*Reich*] is the possible exit from the state-form.[64] Stirner rejects the proposition of a federal state, whatever the features of such a state. Instead, he hopes to exploit the revolutionary situation in order to bring about an Empire, premised no longer on the equality of 'citizens' but on the 'reciprocal relations of compatriots'. The challenge posed by the Empire is a challenge to modernity; like the reintroduction of the imperative mandate,[65] it amounts to a political move intended to salvage difference from the centralism of popular sovereignty's state-principle.

The proposition of a European federalism fascinated Bauer as well. During the 1840s, there arose the possibility of an alliance with the forces of centralisation: the 'hammer of increasing centralisation' was battering the peoples of Europe, thus subjecting them to a common fate and allowing them to recognise each other as fellow Europeans.[66] According to Bauer, centralisation eliminates the remnants of nationality, thereby creating the prospect of a Europe in which the problem of equality can be solved in accordance with the 'dignity and autonomy of the person'. Bauer envisages a new rapprochement of East and West, a Europe extending from the Neva to the Danube and the Tiber.

It is necessary to inquire into the political repercussions of the 1848 revolutions' failure and the effects of this failure on individual biographies. How was the revolutionary rupture experienced by the young Hegelians (who had not been Hegelians for some time, and perhaps never were)? Answering this question would require an in-depth study of issues that came to the fore during the years after the Revolution of 1848. One would have to re-read and carefully analyse Stirner's *Geschichte der Reaktion* and the thousands of pages that Bruno Bauer later produced on the origins of Christianity, on world-politics, and on the new imperialism.[67] Bauer's and Stirner's revolutionary aristocratism would, then, perhaps reveal itself as an intellectual attitude adopted *vis-à-vis* the crisis, a final, desperate attempt to salvage at least one's own individuality from the expanding reach of the forces of *Nivellierung*.[68] Bauer and Stirner both make an extra-philosophical gesture: they try to erect a final bulwark against levelling, even that of their own individuality. As Stirner writes: 'But I am not an ego along with other egos, but the sole ego: I am unique [*Ich bin einzig*]....This is the meaning of the – unique one [*Dies ist der Sinn des – Einzigen*]'; or, in other words: that is the meaning of both my uniqueness

64. Stirner 1848c.
65. Stirner 1848a.
66. B. Bauer 1882.
67. On Bauer's concepts of Empire and imperialism, see Kempski 1992, p. 155.
68. On these aspects of Bauer's and Stirner's thought, see Tomba 2005.

and the book *Der Einzige und sein Eigentum*.[69] By situating himself beyond the distinction between the thoughtless and the meditative ego, Stirner alludes to an extra-conceptual liberation from the iron-cage of conceptual thinking.[70] His extra-conceptual gesture, intended to salvage individuality from the jaws of modernity, concerns individuality in its entirety: the 'unthinkable' and 'unconceivable' ego of the one who makes the gesture. In Stirner, there appears – perhaps for the first time, and closely bound up with his own individuality – the attitude towards modernity that would be characteristic of certain 'katechonic' currents of the nineteenth and twentieth centuries: with regard to modernity's conceptual universe, Stirner summons up the elements of dissolution and allies himself with them, but then, at the decisive moment, he withdraws into his own self, exempting it, by an extra-philosophical gesture, from the effects of levelling. In Stirner, *style* – the extraordinarily innovative style of *The Ego and its Own*, but also the entire life-style of Johann Kaspar Schmidt – imposes itself within philosophy. The swashbuckling exploits of Stirner's Berlin-based circle (the 'Free', *die Freien*) were a way of living and practising the crisis of philosophy: the introduction of an extra-philosophical element, of biography, into philosophical reflection. Here, the performative character of theory coincided fully with the authors' own 'performances'.

The labour of dissolution undertaken in *The Ego and its Own* is only the most visible aspect of the *other unique one*: the book's literary style is identical with Stirner's very individuality. In this sense, that is, to the extent that it destroys, *The Ego and its Own* is also a *katechon*,[71] a means of slowing down history and erecting a final obstacle to the forces of levelling. Bauer was not far-removed from the spirit of this undertaking when he maintained, in his final work, that

> the birthpangs of the Caesarean era coincide with the reawakening of liberty and personal action. In the midst of battle and party-political confusion, there is nothing to stop anyone from surveying the wealth of history and appropriating whatever suits them best; the fear of centralisation does not preclude an autonomous attempt at reform – although such attempts are very difficult.[72]

---

69. Stirner 1907, p. 482 ff.
70. Stirner 1907, p. 198.
71. In his comparison of Stirner and Carl Schmitt, Laska arrives at a different conclusion. He maintains that 'the figures of the *katechon* and of the owner belong to different worlds': Laska 1996, p. 54.
72. B. Bauer 1979, p. 241.

This is conservative thought's most extreme gesture: an individual effort to withdraw from modernity's nihilist drift. It is a gesture that knows itself to be conceptually inappropriate and must, therefore, express itself by a certain manner of living and a certain style. In fact, this mode of thinking is not genuinely conservative (for there is nothing to be conserved in modernity, except one's own individuality); rather, it represents a reaction to modernity, a desperate attempt to swim against the current so as to be able to affirm that a brake, even if individual, remains possible, and that modernity has not triumphed. Stirner recognised this amalgam of biography and intellectual reflection in Bruno Bauer:

> It is precisely the keenest critic who is hit hardest by the curse of his principle. Putting from him one exclusive thing after another, shaking off churchliness, patriotism, etc., he undoes one tie after another and separates himself from the churchly man, from the patriot, etc., till at last, when all ties are undone, he stands – alone.[73]

The solitude of Bruno Bauer, his fate of becoming the 'hermit of Rixdorf',[74] is implicit in his thinking: it is nothing but the outcome of an intellectual career. It is an outcome openly announced as early as 1844, when Bauer stated that the critic must abstain from participating in the sufferings and joys of society, and that nothing can perturb the stoic calm of his solitude.[75] Marx wryly commented on Bauer's position:

> This criticism thus regards itself as the only active element in history. It is confronted by the whole of humanity as a mass, an inert mass, which has value only as the antithesis of intellect. It is therefore regarded as the greatest crime if the critic displays feeling or passion, he must be an ironical ice-cold sophos.[76]

Bauer considered the rise of the masses a reason to withdraw and salvage one's own individuality; Marx saw it as opening up new possibilities. The concept of the individual also had to be superannuated. Marx would take a different view of anachronisms, later proving decisive. For Bauer, the peasantry was the 'rock' capable of putting a brake on the process of levelling,[77] and obstructing the linear course of its temporality. This is the

---

73. Stirner 1907, p. 177.
74. D.M. Bennett, who visited Bauer in his study (a converted barn) when the latter was in his seventies, wrote that Bauer liked to describe himself as the 'hermit of Rixdorf'. See Fischer 1932, pp. 65–8.
75. B. Bauer 1844b, pp. 31–2.
76. Marx 1975a, p. 65; Marx 1975b, p. 356.
77. Marx 1983a, p. 562.

reactionary approach to the non-contemporaneous. It was employed by the conservative revolution of the twentieth century; the conservative revolution of the twenty-first century is preparing to do the same, albeit by different means.

The figure of the historical materialist

Bruno Bauer sought refuge in rural Rixdorf; Marx went to London. He chose to move in the opposite direction. Marx was convinced of rural life's stultifying effect, and left for the metropolises of Europe, where he established contact with working-class groups. *Kritik* abandons the pathos of distance and becomes a weapon, 'criticism in *hand-to-hand combat*'.[78] Marx attacked the 'dispassionate contempt' evident in the critique penned by his 'friend of many years standing', a disdain that gave rise to a 'sad and supercilious intellectualism', yet continued to exercise a certain fascination over German intellectuals.[79] The polemic between Marx and Bauer developed from here. The year was 1844.

In November 1844, Engels began to write *The Condition of the Working Class in England*, published in March 1845. He discovered a new revolution: 'an industrial revolution, a revolution which altered the whole civil society; one, the historical importance of which is only now beginning to be recognised'.[80] Pauperism began to be read as part and parcel of this revolution, with attention paid to the horrors of working-class neighbourhoods. The Feuerbachian notion of an ontological loss of humanity was applied to the study and interpretation of a specific subject – the proletariat – at a precise moment in history – the Industrial Revolution. Analysis of atomism is placed within a new context:

> The dissolution of mankind into monads, of which each one has a separate principle, the world of atoms, is here carried out to its utmost extreme. Hence it comes, too, that the social war, the war of each against all, is here openly declared.[81]

Engels observes the realisation of the type of social relation represented by Stirner. People consider one another only as 'useful objects'; everyone exploits

---

78. Marx 1975c, p. 178.
79. Marx 1975a, p. 64 ff.; Marx 1975b, p. 356.
80. Engels 1975, p. 307. See also Stedman Jones 2006. According to Stedman Jones, Engels's text represents a combination, in an original narrative form, of the German theme of pauperism, the French literature on the Industrial Revolution, and the Feuerbachian notion of humanity's dissolution and regeneration.
81. Engels 1975, p. 329.

everyone else, and the weakest are left with nothing but 'bare life [*das nackte Leben*]'.[82] Atomism was examined as the product of specific social relations – as resulting from the very relations that also determine competition between mutually hostile individuals.

An analysis of society from the point of view of the proletariat gave rise to a new image of social relations and their atomist imaginary. Marx focused on this new perspective in his *Theses on Feuerbach*, where he distanced himself both from materialism – which is capable of grasping reality only in the form of the *Objekt*[83] – and from idealism, which abstractly develops the active aspect [*tätige Seite*] of the real, the side neglected by materialism. Neither of the two points of view is correct, because neither of them is capable of understanding the object *qua* praxis, that is, *subjectively*. In the *Theses on Feuerbach*, written between the *Holy Family* and the *German Ideology*, probably in the spring of 1845, truth assumed a new conceptual status in relation to *praxis*. The truth of reality discloses itself in the possibility of transforming reality, in the revolutionary praxis of subjects that operate in reality and interpret it with an eye to its transformation. This is the meaning of the famous eleventh thesis, which does not amount simply to charging philosophers with the interpretation of the world and revolutionaries with its transformation, but which aims, rather, at developing a different manner of interpreting the world: one capable of disclosing the possibility of transformation by assuming the subjective perspective on the real, the perspective of the subjects who really are producing transformation. From this point of view, the concept of atomism, understood as the dissolution of Europe's traditional social structure (that of societies divided into social estates), turns out already to constitute a judgement about reality. It is a political image that can be used to produce counter-concepts. This is precisely what the reactionaries would go on to do, opposing rootedness to modern rootlessness and the organic community to individualism. However, while there is a nihilist side to modernity, emphasised frequently in reactionary thought, nihilism needs to be defined by reference to what it is concretely annihilating. When nihilism consists in the destruction of relations based on social estate and the production of equality, when it amounts to the destruction of slavery and to the creation of contractual relations between formally-free workers, then it represents the positive content of the struggle of the oppressed classes. If this equality and the contracts between formally free workers are ambivalent, such that equality becomes political indifference, while the sale and purchase of labour-power turns into the extortion of

---

82. Ibid.; translation modified.
83. Marx 1975d, p. 3, first thesis.

surplus-value, then it is on the basis of this new historical stratification that new forms of liberation can be developed – something that can certainly not be done starting from the reactionaries' nihilist image of modernity. What needs to be grasped are the historical statifications of modernity, produced by the struggles of the oppressed class, not the false image of modernity as an undifferentiated, smooth surface. Yet producing the new image of modernity requires a new perspective.

The experience of the 1844 Silesian weavers' revolt played a crucial role in determining this change of perspective.[84] Engels followed the development of the revolt and reported on it for the *Northern Star*. As for Marx, the revolt was the backdrop against which he began to reflect upon the condition of the working class.[85] At the same time, Marx drew attention to the urgent need for a reckoning with the German ideology, that is, with the tendency of German intellectuals to separate themselves from the labour-movement. Marx criticised a manner of conceptualising philosophy that was widespread among the radical intellectuals of the *Vormärz*. In the *German Ideology*, he attempted to bring critical theory into syntony with the historical process of German society's transformation, by relating the country's intellectuals and its working class to one another. The working class was not only more advanced, in practical terms, than the radical intellectuals; it also represented a powerful impetus toward social transformation that already went beyond the positions of the revolutionary bourgeoisie, at least in Germany. Marx and Engels's political intervention opened up a temporal tension within the revolutionary tension: into the tension between the German situation and the revolutionary bourgeoisie, it inserted the praxis of the workers, with whom Marx hoped to make the radical intellectuals associate themselves. German intellectuals were the 'greatest conservatives', Marx wrote in a June 1846 note for the *German Ideology*'s chapter on Feuerbach, because they were unable to think in step with the political temporality of the proletariat. In their pretensions to represent the vanguard of history, they were part and parcel of Germany's anachronisms, which they sought to synchronise abstractly. It was primarily this removal from the reality of the proletariat that Marx attacked in Bauer and Stirner. It was a removal that had been theorised by, and which exercised a certain fascination over, Germany's intellectuals. Both the *Critique of Critical Criticism* (which the publisher Löwenthal decided to issue as the *Holy*

---

84. Löwy 2002.
85. Ernie Thomson has emphasised the role played by Engels in the development of Marx's interest in political economy and the condition of the working class. Thomson also stresses the role played by Engels in Marx's decision to make contact with the leaders of the English working class from 1845 onward: Thomson 2004, p. 173.

Family) and the unpublished *German Ideology* addressed Germany's intellectuals. They did not yet address the proletariat. The *Critique of Critical Criticism*
had still to be completed when Engels pointed out the urgent necessity of
developing a critique of Stirner also, for he was, without doubt, 'the most
talented, independent and hardworking of the "Free" '.[86] Engels believed the
egoism radicalised by Stirner could be turned on its head and transfigured
into communism. He believed that once he had turned the unilaterality of
Stirner's thought on its head, he could put it to good use, as if the Stirnerian
egoists would necessarily be driven, by their egoism, to 'become communists'.
Engels meant to use Stirner's theoretical positions strategically, drawing the
intellectuals of Berlin away from their abstractions and involving them in the
struggle for communism. By contrast, Marx believed that it would be more
opportune to break definitively with Stirner's theoretical elaborations. Both
Marx and Engels meant to engage Germany's radical intellectuals in debate,
yanking them out of their isolation and involving them in a common struggle
on communism's battlefront. Both the *Critique of Critical Criticism* and the *German Ideology* were intended less as a philosophical reckoning with Germany's
Hegelian currents than as an attempt to nip in the bud the emergence of a
political movement of intellectuals without any grounding in social reality.

Georg Jung, who provided Marx with information about the Silesian revolt,[87]
sent him the most recent issues of the *Allgemeine-Literatur Zeitung* and invited
him to develop his critique of Bauer in such a way as to prompt Bauer to come
out into the open and express himself clearly on the revolt:

> Your observations on Bauer are certainly correct. It seems to me it would
> be a good thing if you would develop them into a critical article for a
> German newspaper so as to prompt Bauer to abandon his enigmatic
> reservedness.... Bauer is completely taken with the mania of criticising
> everything, to the point that he wrote to me recently one ought to criticise
> not just society, privileged persons, proprietors, and so on, but also –
> something no-one has ever thought of before – the proletarians. As if
> criticism of the rich, property, and society didn't result from criticism of the
> proletarians, that is, from their inhuman and undignified condition. Write
> to me soon what you believe ought to be done against Bauer. If you don't
> want to devote any time to him, Hess and I will edit your letter so it can
> be published as an article.[88]

---

86. Engels 1982a, p. 13.
87. Jung 1975a, p. 432.
88. Marx's letter has been lost, and we have only Jung's reply, dated 31 July 1844:
see Jung 1975b, pp. 436 et sq.

Jung sided with Marx, but he did not understand that Bauer has chosen an altogether different side. For Bauer, if criticism needs to be directed against the proletariat as well, then this is not so as to denounce the proletariat's material circumstances, but because the proletariat is simply one more element of the old world (to use Bauer's jargon). From 1844 onward, Bauer's position was contrary to that of Marx. For Bauer, the proletariat appertained to those 'masses' from which he intended to distance himself in order to preserve the purity of *Kritik*. Marx attacked this aristocratic withdrawal from the world because it expressed itself politically in German intellectuals' detachment from communism. It is the context, here, that is interesting. The observations contained in the lengthy draft of a review of Bruno Bauer's 'Charakteristik Ludwig Feuerbachs',[89] observations Marx meant to include in a chapter titled 'Feuerbach and History', were torn from their context by the editors of Marx's collected works, who inserted them into the chapter on Feuerbach in the *German Ideology*;[90] a chapter which does not exist as such. It is only by dismantling this text and reading its various parts in their proper context that one can understand the polemical referents of Marx and Engels's arguments. Bruno Bauer and the group associated with the *Allgemeine-Literatur Zeitung* were working to create a massive rift between Germany's radical intellectuals and the proletariat. Marx had already commented on the separation between the two by stating that German philosophy was the head of emancipation and the proletariat its heart.[91] The comment was political, formulated from within the contingency of a confrontation. For Marx, it was a question of winning Germany's radical intellectuals over to the cause of the proletariat and dismantling the German ideology that perpetuated the aloofness of critique.

Written as communist meetings were being organised all over Germany,[92] the pages of the *German Ideology* were intended as a response to critical attacks on the conceptual nexus *Feuerbach-Gattung-Kommunismus*. In the concluding section of his 'Charakteristik Ludwig Feuerbachs',[93] Bauer in fact attacked

---

89. See Marx and Engels 2004, p. 6; according to the *Entwurf*, the article was 29 pages long; the third and seventh pages have, however, been lost.

90. See 'Einführung zur Vorabpublikation der *Deutschen Ideologie*', pp. 5–28 in Marx and Engels 2004. The chapter on Feuerbach familiar to Marxists is the product of major liberties taken by the editors of the German edition of Marx's works (*Marx Engels Werke*, MEW), who 'completed' Marx and Engels's text without offering any sort of justification for their editorial intervention (Marx and Engels 2004, p. 12). See also Weckwerth 2009.

91. 'The *head* of this emancipation is *philosophy*, its *heart* is the *proletariat*': Marx 1975d, p. 187.

92. Engels 1982b.

93. B. Bauer 1845; the section in question is titled 'Feuerbach und der Einzige. Die Consequenzen Feuerbachs und ihr Kampf gegen Kritik und den Einzigen'. This is the

not just Feuerbach, but also Moses Hess and the authors of the *Holy Family*. As Marx emphasised polemically, this was not the only text in which Bruno Bauer appropriated arguments developed by Stirner. Bauer's 'Charakteristik' revealed how polarised the debate had become, with Bauer and Stirner on one side, and Feuerbach, Marx, Engels, and Moses Hess on the other. The philosophical controversy began to assume political features. In his review of the *Holy Family*,[94] the socialist Otto Lüning presented the contentious issues in schematic terms: 'In order to get rid of the French Revolution, communism, and Feuerbach, he [Bruno Bauer] shrieks "masses, masses, masses!", and again: "masses, masses, masses!"'[95] The opposition had become manifest; it was no longer just theoretical. On one side, there were the French Revolution, communism, and Feuerbach; and on the other, criticism of the Revolution, of the masses,[96] and of *Gattung*.[97] Whether Feuerbach could, indeed, be assimilated to communism and the Revolution had become a secondary issue.

In any case, the 1845 confrontation with Bauer and Stirner helped Marx critically reconsider the organicist logic of *Gattung* without falling back into an individualistic approach.[98] The confrontation with Stirner was indispensable for developing an understanding of Feuerbach's limits.[99] In order to respond to the criticisms of Stirner, who viewed the communist concept of class as a variant of Feuerbach's *Gattung* under which individuals are subsumed, Marx was forced to rethink his own position. He criticised the Feuerbachian positions that Bauer and Stirner identified within communism, and distanced

---

text that Marx intended to review. However, he did not complete his review, and his drafts were included in the *German Ideology*'s so-called 'chapter on Feuerbach'. See Marx and Engels 2004, p. 6.

94. Lüning 1845.

95. Lüning 1845, p. 212.

96. B. Bauer, 1844c.

97. See B. Bauer 1845, where Bauer attacks the Feuerbachian concept of *Gattung*, defining it as the new divinity to which the individual is subordinated. Bauer's polemic against Feuerbach turns on the concept of *Gattung*. Marx would go on to defend Feuerbach against Bauer: Julius 1845, p. 320.

98. More specifically, Kojin Karatani maintains that Stirner's critique of the 'spectral' character of the Feuerbachian abstraction 'man' compelled Marx and Engels to redefine the reality of the individual starting from the totality of the individual's social relations (Karatani 2003, p. 172). See also the comments of Kouvelakis, according to whom Marx does not use the term 'species' in the original Feuerbachian sense (intersubjectivity) but relates it, rather, to the Hegelian concept of *vie du peuple*. According to Kouvelakis, Marx sought to redefine the concept of *vie du peuple* in accordance with a notion of 'true democracy' *qua* expansive process of the political form; see Kouvelakis 2003, p. 329 ff.

99. On this point, see Thomson 2004, pp. 13, 151–5, 163.

himself from these positions.[100] There began the labour of expunging Feuerbachian positions from communism.[101]

The social revolution

The Silesian revolt – or, rather, the task of comprehending its political significance – required a new 'point of view',[102] a break with the point of view emphasising the 'isolation of man from the community'.[103] Isolation was understood as the product of a specific 'organisation of society', not concerning the political community or the individual's separation from the state, but rather the worker's isolation from life and from the 'true community of human beings'.[104] In fact, the community from which the worker is isolated is that of 'life itself, physical and mental life, human morality, human activity, human enjoyment, *human* essence'.[105] The worker is isolated from the human community, and hence from humanity's very essence; he is isolated from the true community, in which the worker's human essence is free to develop itself both spiritually and physically, by means of the pleasures of the mind and the body. The revolt of industrial workers, the *soziale Revolution*,[106] displays the universal character of humanity's protest against 'dehumanized life'.[107]

---

100. Bauer writes: 'What has Feuerbach done by transforming theology into anthropology? Nothing but what Hegel did when he elevated theology to the rank of philosophy. In anthropology as in philosophy, theology is consecracted, sanctified, overcome. Anthropology is religion; the *Gattung* is a force that exists independently from man, one that exists for itself, outside the individual's personality': B. Bauer 1845, p. 109.

101. Obviously, the presence of Feuerbachian positions within Marxian theory is more than merely a matter for the philosophy of history. The issue directly concerns the way we conceive of individuality and politics. Roberto Finelli has drawn attention to the problem by pointing out the presence, in Marx's work, of a symbiotic and fusional anthropology that derives from Feuerbach and displays markedly organicist and palingenetic features: see Finelli 2004. It is not simply a question of determining whether, how, and when, Marx freed himself from this powerful young-Hegelian legacy; one needs also to work towards its definitive correction, as Finelli seems to be willing to do.

102. Marx 1975e, p. 197.

103. Marx 1975e, p. 204.

104. Marx 1975e, pp. 199, 204; translation modified.

105. Ibid.; translation modified.

106. Marx 1975e, p. 205.

107. Ibid. Andrew Chitty maintains that the concept of 'life' represents the systematic link between Marx's 1842 works and those penned after 1845: Chitty 2003, p. 236 ff. Yet while Marx continued to use the concept of 'life', including in his discussion of modes of production, the mid-1840s saw him beginning to introduce theoretical elements that do not belong to the idealist tradition, thus altering the semantics of this concept.

It is something more than merely moral condemnation; what is condemned is the very organisation of society, a society that produces and reproduces inhuman conditions of existence and denies the worker all pleasure. Marx's discourse is always also a discourse on the body; hence his references to the 'shrunken flesh of the women, undermined by labour and poverty', the 'children crawling about in the dirt', and 'deformity resulting from excessive labour in the monotonous mechanical operations of the factories'.[108]

Everything appears as in a negative image, as in a *camera obscura*:[109] the image of isolation is the product of relations of competition. A relation – namely, that of competition – is, in fact, what isolates individuals.[110] While it originates in the 'co-operation of different individuals', the 'social power' of the capitalist forces of production presents itself to these individuals as an 'alien force' that does not just exist independently of their will, but is in fact capable of governing 'the will and the action of man'.[111] This is the 'illusory' community [*die scheinbare Gemeinschaft*]:[112] a form of communal life that represents both a bond between individuals and their separation, and which becomes autonomous *vis-à-vis* the individuals. In this form of communal life, individuals find themselves fatefully cast into a class, within which they 'find their conditions of existence predestined' and within which they are 'subsumed',[113] like the ball tossed into one of those *roulettes* that began to become popular during the early nineteenth century. What Stirner attributes to communism actually constitutes the normal state of affairs under existing social relations: the 'subsuming of individuals under definite classes cannot be abolished until a class has taken shape, which has no longer any particular class interest to assert against the ruling class'.[114] New possibilities open up as soon as one changes one's perspective, assuming the point of view of a class

---

108. Marx 1975e, p. 193.
109. Marx and Engels 1975, p. 36.
110. 'Competition separates individuals from one another, not only the bourgeois but still more the workers, in spite of the fact that it brings them together. Hence it is a long time before these individuals can unite, apart from the fact that for the purposes of this union – if it is not to be merely local – the necessary means, the great industrial cities and cheap and quick communications, have first to be produced by big industry. Hence every organised power standing over against these isolated individuals, who live in relationships, daily reproducing this isolation [*die Isolierung*], can only be overcome after long struggles': Marx and Engels 1975, p. 75. On the individual and the community, see Basso 2008.
111. Marx and Engels 1975, p. 48.
112. Marx and Engels 1975, p. 78.
113. Marx and Engels 1975, p. 77.
114. Ibid.

of individuals who cannot 'abolish the...condition of their existence' without also abolishing that 'of all society up to the present'.[115]

It is not enough to draw attention to a certain form of communal life; the very concept of the individual needs to be redefined. Marx distinguishes not just between two types of community, but also between two types of individuality. One community presents itself as a 'form...indifferent to the intercourse of individuals as individuals', whereas in the other, individuals are 'put into a position to enter into relation with one another *as individuals*'.[116] Until now, that is, under conditions characterised by the individual's separation from the totality, there have been only 'substitutes for the community': there has only been an 'illusionary community [*scheinbare Gemeinschaft*]'.[117] The 'real community [*wirkliche Gemeinschaft*]' is not something projected back from the future; it is not created from nothing, but already given in the 'community of revolutionary proletarians',[118] in which individuals participate 'as individuals',[119] without sacrificing their own individuality. In paying attention to what anticipates communism, Marx proceeds in such a way as always to conceptualise the individual from the starting point of its relations, and as such, every change in the individual's anthropology as starting from a change in the individual's relations:

> When communist *artisans* associate with one another, theory, propaganda, etc., is their first end. But at the same time, as a result of this association, they acquire a new need – the need for society – and what appears as a means becomes an end. In this practical process the most splendid results are to be observed whenever French socialist workers are seen together. Such things as smoking, drinking, eating, etc., are no longer means of contact or means that bring them together. Association, society and conversation, which again has association as its end, are enough for them; the brotherhood of man is no mere phrase with them, but a fact of life, and the nobility of man shines upon us from their work-hardened bodies.[120]

What is being described, here, is a new individuality. This new, post-individual individuality, for which Marx does not yet have a name, takes shape within the abolition of the rule of segregated parts, by which people become proletarians.

---

115. Marx and Engels 1975, p. 80.
116. Marx and Engels 1975, p. 86 ff.
117. Marx and Engels 1975, p. 78.
118. Marx and Engels 1975, p. 80.
119. Ibid.
120. Marx 1975f, p. 313.

There is no individuality to be restored, because the modern individual, engendered by the modern, capitalist division of labour, belongs to a class that is subject to accidental living conditions: it is an 'average individual [*Durchschnittindividuum*]'.[121] Marx posits an ulterior 'division between the personal and the class individual [*persönliches Individuum, Klassenindividuum*]', explaining that 'the accidental nature of the conditions of life for the individual, appears only with the emergence of the class, which is itself a product of the bourgeoisie'.[122] This multiple declination of the concept of the individual indicates the existence of a Marxian problem. To put it in negative terms: Marx wants to restore neither the *average individual*, that is, the member of a class who is determined by the class to which he belongs, nor the *personal individual*. The difference between the two is, in fact, an imaginary one. It is only in the imagination that the individuals of the bourgeois world 'seem freer under the dominance of the bourgeoisie than before, because their conditions of life seem accidental; in reality, of course, they are less free, because they are to a greater extent governed by material forces'.[123] The more the modern individual presents itself as free, as a personal individual, the more it is in fact driven by social forces it does not control and becomes subject to the alien fate of the 'class individual'. The various meanings of the term 'individual', multiplied in order to survey its spectral radiance, become the ray of light by which to expose what would otherwise remain hidden. Marx aims at a *different* concept of the individual, which we can refer to as such only for want of a more precise term.[124] It is an individual that boasts a wealth of relations and waxes in power to the extent that the species does, an individual that 'embraces a wide circle of varied activities and practical relations to the world'.[125] Yet the development of this individual, who is no longer an individual, is possible only in a context in which life is no longer separated from the proletariat. It is in light of this problem that we should read Marx's more utopian pages, such as those describing a communist society 'where nobody has one exclusive sphere of activity' and in which society, by regulating general production, makes it possible for everyone to 'do one thing today and another tomorrow, to hunt in the morning, fish in the afternoon, rear cattle in

---

121. Marx and Engels 1975, p. 80.
122. Marx and Engels 1975, p. 78.
123. Marx and Engels 1975, p. 78 ff.
124. Jacques Camatte proposes a concept of anthropological discontinuity, that of *l'homme Gemeinwesen*, as an alternative to those of the individual and of *homo sapiens*, thanks to whom humanity is approaching a catastrophic transformation of the biosphere. See Camatte 2002, p. 84 ff.
125. Marx and Engels 1975, p. 263.

the evening, criticise after dinner'.[126] Such passages, whose anti-philosophical character has embarrassed Marxists, and which have provoked the sarcasm of anti-Marxists, reach out towards the non-conceptual image of a post-individual horizon.

Phases and counterphases of the revolution

Marx begins with an analysis of bourgeois revolutions that are already characterised by a certain proletarian presence. Such revolutions are always in danger of being reversed, that is, of becoming counterrevolutions, but they may also be turned into proletarian revolutions. Marx's approach has prompted the claim that he always proceeds 'from the fact that, historically, ... revolutions have not been brought about by the proletariat, but have been facts imposed by the bourgeoisie'.[127] Revolutions already exist, namely as bourgeois revolutions, and the proletariat has to transform them into proletarian revolutions. Such a transformation cannot but alter the nature of the very concept of revolution: 'Only in the name of the general rights of society can a particular class vindicate for itself general domination'.[128] A particular class that represents itself as universal and acts in the name of the whole – this is the model of the bourgeois revolution, from which Marx tries to arrive at that of the proletarian revolution.

> For the *revolution of a nation*, and the *emancipation of a particular class* of civil society to coincide, for one estate to be acknowledged as the estate of the whole society, all the defects of society must conversely be concentrated in another class, a particular estate must be the estate of the general stumbling-block, the incorporation of the general limitation [*allgemeine Schranke*].[129]

The way Marx shifts back and forth between the terminology of social estate [*Stand*] and that of class [*Klasse*] shows that his lexicon is still in the making – even if the term *Stand* seems to refer to social position, whereas *Klasse* is defined dynamically, in terms of opposition. In the French Revolution, '[t]he negative general significance of the French nobility and the French clergy determined the positive general significance of the nearest neighboring and opposed class of the *bourgeoisie*'.[130] But the true problem, which Marxism inherited, lies in Marx's projection of the bourgeois revolution's development

---

126. Marx and Engels 1975, p. 47.
127. Krahl 1971, p. 389.
128. Marx 1975c, p. 184.
129. Marx 1975c, p. 185.
130. Ibid.

onto the proletarian revolution. The problem can only be resolved by rethinking the historicity proper to the proletarian revolution.

The 'historical method'[131] of German post-Hegelianism involves a peculiar 'inversion':[132] the 'consciousness of a later age' is foisted on earlier periods of history, such that it becomes 'possible to transform the whole of history into an evolutionary process of consciousness'.[133] This amounts to a reverse-teleology that ignores history's real foundation:

> the real production of life appears as non-historical, while the historical appears as something separated from ordinary life, something extra-superterrestrial. With this the relation of man to nature is excluded from history and hence the antithesis of nature and history is created. The exponents of this conception of history have consequently only been able to see in history the spectacular political events and religious and other theoretical struggles, and in particular with regard to each historical epoch they were compelled to *share the illusion of that epoch*.[134]

The 'illusion' of the modern epoch is that of the single, isolated individual, which is treated *not* as a historical product, but as history's starting point. Robinsonades, or the projection of present circumstances onto an ahistorical state of nature, develop from here: Smith and Ricardo start from an 'individual and isolated hunter or fisher', and Hobbes and Rousseau take as their starting point the free individuals in the state of nature.[135]

The challenge confronted by the *German Ideology* was that of eliminating the 'phrases' associated with the representations produced by religious, post-Hegelian historiography. It was a question of eliminating the imagination that 'puts the religious production of fancies in the place of the real production of the means of subsistence and of life itself'. This task could be achieved not by virtue of a new (materialist) conception of history, but by means of 'practical dissolution of these phrases', this dissolution requiring a change of perspective: 'For the mass of men, i.e., the proletariat, these theoretical notions do not exist'.[136] It was necessary to abandon the atomist point of view, considering it as the product of a particular 'organisation of society'.[137] According to Marx's

---

131. Marx and Engels 1975, p. 62.
132. Marx and Engels 1975, p. 89.
133. Ibid.
134. Marx and Engels 1975, p. 55.
135. Marx continued to reflect on this throughout his work. See the 'Introduction' in Marx 1986a, and also the chapter on fetishism in *Capital*.
136. Marx and Engels 1975, p. 56.
137. Marx 1975e, p. 199 (translation modified). On Marx's abandonment of the atomist perspective following the writing of 'The Jewish Question', see Jaeck 1979, p. 103 ff.

reasoning, the atomist conception is doubly abstract. Not only is atomism understood to be the product of a particular organisation of society; it also treats the political isolation of the single person as absolute, that is, it is blind to class-distinctions. Not everyone is isolated in the same way. The single person's isolation from the state, that is, his relationship of alterity *vis-à-vis* state-power, is not the same as the worker's isolation from life. For Marx, these two forms of isolation – the citizen's isolation from the state and the worker's isolation from life – entail different practices: protest against isolation from the state in the first case, and protest against dehumanised life in the other. Here is the subjective side of the real. The two forms of protest represent the axis capable of maintaining tension within the real, opening it up to new possibilities. This was why Marx made the concept of revolution a twofold one, distinguishing between *social* and *political* revolution. Marx did not think of these two revolutions as relating to each other diachronically, with one succeeding the other. Nor did he consider the relationship between them a teleological one. Rather, they need to be conceptualised as synchronic and from within a given situation. With this perspective in mind, Marx sought to render visible the disjunction between an industrial workers' revolt and a political revolution. The latter involves classes that are deprived of political influence and react against their isolation from the state and from power. It involves a form of isolation that is only partial, that of the 'citizen'. The other involves isolation from life – and not only that. Political revolution expresses the 'political soul of the revolution', and '[i]ts point of view is that of the state',[138] that is, its point of view is always a limited one: 'it regards the *will* as the cause of all evils and *force* and the *overthrow of a particular* form of the state as the universal remedy'.[139] From this point of view, pauperism results from the counterrevolutionary attitude of the proprietors; thus the National Convention beheaded the proprietors. Or, it results from the bad will of the poor; thus England punished the poor by locking them into workhouses, and Napoleon by locking them into *dépôts*.

Seen from the new perspective introduced by Marx, Germany's backwardness also acquired a new meaning. Germany did not necessarily have to undergo a political revolution in order to arrive at a social revolution. Leaps are possible. By virtue of its social revolutionary features, the Silesian revolt was an advanced, not a backward, expression of Europe's revolts.[140] Germany's anachronistic condition, characterised by political backwardness, but also by the presence of a factory-proletariat, gave rise to an unfortunate

---

138. Marx 1975e, p. 205.
139. Marx 1975e, p. 204.
140. Marx 1975e, p. 201.

disproportion between its various different levels of development. Thus the difficulty of bringing about a German political revolution did not justify denouncing the Silesian revolt as inconsistent; on the contrary, it was what rendered possible the leap forward to social revolution. Social revolution traverses every political revolution, in the sense that it dissolves not just the old powers, but also the old society.[141] Not only is there no diachronic relationship between the two revolutions, but anachronism can actually be used as a springboard from which to leap.

The imagery of atomism having been discarded, a new imagery was produced, one capable of setting the social revolution in motion once more. To do this, the past had to be cleared away in such a manner as to create a new tradition: 'The Lyon workers believed that they were pursuing only political aims, that they were only soldiers of the republic, whereas actually they were soldiers of socialism'.[142] Striving to arm present struggles with a tradition of class struggles for socialism, Marx employed the various historical temporalities of the revolution within the revolution. Social revolution traverses political revolution; it emerges from the cracks opened up by class-dynamics that cannot but remain mysterious to those who consider only the relationship between the individual and the political community. For Marx, the revolt of the Silesian weavers was more than merely a stimulus for theoretical reflection; it exercised a practical influence on his approach to politics. The Silesian revolt contained a practical anticipation of theory. It was an event demanding reflection. Working through this event, theory was constrained to reorganise its conceptual tools.

Re-reading the Terror

A new reading of the revolutionary period of 1792–3 becomes possible once the Revolution's multiple temporalities are probed. This involves abandoning the notion of a single historical process and the point of view of those who, stumbling upon the Terror, interpreted it in Hegelian terms, as 'absolute freedom' *qua* 'fury of destruction'. Marx was fascinated by this model: it allowed one to trace the Terror, understood as a hypostasis of the political, back to the '*classical* period of political intellect',[143] that is, to the notion of 'omnipotence of the will', which is political to the extent that it remains within the bounds of politics and abstracts from the concrete organisation of society. From this abstract point of view, pauperism was attributed either to

---

141. Marx 1975e, p. 205 ff.
142. Marx 1975e, p. 204.
143. Marx 1975e, p. 199; translation modified.

the bad will of the poor, or to the unchristian feelings of the rich, or to the counterrevolutionary attitudes of the proprietors. As the diagnosis varied, so did the remedy: the English government punished the poor, the Prussian government exhorted the rich and the National Convention beheaded the proprietors.[144] But Marx's reflection was already more advanced than this historiographical model. Within one year, he had turned it on its head. In conceptualising the Terror, he started from the social tensions that traversed it. He thought of it as that which escaped the bourgeoisie: an expression of the 'the class which *alone* was truly revolutionary, the 'innumerable' masses'.[145] *Pace* Stirner, who invoked the Hegelian model of 'absolute freedom', the Terror did not express the rule of an idea ('clericalism', in Stirner's terminology). Marx's reply to Stirner was that, 'with this sort of conception of history, "all cats become grey", since all historical differences are "abolished" and "resolved" in the "notion of clericalism"'.[146] The Terror could not be explained by reference to the rule of an abstraction. If heads were cut off, then this was done on the basis of 'extremely worldly interests, though not, of course, of the stockjobbers, but of the "innumerable" masses'.[147] The Revolution met with revolutionary insurgencies: not only would it not have been possible without the support of the innumerable masses, who were neither inert nor passive, but that support entered into conflict with other revolutionary interests. The Terror and the guillotine were the expression not of a particular class, but of a conflict between different revolutionary interests. Robespierre's dictatorship was not the rule of an abstraction, but the expression of 'the class which *alone* was truly revolutionary'.[148] The Terror was not the symptom of a bourgeois revolution run amok, nor the epiphenomenon of an abstract universal freedom: its terrorist violence was the expression of a revolution within the Revolution, of the 'innumerable masses' acting to shape the course of the Revolution. It was not a question of defining to which class the Girondists and the Montagnards belonged, nor even what interests they represented. It was necessary, rather, to look at the 'driving forces behind the driving forces', that is, at that which pushed certain endeavours in certain directions.

Within the revolutionary trajectory that began in 1789, one finds a revolutionary insurgency. It expressed elements of emancipation that refused to be confined within the historical temporality of the 'bourgeois' Revolution, but which were open to new temporalities. From this point of view, the

---

144. Marx 1975e, p. 197 ff.
145. Marx and Engels 1975, p. 178.
146. Marx and Engels 1975, p. 177 ff.
147. Marx and Engels 1975, p. 178.
148. Ibid.

period between 1792 and 1793 marks neither the beginning nor the end of the Revolution. It was Engels, in London, who grasped the importance of this tradition. At the Festival of Nations, held in 1845, Engels gained an impression of the mood of the Chartist workers' movement, which was celebrating the establishment of the French Republic on 22 September 1792. Engels saw French communism and English Chartism as the heirs of the struggle for democracy that began with the French Revolution. The Chartists reconstructed the pieces of the working-class tradition, and Engels pushed forward with theoretical reflection, demonstrating that the revolution goes beyond the struggle for a particular form of state.[149] And not only that: if the Chartists latched onto a revolutionary tradition whose roots went back to 1792, then all Engels needed to do was to rewrite the history of that historical moment from the specific point of view of the Chartists: the 1793 constitution and the Terror should be interpreted as expressions of the party that supported the insurgent proletariat, and the fall of Robespierre as the victory of the bourgeoisie over the proletariat.[150] 'There can be no true reform as long as sovereignty does not wholly belong to the nation; there is no national sovereignty as long as the principles of the constitution of 1793 are not a reality'.[151] Engels hailed a democratic-communist tradition whose essential moments of passage were the 1793 insurgency and the adoption of the French constitution of that year, which was never applied.

The Chartist re-evaluation of the Terror imposed a clear-cut alternative: one could either continue working from the pages of Hegel's *Phenomenology* and the post-Hegelian tradition, considering the Terror as the product of a hypostasis of the political intellect, or strike a new path and begin formulating an apology of what occurred in 1793. Marx chose the third option, that of critically re-reading the Terror from the point of view of the working class. It was necessary to find new teachers. Having drunk from the springs of liberal and conservative historiography, Marx and Engels began taking lessons from the English Chartist George Julian Harney. Engels listened to his speech at the Festival of Nations and patiently transcribed it. The French Revolution revealed its true social nature to the extent that the English labour-movement appropriated it as a part of its own history – an appropriation that was undertaken not at the desk, or through theory, but in the labour-movement's everyday political work.

Marx was quick to learn how to combine two historiographical registers: communist criticism of the Revolution's limits, which he had learned to

---

149. Engels 1976a.
150. Ibid.
151. Engels 1976b, p. 363.

formulate from Babeuf, Buonarroti, and Hess, was meshed with the class-analysis of the historians of the Restoration period, such as Guizot, Thiers, Thierry, and Mignet.[152] Unmasking the concept of the people as a fiction elevated to the rank of the modern state's sovereign-subject is a move that Marx's criticism shares with aristocratic and counterrevolutionary criticism. The Revolution, which bore within it both the third estate's struggle against the privileged orders and the plebeian struggle against the bourgeoisie, could not be read as a process governed by a single political temporality. Nor could the period of the Terror be reduced to a mere totalisation of the political *vis-à-vis* the social. In the December 1848 issue of the *Neue Rheinische Zeitung*, with the Revolution behind him, Marx reinterpreted the French revolutionary period of 1793–4 as expressing a struggle between non-bourgeois social strata, a struggle for the interests of the bourgeoisie conducted in a non-bourgeois manner: '*All French terrorism* was nothing but a *plebeian way* of dealing with the *enemies of the bourgeoisie*, absolutism, feudalism and philistinism'.[153] This struggle assumed a 'plebeian' character because the proletariat had not yet constituted itself as an autonomous class with distinct interests opposed to those of the bourgeoisie. The 'mighty hammer blows' of the Terror expressed the 'bloody action of the people', by which the ruins of feudalism were spirited away, a task 'the timidly considerate bourgeoisie would not have accomplished... in decades'.[154] There emerged a revolution within the 'bourgeois revolution'. It assumed the tasks of the bourgeois revolution, and accomplished them with greater resoluteness, but it also began to enter into conflict with the bourgeoisie. 'The first manifestation of a truly active communist party is contained within the bourgeois revolution, at the moment when the constitutional monarchy is eliminated'.[155] The most consistent republicans – the English Levellers, Babeuf, and Buonarroti – were the first to raise the social question. The social question was, however, not simply their brainchild; it was discovered by them in the revolutionary-social movement that interacted with the bourgeois revolution. Here was a new 'insight',[156] by means of which these consistent republicans were led to the praxis of revolution: 'the disposal of the social question of *rule by princes* and *republic* did not mean that even a single "social question" has been solved in the interests of the proletariat'.[157] This is Marx's

---

152. See Löwy 1989, p. 234. See also Hobsbawm 1990.
153. Marx 1977a, p. 161.
154. Marx 1976a, p. 319.
155. Marx 1976a, p. 321.
156. Ibid. translation modified.
157. Marx 1976a, p. 322.

insight; he drew attention to a communist tradition that had been at work within the bourgeois revolutions, and which conflicted with them.

The Terror was not the expression of a proletariat organised as a class – for such a proletariat did not yet exist – but rather of radical tendencies among certain strata of the population, tendencies that conflicted both with the aristocracy and with the bourgeoisie. The Terror was the result of this conflict. For Marx, neither the French Revolution nor the Terror represented a model for the proletarian revolution. The Terror was a revolutionary temporality *within* the bourgeois revolution: its anti-bourgeois features guaranteed the bourgeoisie's social and political triumph.[158] Marx reasoned according to a plural semantics of history. The problem that he examined was not so much whether the French Revolution constituted a rupture or not,[159] but rather, that of identifying the revolution within the Revolution, a discontinuity *vis-à-vis* the historical process by which the modern state waxes in strength. Marx posed the question clearly in the *Eighteenth Brumaire*: on the one hand, there is the centralisation of modern political power, begun by absolute monarchy and continued by the Revolution – the construction of the state-machine,[160] which the revolutions of the past have not broken but perfected; on the other hand, there is the revolution capable of interrupting this history.*

---

158. Löwy 1989, p. 241.

159. According to Kouvelakis, Marx, in writing on the Paris Commune, rehabilitated the Revolution as a moment of rupture and abandoned the model that he had developed in the *Eighteenth Brumaire*, which was derived from Tocqueville. I do not fully agree with Kouvelakis's claim that these reflections involved Marx further developing the analyses of power that he had conducted in Kreuznach. See Kouvelakis 2003 and Kouvelakis 2007.

160. Marx 1979a, p. 186.

* Translated by Max Henninger.

Appendix

Political Historiography.
Re-Reading the *Eighteenth Brumaire*

Freeing history from history

'Hegel remarks somewhere that all the great events and characters of world history occur, so to speak, twice. He forgot to add: the first time as tragedy, second as farce'.[1] This is the famous opening to the *Eighteenth Brumaire of Louis Bonaparte*. The passage was suggested by Engels, in a letter dated 3 December 1851, when Marx was preparing to write his text. Engels wrote:

> It really seems as if old Hegel in his grave were acting as World Spirit and directing history, ordaining most conscientiously that it should all be unrolled twice over, once as a great tragedy and once as a wretched farce, with Caussidiere for Danton, Louis Blanc for Robespierre, Barthélemy for St. Just, Flocon for Carnot and that mooncalf with the first dozen debt-encumbered lieutenants picked at random for the Little Corporal and his Round Table of marshals. And so we have already arrived at the Eighteenth Brumaire.[2]

1. Marx 1960a, p. 115; Marx 1979a, p. 103.
2. Engels 1982c, p. 505.

The iteration, the repetition of the Hegelian form of repetition [*Wiederholung*] produces a difference.[3] Repetition is redefined in the shift of the formula *Tragödie-Farce*.[4] This also applies to the 'Hegel' mentioned in the *incipit* of what Marx wrote: the quotation is in a form that deprives it of authority. Not only is Hegel's remark taken from some indeterminate place – 'somewhere' – that is apparently not important enough to acknowledge, but Hegel even forgets to add the most important thing: the *Tragödie-Farce* model, which Marx takes from Heine. The form of repetition redefines the very form of Hegel's quote itself: the formula of *repetition* of the story renders 'Hegel' a *farce* himself; not because history, due to some mysterious law, is supposed to repeat itself in the form of farce, but because *there is no repetition*.[5]

There is a tone in Engels's letter that later also pervaded Marx's writings: the comedy in which 'it really seems as if old Hegel in his grave were acting as World Spirit and directing history'. It is certainly not Hegel, but, rather, the Hegelian tradition, that works from the realm of the dead; it does not work directly on history, but on historiography, and thus on history itself. In the 1850s, the image of historical parallels was spreading, and not only between 2 December 1851 and 9 November 1799, the real eighteenth Brumaire.[6] Democracy and dictatorship under Napoleon III are shown to be two sides of the same coin. The defenders of Napoleon were quite right, according to Bauer: Empire and popular sovereignty are 'two great, mutually related, things'.[7] It was Proudhon, instead, who was wrong in thinking that the historical alternative was to be played out between anarchy and Caesarism.[8] 'Empire' and 'Caesarism' are the keywords of the rhetorical arsenal of the historical parallel against which Marx argues. In the 'Preface' to the 1869 second edition of the *Eighteenth Brumaire*, Marx attacks the neologism 'Caesarism',[9] inasmuch as the latter is the bearer of superficial historical analogies, which, instead of

---

3. Hegel writes that, 'By repetition, that which at first appeared merely a matter of chance and contingency, becomes a real and ratified existence.' Hegel 1971, p. 403; Hegel 1991, p. 313.

4. On the aspect of repetition as a symptom of the incapacity to take hold of the present and, at the same time, as a modality of reappropriation of the present, see Barot 2007, pp. 82–4; Fietkau 1978, pp. 138 et sq.

5. On the structure of repetition in the *Eighteenth Brumaire*, see Riquelme 1980. Repetition produces an excess, a heterogeneous element: Mehlman 1977, p. 14.

6. See Marx 1985d, p. 679.

7. B. Bauer 1972c, p. 80.

8. Proudhon 1852; see B. Bauer 1972c, pp. 79–80.

9. The term was born in July 1850, the year of publication of Auguste Romieu's work *L'Ère des Cèsars*. See also, for bibliographical references regarding this term, Cassina 2001, pp. 18, 41 n. 4.

explaining an event, tend to obscure the specific differences between different forms of class-struggle.

In the same 'Preface', Marx cited Victor Hugo and Proudhon, synecdoches for examples of radically polarised historiographical positions. Victor Hugo, in the act of writing his *Napoléon le petit,* saw nothing but the personal violence of Louis Napoleon, therefore magnifying that figure instead of minimising him; on the other side, Proudhon, in his *Coup d'état,* made the symmetrically opposite error, that is, the error of objective historiography that represents Napoleon III's Empire merely as the outcome of previous historical developments.[10] Hugo thought in terms of historical personality, but Proudhon only saw the historical development of circumstances that eventually led Louis Napoleon to power. The same historiographical models are at work in many accounts of Hitler and Nazism, so much so that one could put together fine analyses of the present based upon the historiographical model dominant at this or that point in time. For the historical materialist, both positions are false. It is, instead, a question of showing how the *history*[I] of the class-struggle interacted with the *history*[II] of French politics from February 1848 onwards, preparing the conditions that allowed 'a mediocre and grotesque character to become the hero'.[11] Napoleon III was not an innovator, but the radically new situation made him appear as such.

In writing the *Eighteenth Brumaire*, Marx chose the genre of apology as a genre of refusal and an altered point of view, providing a vision that is free of resignation, but is, instead, tragicomic: Cromwell had dissolved Parliament while holding a watch in his hand; Napoleon had read a death-sentence to the National Assembly; Louis Napoleon proceeded with theft, lies and public expressions of charlatanism.[12] Napoleon Bonaparte was followed by the grotesque and mediocre figure of Napoleon III. Repetition is a rhetorical device in which the representation employed is the representation of farce. The novelty comes from the new configuration of class-struggle, ever since the red flags on the barricades of Lyon signalled the end of the dream of any national homogeneity.

Marx's historiographical and political intention was to represent as a farce the history of the aftermath of the Revolution of 1848, so as to liquidate 'any faith in the superstitious past', and to get rid of that 'tradition of all the dead generations' that 'weighs like a nightmare [*Alp*] on the brain of the living'.[13] History can be freed from history only if tradition ceases to oppress the

---

10. Marx 1960a, p. 559; Marx 1985e, p. 57.
11. Marx 1960a, p. 560; Marx 1985e, p. 57; translation modified.
12. Ibid.
13. Marx 1960a, pp. 191–2; Marx 1979a, p. 103.

living, only if the ghosts of the past are cleared away. The *Alp*, the *incubus* that weighs on the brains of the living, is, in the Germanic tradition, also a vampire who enters houses disguised as a butterfly in order to rest on the chest of the sleeper. It is a ghostly presence, because it was spectres that filled the post-revolutionary imaginary, and, specifically, haunted the dictatorship of Napoleon III. The vampire has a political dimension that is typically modern: it represents the past that does not want to die; that which torments the living or is even resuscitated in mythical form in the reactionary politics of nationalism and fascism.[14] To liberate the living from the rule of the dead, and thereby liberate the true potentialities of the present moment, Marx, recalling the passage from the *Gospels*, writes that we must let 'the dead bury their dead'.[15] The writing of history puts on stage 'a population of the dead' acting out a burial-rite.[16] This has a symbolic function: making a place for the dead allows a society to give itself a past in language, thus redistributing 'the space of possibility'.[17] Burying the past defines that which will not be done again, thereby opening a present for that which is yet to be done. What Marx's text eminently demonstrates is the performative character of this historical text. 'Language allows a practice to be situatated in respect to its *other*, the past'.[18]

After the defeat of the revolutionary proletariat, the social imaginary is thus occupied by the spectre of revolution.[19] The 'red spectre [*rotes Gespenst*]' evoked by Vaissé is the bugbear of the counterrevolutionaries.[20] It takes the place of the true revolution and manifests itself not with the 'Phrygian cap of anarchy on the head, but in the uniform of order, in a *soldier in red pants*'.[21] The spectre, the *Gespenst*, is the image that the victors give to communism. This point also holds for the opening of the *Manifesto*. The Marxian approach seeks to overturn these images. If all 'of the powers of Old Europe have entered into a Holy Alliance to exorcise the spectre: Pope and Czar, Metternich and Guizot, French Radicals and German Police-Spies',[22] this means that the 'powers of Old Europe' are really afraid of the spectre. The oppressors fear the oppressed. The image is thus overturned: 'Communism is already acknowledged by all European Powers to be itself a Power'.[23]

---

14. See Neocleus 2005.
15. Marx 1960a, p. 117; Marx 1979a, p. 106.
16. De Certeau 1988, pp. 99–100.
17. De Certeau 1988, p. 100.
18. De Certeau 1988, p. 101.
19. Marx 1960a, p. 117; Marx 1979a, p. 106.
20. Marx 1960a, p.174; Marx 1979a, p. 162.
21. Marx 1960a, p. 136; Marx 1979a, p. 125; translation modified.
22. Marx and Engels 1959, p. 461; Marx and Engels 1976, p. 481.
23. Ibid.

Only by escaping the sense of weakness and the air of defeat is it possible to take up the battle anew. This is the case in both the *Manifesto* and the *Eighteenth Brumaire*. The classes that have defeated the proletariat have, for a long time, occupied the imaginary of spectres, and the void left by the revolutionary subject has been filled with fear. It is fear that acts as a binding agent for different classes to unite against a sinister and elusive enemy; fear also that occupies the imaginary of the proletariat, by crushing it under its own defeat and tying it to the world of the dead. The problem is, then, to write this history so as to free history from a tradition and an imaginary: what Marx seeks to evoke is the spirit [*Geist*] of the revolution, not its ghost [*Gespenst*].[24]

'Men make their own history, but they do not make it just as they please; they do not make it under circumstances chosen by themselves, but under circumstances directly found, given and transmitted from the past'.[25] For the historical materialist, circumstances are not inert elements of action, as the water is to the swimmer. The latter only has to know the currents in order to be able to use them to his own advantage. However, just as the pirate must know the lore of the seas in order to choose the best time to launch an attack, the historical materialist must know the burden of tradition that weighs down the symbolic horizon of circumstances. The imaginary of politics must deal with what it inherits from tradition. The entire superstructure of illusions and ways of thinking, expressed by certain social conditions of existence, reaches the individual through 'tradition and upbringing',[26] and contributes to the construction of that very imaginary that he or she believes to be the starting point and destination of his or her action. This is why the symbolic register of tradition must be taken in hand and its signal changed.

The tragicomic model is functional to the new revolutionary historiography: it is not a descriptive model, but a performative one.[27] This Marxist historiography matures along with its commitment to political struggle. We find it for the first time and in an embryonic form in the *Critique of Hegel's Philosophy of Right*, written between December 1843 and January 1844, and published in the *Deutsch-Französische Jahrbücher* in February 1844. Here, the German system is called an 'anachronism', a modern *ancien régime* which is nothing but the comic figure of a world-order whose real heroes are dead: 'The last stage of a world-historical form is its *comedy*'.[28] The representation of

24. Marx 1960a, p. 116; Marx 1979a, p. 105.
25. Marx 1960a, p.115; Marx 1979a, p. 103.
26. Marx 1960a, p. 139; Marx 1979a, p. 128.
27. The following works are insistent on the performative aspect of this Marxian writing: Petry 1988; Carver 2002; Martin 2002; Jessop 2002, which defines Marxian prose as 'performative at several levels'.
28. Marx 1956b, p. 382; Marx 1975c, p. 179.

the German system as an *ancien régime* of clowns is made in order happily to take leave from a past.[29] The shape, the style of this political history[30] by Marx only makes sense if it was meant to be addressed not to an abstract, neutral and disinterested reader, but to a concrete reader with political and economic interests. Marx learnt at the school of workers' struggles a new way to read the various historical temporalities found in revolutions.

Breaking with bourgeois historiography does not simply involve telling another story, but breaking with the form of its representation. If the media-era has allowed us to believe, for a moment, that a literary production aimed at a disinterested audience is possible, Marx repoliticises this sphere,[31] marking its partiality, and turning to a precisely determined interlocutor: the working class in struggle. The point of view from which Marx writes history is openly particularist. Nothing is more ideological than claiming to write independently from every particular point of view and for a universal audience, which only exists in the cunning rhetoric of the self-styled disinterested or objective historian. Every historicism is also a rhetoric, although not in the sense suggested by Hayden White. For the materialist, the past is never reducible to mere speech: it is not a question of representing the past 'in a convincing narrative'.[32] There is an opposition between the essence of fascist historiography that rewrites the past in its own image and likeness, and the materialist historiography that rewrites the past in order to release the revolutionary possibilities for the present. Past revolutionary opportunities, which have, thus far, been negated by the victorious classes, are revitalised in the struggles of the present. Revenge is not a secondary political category. The materialist historian is not looking for an objective description. He knows not only that traditions are always constructions, but also that the facts themselves are interpretations. The materialist historian highlights the subjective of the object, the constitutional force of a class-practice within a historical phenomenon. His history is partisan and takes the side of one of

---

29. Ibid.

30. On the changes in form, style and interpretive models between the writings on the *Class Struggles in France*, and the *Eighteenth Brumaire*, see Moss 1985, pp. 555 et sq.

31. Peter Osborne writes: 'If Dadaism was an attempt to match the effects of film within the (technically obsolete) medium of painting, so the *Manifesto* may be understood as an attempt to invent a literary form of political communication appropriate to a period of mass politics on an international scale': Osborne 1998, p. 198.

32. White 1973, p. 320. According to White, Marx utilises 'two fundamentally linguistic protocols, metonymical on the one hand and synecdochic on the other' (p. 310). Adamson discusses the writings of White, integrating these with his own interpretation of the co-presence of four historical registers in Marx: 'anthropological', 'pragmatological', 'historiographic' and 'nomological': Adamson 1981, pp. 400–1.

the subjects of the struggle. He does not just sympathise with the latter, but reads history itself from that point of view. He takes part in that conflict by politicising historiography. This is not meant to be an objective history, nor does it represent history as such: instead, it shows how things went for the oppressed, and how they tried over and over to redeem themselves. He wants to build a tradition from past attempts at liberation that is able to join in a fight in the present.[33]

Marx's historiographical interventions serve to force solutions beyond the immediate political and economic possibilities of the moment. From this per- spective, we can discern the difference between the writings on 1848 in the *Neue Rheinische Zeitung* and the *Eighteenth Brumaire*.[34] The *Neue Rheinische Zeitung* was still an organ of democracy. Its pages revealed the incapacity of the French proletariat to make its own revolution. Marx pushed for a full affirmation of bourgeois rule, able to break up the material roots of feudal society; he tactically joined the proletarian struggle up with the success of a full bourgeois revolution. In the course of the Revolution, Marx observed that the alliance with liberal democrats was impossible. The German and French events followed parallel courses, and each of these two cases saw the bourgeoisie retreat in the face of reaction, abandoning and attacking the proletariat which had fought side-by-side with it. After a year of experience with the democratic struggle, Marx and Engels declared themselves for a dis- tinct organisation of the proletariat. Thus, in September 1848, confronting the constitutional hesitations of the liberal minister Ludolf Camphausen, Marx invoked an 'energetic dictatorship' able to defend the bourgeois Revolution from the counterrevolutionary clique constituted by the aristocracy, military and bureaucracy;[35] and, in January 1850, he called for the overthrow of the bourgeoisie and the 'dictatorship of the working class!'[36] In March 1850, in the *Address of the Central Committee to the Communist League*, Marx and Engels summarised the results of the revolutionary years 1848–9. Reconsidering the advantages obtained by the democratic party and by the workers' party, they advanced the watchword 'independence of the workers'.[37] Not only were the interests of the workers' party no longer to be subordinated to those of the democratic party, unless instrumentally so against common enemies, but two different revolutionary perspectives presented themselves: the interest of the

---

33. On the possibility of 'revolutionary inventions of traditions', see also Callinicos 2004, p. 242.
34. See Moss 1985, pp. 555–7.
35. Marx 1959d, p. 402; Marx 1977c, p. 431.
36. Marx 1960b, p. 33; Marx 1979b, p. 69.
37. Marx and Engels 1960a, p. 244; Marx and Engels 1978a, p. 277.

bourgeoisie was to bring the Revolution hurriedly to a close; the interest of the workers' party was to make it 'permanent',[38] leading to the conquest of state-power and its expansion to other countries. Marx reiterated with emphasis the proletariat's need to create itself an 'autonomous organisation', in an *Arbeiterpartei*. He did so again in the *Address* of June 1850.[39] He continued to refer to this party as if it already existed. 'It is as if he wanted to create reality by use of the word', writes Attali.[40] However, to realise this performative party, he needed to dissipate the air of defeat that enveloped the proletariat following the revolutions of 1848. He needed to produce a new image able to uproot the spectral scenario of the counterrevolution. It was in this spirit, and with his son on his knee, that Marx wrote the *Eighteenth Brumaire*.

The *tragedy-farce* model has no heuristic goal, but only a practical one: it corresponds to an analysis of reality that can open new possibilities for change, the only analysis that the historical materialist can consider scientific. Representing the past as a farce aims to destroy one of its registers, so that the revolutionary act of creation of the not-yet-existing will not end up duplicating the old tradition by borrowing from the traditional watchwords and costumes.[41] Nonetheless, reviving a tradition does not necessarily mean reproducing the old. Tradition is not always, nor solely, a weight and a block: it can also serve to glorify the new struggles, to push them forward, to exalt the new tasks; tradition can also be a revolutionary trigger. The parody of the past can be a brake on action, but it can also be an impulse capable of dissolving the shackles of another tradition. The parody of the Empire by Napoleon III did not block its action, but functioned as a powerful chemical reagent.

When the heroes, parties and masses of the French Revolution established – 'in Roman costume and with Roman slogans' – modern civil society, the revival of tradition was not a brake on the Revolution, but rather a stimulus for new struggles. The gladiators of the Revolution 'found in the stern classical traditions of the Roman republic the ideals, art forms, and self-deceptions they needed in order to hide from themselves the limited bourgeois content of their struggles and to maintain their enthusiasm at the high level appropriate to great historical tragedy'.[42] In a similar way, Cromwell and the English revolutionaries borrowed from the Old Testament words, passions and illusions for their bourgeois revolution. In both cases, the resurrection of the dead

---

38. Marx and Engels 1960a, p. 254; Marx and Engels 1978a, p. 287: 'Their battle cry must be: The Revolution in Permanence'.
39. Marx and Engels 1960b, pp. 306–12; Marx and Engels 1978b, pp. 371–7.
40. Attali 2005, p. 114.
41. Marx 1960a, p. 115; Marx 1979a, p. 104.
42. Marx 1960a, p. 116; Marx 1979a; translation modified.

was not a block; it did not serve as a parody of the old fights, but exalted the new one, by putting back into movement the true spirit of the revolution. This contrasts with the historical situation in which Marx wrote, because now the tasks of the revolutionary proletariat are different. The politicised historiography of Marx is a historiography of the revolutionary crisis: Marx writes history so that men cease to evoke the spirits of the past and enlist them in their service,[43] as happened when the revolutionaries of 1848 parodied the 'revolutionary tradition' of 1793–5.[44]

The proletarian revolution needs a different symbolic horizon from that of the bourgeois revolutions. The historical materialist cannot make such an horizon, but he can work for the destruction of a tradition that is a barrier to it, in order to reconnect today's struggle to its true tradition, the one that the historiography of the victorious classes will do anything to forget. Whoever participates in this, writing hymns to the obliteration of memory while thinking that such a loss of memory can itself have revolutionary potential, becomes a participant in the construction of the dominant imaginary that, through the erasure of that tradition, pushes the working class offstage. The current erasure of memory, like its institutional museumification, is, likewise, part of the postmodern saga of its mystification, which is not only a direct and unprejudiced falsification of history, but also the production of an imaginary in which the various narrations are of equivalent value, and thus indifferent. An archive of working-class memory must not throw that history into a museum, but, instead, evoke the past tradition in order to call for revenge. Tradition, the notion that traditionalists used as a political weapon in the crisis of the tradition and society of the *ancien régime*, should be used to reconnect the struggles of the past to those of the present, to load the past with a revolutionary charge whose fuse is to be triggered in the instant of a struggle today.[45] It is the struggles of past generations that must be remembered, because they are still asking to be freed from the tyranny of the past – and of the present. If the concept of tradition is a weapon to oppose to the Revolution for traditionalists, continuity's distinctive feature,[46] in Marx the working-class tradition triggers a break with the tradition of the ruling classes.

The great innovation of Marx's *Eighteenth Brumaire* is the duplication of historiographical registers. Instead of relegating the tradition into the past,

---

43. Marx 1960a, p. 115; Marx 1979a, p. 104.
44. Ibid.
45. In contrast, Assoun, denouncing the conservative and anti-Enlightenment character of the idea of tradition, argues that its use on Marx's part constitutes a movement beyond materialism: Assoun 1978, pp. 119–21.
46. On the concept of tradition as *'Merkmale der Kontinuität'* for the counterrevolutionaries Bonald and Adam Müller, see Wiedenhofer 2004, pp. 638–9.

he grasps its specific temporality as the past-present. The focus on this past, which is present in the present as tradition, is an advance in comparison to his thought in 1845.[47] Marx now explored the different temporalities of the present praxis, since the past-present – namely tradition – is a weapon to be salvaged from the grip of the traditionalists. For them, tradition is a mode of historical continuity and the search for social cohesion; for Marx, it becomes the energy of discontinuity and rupture. Traditionalists build the past in order to impose it and legitimise it in terms of continuity; the historical materialist is working with tradition in order to show the fault-lines throughout history and thus to pose the problem of the true revolutionary discontinuities that can rupture the story of exploitation. Marx is concerned, here, with the interplay of tradition with the praxis of the present, including its ambivalences.

> Historical tradition produced the French peasants' belief in the miracle that...a man named Napoleon would restore all their glory. And an individual turned up who pretended to be that man, because he bore the name of Napoleon....After twenty years of vagabondage and a series of grotesque adventures the prophecy was fulfilled and the man became Emperor of the French.[48]

Tradition interacts with the present circumstances. If an 'everyman' can become Emperor of the French, it is because his praxis intersects with a tradition present in the most numerous class of the French population: the peasants. This tradition ensures continuity even at the cost of discontinuity. Tradition can, in fact, contribute to the production of discontinuity: 'the parody of imperialism' served to liberate the French nation from the burden of one 'tradition' and to bring out 'the antagonism between the state-power and society in its pure form'.[49] The new 'state-centralisation', fuelled by reference to the imperial tradition, could succeed only through a discontinuity with the most recent republican tradition. This intersection of continuity and discontinuity, in the twentieth century, has allowed the birth of the legends of a revolutionary Mussolini and of a left-wing National Socialism. But neither Italian Fascism nor German Nazism constituted any actual break with the mechanism of the modern state. Rather, they produced its modernisation. It is crucial to determine the position of the bourgeoisie in the face of the crisis.

---

47. Similar, though coming to an opposed conclusion, is Assoun 1978, pp. 130–1. The scheme of the *Eighteenth Brumaire* is no longer that of the 'world-praxis' of the *German Ideology*, in which the dominant ideas are those of the dominant classes; instead, in *The Eighteenth Brumaire*, the relationship between a symbolic horizon lived ideologically and its social status is developed: see Assoun p. 128.
48. Marx 1960a, p. 199; Marx 1979a, p. 188.
49. Marx 1960a, p. 203; Marx 1979a, p. 193.

The crisis between the two World-Wars, together with the workers' struggle and the Red Terror, forced the bourgeoisie to accept the planned economy, thereby intensifying its internal contradictions. The crisis today forces the bourgeoisie to renounce the rule of law, and to suspend certain constitutional guarantees. The bourgeoisie even becomes critical of democracy, but in a different sense than the oppressed classes are. Social democracy, by contrast, sees its task as that of *preserving* the rule of law.

The parody of the present is the means that Marx uses to rescue it from those spectral presences that belong to the nightmare [*Alp*] that sucks away its energy like a vampire. The parody of every single character is built around the formula *Tragödie-Farce*: Marrast is the 'Republican in yellow gloves' disguised 'with the mask of the old Bailly'; Louis Napoleon is 'the adventurer who is now hiding his commonplace and repulsive countenance beneath the iron death mask of Napoleon'.[50] The image of the parallel is used in a double register that deconstructs their meaning, turning it into farce. If the uncle 'recalled the campaigns of Alexander in Asia, the nephew recalled the conquests of Bacchus' in the same lands.[51] The different registers of memory – Alexander and Bacchus – redeploy figures of the two Napoleons: if Alexander was only a demigod, 'Bacchus was a god, in fact, he was the god of the Society of 10 December',[52] the protector of the private army of Bonaparte, which consisted of ten thousand beggars, 'roués of doubtful origin and uncertain means of subsistence', 'corrupt adventurers',

> vagabonds, discharged soldiers, discharged criminals, escaped galley slaves, swindlers, confidence tricksters, lazzaroni, pickpockets, sleight of hand experts, gamblers, macquereaux, brothel-keepers, porters, pen-pushers, organ-grinders, rag and bone vendors, knife-grinders, tinkers and beggars: in short, the whole indeterminate fragmented mass, tossed backwards and forwards, which the French call *la bohème*.[53]

The bohemian Emperor puffs with 'cigars and champagne, jelly chickens and garlic sausages', the 'higher powers which man, and the soldier in particular, cannot withstand'.[54] The curtain falls on the *Scènes de la vie de bohème*, Henry Murger recedes, and Napoleon III paves the way for the 'princely lumpenproletariat'.[55]

---

50. Marx 1960a, p. 116; Marx 1979a, p. 105.
51. Marx 1960a, p. 163; Marx 1979a, p. 151.
52. Ibid.
53. Marx 1960a, p. 161; Marx 1979a, p. 149.
54. Marx 1960a, p. 163; Marx 1979a, p. 151.
55. Marx 1960a, p. 169; Marx 1979a, p. 157.

In the grotesque repetition, however, there emerges a gap, a heterogeneous element: the underclass, which Napoleon III is able to draw to him. This spell, which is part of the arcane appeal of Louis Napoleon's power, is possible because the rule over the present happens in the name of what is past. Everything is full of ghosts, and a sorcerer [*Hexenmeister*], who is not even that, can cast his spell [*Bannformel*],[56] and make vanish like a phantasmagoria the sacred principles of democracy: *Liberté, Egalité, Fraternité*. These same principles, in the phantasmagoria of democracy, are transformed into 'Infantry, Cavalry, Artillery'.[57] The democrats have no defence against Napoleon's spells, as Napoleon is the democracy that laughs in the face of democracy.

Marx arranges this new representation with a theatrical lexicon. The script is displayed in the first paragraph of the *Eighteenth Brumaire*. 'The prologue of the revolution' covers the period from the fall of Louis Philippe to May 1848, and sees all the social forces rush on to the 'political stage'. The period from May 1848 to May 1849 is that of the foundation of the bourgeois Republic; the leaders of the proletarian party are removed from the 'public stage'. The climax is reached with the June Insurrection, 'the most colossal event in the history of European civil wars', after which the proletariat, left isolated by other social forces, is massacred and repressed. With this defeat, it withdraws to the 'background of the revolutionary stage'. Marx's lexicon of theatrical representation sought to intervene in the symbolic self-representation of the various classes after the proletariat's defeat in 1848. Marx did not intend to describe the human comedy of a dramatised history,[58] but, on the contrary, wanted to write a parody of the parody as to show the absurd normality of that history of simulacra. What allowed him to make history spectacular, portraying it in a theatrical manner, was removing of class-conflict from the historiography of the Second Empire. The viewpoint of class-struggle as an external perspective on this representation does not serve to distinguish between fictional and real, because it is, by now, obvious that the imaginary has more real implications than reality. Rather, this point of view allows an access to the imaginary and symbolic constructions, which are actual elements of the making of history.

The representation of representation

Phantasmagoria is the representation of a society without a body, without substance. In *Capital*, phantasmagoria characterises the specifically capitalist

---

56. Marx 1960a, p. 119; Marx 1979a; translation modified.
57. Marx 1960a, p. 148; Marx 1979a, p. 137.
58. See, conversely, Mehlman 1977, p. 13.

form of society. Phantasmagoria is also the Second Empire,[59] in which the Constitution, the National Assembly and law – in short, everything that the middle-class had held up as essential principles of modern democracy – disappear. The *Eighteenth Brumaire*, by describing in diabolic terms that Bonapartist ideology which re-launched the spectre of communism, works with different rhetorical registers in order to comprehend a social imaginary able to have concrete, real effects on social reality. The phantasmagoria of the Second Empire is not a solely bourgeois product; rather, it is the product of an anti-class struggle. It is part of that struggle. For this reason, the phantasmagoria is reflected onto the different social classes without ever belonging to one class alone. It re-projects the real social conflicts in distorted forms onto the different classes, producing anti-bourgeois effects alongside immediately anti-proletarian ones. This new form of phantasmagorical imagination reacts to the impact of the revolutionary fracture by domesticating it, just as when Robertson's phantasmagorias turned the image of the revolutionary nightmare into evening-entertainment.[60]

Phantasmagorias, spectres, vampires and the living dead became constituent elements of Marx's prose through the same gothic scenario: the deathlike scenario of capitalist modernity. It is a world of shadows without body. It is a Peter Schlemihl history turned upside down.[61] A story of shadows without body is also a history represented without the class-struggle. The phantasmagoria of the Second Empire constitutes the spectral imaginary of the class-struggle. The principles of the Revolution and of the Republic are sacrificed to the struggle against the class-struggle. 'The revolution paralyzes its own representatives and endows only its opponents with passion and forcefulness'.[62] This history is a history without events, where the passing of time is marked only by the mechanism of the clock-hand. Against this historical temporality of a history without class-struggle, Marx counterposes the other historiography of the class-struggles with their syncopated temporality.

For Marx, revolutionary events like the February Days are only real events to the degree that the workers play their role. The temporality and the substance of the Revolution are given by the syncopated time of the class-struggle, which traverses it like a revolution within the Revolution. If, in the *Manifesto*, Marx wrote an apology for the revolutionary bourgeoisie, tracing its history

---

59. Marx 1960a, p. 119; Marx 1979a, p. 108.
60. On the concept of *'phantasmagoria'*, see Castle 1988.
61. Marx 1960a, p. 136; Marx 1979a, p. 125: 'If any section of history has been painted grey on grey, it is this. Men and events appear as Schlemihls in reverse, as shadows which have become detached from their bodies'.
62. Marx 1960a, p. 163; Marx 1979a, p. 152.

in terms of a grandiose epic, in the *Eighteenth Brumaire* what he represents is
a macabre dance. The great bourgeois political forms – parliamentary democracy, universal suffrage, the universalism of rights – have lost, in a moment,
their presumed progressive character, and nothing remains of them but artificial fireworks. This critical practice had already been expressed on 15 May
by the Paris proletariat's revolt against the National Assembly that emerged
from the national elections, and which was, therefore, formally representative
of the entire nation. The Paris proletariat saw in it 'a living protest against the
aspirations of the February days',[63] and, for this reason, rebelled. The proletariat was advanced enough to put into question the very idea of national representation. Marx took up the theoretical content of this praxis and developed
it into a critique of the system of parliamentary representation.

Universal direct suffrage, proclaimed by the February Revolution, was
investigated in all its ambivalence. If, on the one hand, it was a revolutionary
conquest that broke up the electoral privileges of the July Monarchy, on the
other hand, it introduced a metaphysical relationship between the National
Assembly and the nation that elected it. Every deputy represents a seven-
hundred-and-fiftieth *anybody* of the nation, whose reality, as a political agent,
exists only by means of their representation. However, to be able to carry out
its own function, the parliamentary Republic must unceasingly produce and
reproduce, in the decisions of the majority of the National Assembly, the fiction of an undivided people. The majority acts in the name of the people, in
its totality, whose power is subordinated to the *Konstitution* itself.[64] Inasmuch
as it is an expression of the people, the decisions of the Assembly no longer
have any limitations on them, as had been the case under the monarchy. The
monarchical element is not, however, eliminated by the parliamentary form:
its removal does not correspond to its elimination. It reappears in the figure
of the President elected by direct suffrage by all the French. Here, the unity
of French nation is expressed in its maximum-concentration. The President
incarnates the national spirit, and, being President 'by the grace of the people', 'against the Assembly he possesses a sort of divine right'.[65] All that he
does is just, because he does it in the name of the people, of whose spirit he
is precisely the *incarnation*. The ascension of Napoleon III, including the *coup
d'état* of 2 December 1851, does not represent any breakdown of the state-
mechanism, but only brings to light the aporetic nature of the state. The state
of siege [*Belagerungszustand*], that invention periodically applied during crises
'which has found periodic application in every successive crisis in the course

63. Marx 1960a, p. 121; Marx 1979a, p. 109.
64. Marx 1960a, p. 146; Marx 1979a, p. 135.
65. Marx 1960a, p. 128; Marx 1979a, p. 117.

of the French Revolution',[66] becomes the rule, leading to the suspension of Parliament. Thus, democracy becomes a phantasmagoria.

In the battle against socialism and to 'save society' once and for all, without having to have repeated recourse to the state of siege, bourgeois society liberates itself from the trouble of governing itself. Marx expounds the point of view from which the historical materialist views the state: the state of exception as the rule. He is, at the same time, working with a double historiographical register: on the one hand, he is writing his own revolutionary historiography, throwing it back in the face of the bourgeoisie and its amazement when faced with Louis Napoleon's *coup d'état*; on the other hand, he digs with the tools of proletarian historiography to show the syncopated cadence of the revolution within the Revolution. The bourgeois Republic, which triumphed by its undoing of the proletariat, in its struggle against the proletariat, destroyed parliamentary power. Seeking to block the power of the President, instead they pave his way. 'Parliamentary cretinism, which holds its victims spellbound in an imaginary world and robs them of all sense, all memory, all understanding of the rough external world',[67] is the belief in defending parliamentarianism from the proletariat by destroying Parliament and reinforcing the executive. This same cretinism affects also those who, like Thiers in attempting to bring the President back within the restraints of the Constitution,[68] seek to oppose the destruction of Parliament with the rules of parliamentarianism and the Constitution. The outcome was not given, however: it would have sufficed, in fact, for the Assembly, instead of letting itself be intimidated 'by the executive power with likelihood of new disorders', and instead of ceding to the temptation of the state of emergency, to have left itself 'a little free space for the class struggle', so that the executive power would remain dependent on it. The collapse of the state could have been avoided by bringing the class-struggle into the constitutional dynamic. Because the Assembly 'didn't feel itself equal to the task of playing with fire',[69] the constitutional dynamic continued to oscillate between the state of exception and parliamentary cretinism. The decomposition of the party of order followed from the history without events.

The pompous catalogue of freedom to which the Revolution of 1848 had given birth was made inviolable by the Constitution and through its very ambiguity.

66. Marx 1960a, p. 130; Marx 1979a, p. 119.
67. Marx 1960a, p. 173; Marx 1979a, p. 161.
68. Marx 1960a, p. 190; Marx 1979a, p. 179.
69. Marx 1960a, p.174; Marx 1979a, p. 162.

> Each of these liberties is proclaimed to be the unconditional right of the French citizen, but there is always the marginal note that it is unlimited only in so far as it is not restricted by the 'equal rights of others and the public safety', or by 'laws', which are supposed to mediate precisely this harmony of the individual freedoms with each other and with public safety. For example, 'Citizens have the right to form associations, to assemble peaceably and without weapons, to petition, and to express their opinions through the press or in any other manner. *The enjoyment of these rights has no other restriction than the equal rights of others and the public safety*' [Chapter II of the French Constitution, Paragraph 8]. Or: 'Education is free. Freedom of education shall be *enjoyed* under the conditions fixed by law and the supreme control of the State' [Paragraph 9]. Or: 'The domicile of every citizen is inviolable, *except* in the forms laid down by law' [Chapter. II, Paragraph 3]. And so on. The Constitution therefore constantly refers to future *organic* laws which are to implement the above glosses and regulate the enjoyment of these unrestricted liberties in such a way that they do not come up against each other or against public safety.... Where the Constitution entirely forbade these liberties to the 'others' or allowed them to be enjoyed under the conditions which were simply traps set up by the police, this always happened solely in the interests of 'public safety', i.e. the safety of the bourgeoisie as laid down in the Constitution.... For each paragraph of the Constitution contains its own antithesis, its own upper and lower house, namely freedom in the general phrase, abolition of freedom in the marginal note.[70]

Marx shed light on the limits of the limits: reasons of public security can always limit or even suppress constitutional freedoms. Modern rights exist only because of this contradiction. To the extent that the individuals are holders of rights, to the same degree there exists a coercive power capable of guaranteeing them; that same power, because of a real or imagined threat to public security, can suspend these same rights that it is supposed to protect and that should, at the same time, limit it from committing possible abuses. It is the Constitution itself that is self-contradictory. It must assume the possibility of its own 'violent suppression'.[71] The state-power creates and preserves rights only to the extent that it can suspend them, and this suspension, evoked for reasons of public order and public security, is always justifiable. Having shown the limits of the limits, Marx demonstrates that the true limit is the Constitution itself. The Bonapartist dictatorship does not signal any real exception with respect to the juridical course of the state, but is substantially

---

70. Marx 1960a, p. 126; Marx 1979a, p. 115.
71. Marx 1960a , p. 127; Marx 1979a, p. 116.

tied into the continuum of a state of exception that is the rule. The *coup d'état* of Napoleon III was not a bolt of lightning in a serene sky.

The Constitution is the limit to the new possibilities opened up in a constitutional crisis. With respect to this crisis, Bonapartism 1) can be accepted with pessimistic resignation; 2) can be combated by a defence of legality or 3) can be welcomed with enthusiasm. Marx posits a fourth option: that which is not included in this list of options. Marx captures the ambivalent nature of the crisis, seeing in it not only the birth of the Bonapartist dictatorship, but also the possibility of resuming the class-struggle of the proletariat. Beyond the historical solution, it is the Marxian act that remains of interest: upstanding amidst the crisis and its possibilities of liberation.

Marx was equally distant from the history of ideas that, tracing a certain continuity with the preceding illiberal tradition, exaggerated the exceptional character of the events in which Louis Napoleon Bonaparte was involved; from the historiography *à la* Tocqueville that, working with a process-oriented philosophy of history, inscribed the Bonapartist project within the processes of politico-administrative standardisation and of centralisation; and from that doctrinaire historiography which would later confer on itself *post-mortem* the title of 'historical materialism'. For Marx, there was no automatic relationship between the economic crisis and Napoleon's *coup d'état*: this relationship must be investigated starting with the class-relations that pressure the situation.[72] The commercial crisis brought about a widespread anti-parliamentary sentiment when the bourgeoisie began to accuse the 'parliamentary struggles of being the cause of stagnation and screamed for them to fall silent so that the voice of trade could again be heard'.[73] This anti-parliamentary sentiment, combined with fear of the 'red spectre', constituted the perfect mix for a spark to provoke a chain-reaction.

In *Capital*, Marx inserted the French events in the European context of a civil war between capitalist and working classes over the length of a 'normal working day'. This was a civil war temporarily won by capital – in Britain, after the incarceration of the Chartist leaders, and the abolition of the 10-hours law in 1850; in France, after the June Insurrection in Paris was drowned in blood, and the support for Napoleon III's dictatorship. 1848, and in particular 1 May, the date on which the working class succeeded in imposing the 10-hours law, gave rise to the 'open revolt' of the capitalists who, with 'terroristic energy', began their 'revolt' not only 'against the Ten Hours Act, but against all the legislation since 1833 that had aimed at restricting to some extent the "free" exploitation

---

72. James 2009, p. 129.
73. Marx 1960a, p. 183; Marx 1979a, p. 172.

of labour-power'.[74] In Britain, as in continental Europe, 'all fractions of the ruling classes, landowners and capitalists, stock-exchange sharks and small-time shop-keepers, Protectionists and Freetraders, government and opposition, priests and freethinkers, young whores and old nuns'[75] united under the common cry of the salvation of property. With a language and a style that recall the *Eighteenth Brumaire*, Marx presented classes and antithetical social groupings united as factions of the dominant classes against the proletariat. This common front for the defence of the existing order could stay together only because of an imaginary of terror; in *Capital*, Marx counterposed to this the infernal imaginary of the existing order. After having presented this temporary victory of capital, Marx went on to describe how the class-antagonism immediately resumed with a new, unheard-of degree of tension.[76] In chapter after chapter, he outlines how capital uses and continues to use machines as 'the most powerful weapon for suppressing strikes, those periodic revolts of the working class against the autocracy of capital'. He adds, 'It would be possible to write a whole history of the inventions made since 1830 for the sole purpose of providing capital with weapons against the working-class revolt'.[77] On page after page, Marx moves from describing the struggle over the length of the working day to machines and their use against workers' strikes; he then describes large-scale industry as an infernal place populated by blood-sucking vampires, thereby adding to a representation in which the progressive imaginary of the bourgeoisie falls apart, revealing a world populated by the undead.

The revolution within the Revolution

The theatrical register chosen by Marx stages the representation of representation. Only when intrigues are shown to be superficial appearances that hide the class-struggle is it possible to dissolve the phantasmagoria. The presages of the *coup d'état* have the form of a comedy:

> the Bonapartist newspapers threatened a coup d'état, and the nearer the crisis approached, the louder their tone became. In the orgies at which Bonaparte celebrated every night in company with the men and women of the 'swell mob', when the hour of midnight approached and rich libations had loosened tongues and heated imaginations, the coup d'état was fixed

74. Marx 1962a, p. 302; Marx 1996, p. 290.
75. Ibid.
76. Marx 1962a, p. 309; Marx 1996, p. 297.
77. Marx 1962a, p. 459; Marx 1996, p. 439.

for the following morning. Swords were drawn, glasses clinked, deputies were thrown out the window, and the imperial mantle fell on Bonaparte's shoulders, until the following morning once more exorcized the ghost, and an astounded Paris learned of the danger it had once again escaped from vestals who lacked reserve and paladins who lacked discretion.[78]

But farce hid tragedy. It was the democratic institutions of the Republic that frayed, to the point that they were sacrificed in the struggle against class-struggle. The state is almost never reducible to a committee for managing the affairs of a single determinant class. Rather, it expresses a relative autonomy that aims at stemming the conflictual dynamics of the different classes. This autonomisation of the political, which proceeds via an administrative route through the centralisation of state-power, is anything but peaceful. Its violent nature is the same as the non-neutral neutralisation of conflict: it is the struggle against the class-struggle. For this reason, it can momentarily conflict with the interests of the bourgeoisie. If the first history, that of the autonomy of the political, was represented by the historiography of continuity, the other history calls for an analysis of the class-stratification of unique situations.

Marx does not elaborate a theory of revolution that is valid for every occasion. What interests him is a historiography capable of grasping, in the various temporalities of the Revolution, the chance for true liberation. When he compares the French Revolution with that of 1848, he does so not in order to test an improbable comparative historiography of revolutions.[79] What he intends to put into question is the historiographical model of linear causality. He does so in a beautiful passage, in which the repeated reversals carried out through chiasmata not only disrupt any notion of linear causality, but repaint these situations in tragicomic colours:

> Constitutionalists who openly conspire against the constitution; revolutionaries who are by their own admission constitutionalists...an executive power which draws strength from its very weakness and its respectability from the contempt it inspires; ...passions without truth, truths without passion; heroes without deeds of heroism, history without events [*Geschichte ohne Ereignisse*]; a course of development, apparently only driven forward by the calendar, and made wearisome by the constant repetition of the same tensions and relaxations.[80]

---

78. Marx 1960a, p. 188; Marx 1979a, p. 177; translation modified.
79. Marx 1960a, pp. 135–6; Marx 1979a, p. 124.
80. Marx 1960a, p. 136; Marx 1979a, p. 125.

Time reduces historical law to linear causality: to a driving force that is merely the passing of the days of the calendar, characterised by sameness – the *Geschichte ohne Ereignisse*. Marx is not reasoning according to historical law, but by means of historiographical registers. This is a model of linear causality that Marx intends to show to be inadequate for understanding revolutionary situations. The event belongs to the order of ruptures, 'it cleaves linear homogeneity, and fills the spatial void, it negates the abstraction of modern temporality'.[81] It is not history that is without events; rather, it is the historiographical lenses adopted in order not to grasp them that is without events. We need, instead, a historiography that is up to this task. The materialist historiographer works at this, intervening not only in the history of the present but also in that of the past. History does not, in reality, stand before the materialist historian as an object to be represented objectively, 'as it really happened', but as a *Kampfplatz* in which to intervene. Marx does not limit himself to reporting events and to repeating what has been said, but names the event in order to demonstrate the opening of possibilities that were available in the past, and which the revolutionary class must gather together. The expression 'social republic', though absent in the decrees and proclamations of the Provisional Government, is, nevertheless, for Marx, the seal pressed upon the Republic by the Paris proletariat and the 'general content of the modern revolution'.[82] The revolutionary class for which Marx writes history has its own traditions, which allow it to make the leap into the future embodied in the past and join together with the struggles of the comrades that were defeated.

The nightmare of liberal historiography is that the Revolution seems not to want to end. It is a nightmare produced by the spectres that agitate within the Revolution. Understanding history as a process of *longue durée* constituted the strategy for domesticating historical events, for rediscovering the capacity to formulate diagnoses of the present. Marx did not ignore this historiography of continuity. He, too, works with a concept of history as a process that, as he argues with regard to Tocqueville, leads him to think in terms of processes of *longue durée*. Marx, however, also reasons with a plural semantics of history: he counterposes a notion of history marked with fractures to the history of continuum. This contraposition is political: it grows out of the search for a revolution capable of interrupting that continuum. Marx's problem is not

---

81. Bensaïd 1995, p. 192. The event, continues Bensaïd, is the antithesis of the cinerary: it is the 'living, that, exceptionally, extraordinarily, mysteriously, resuscitates the dead'.

82. Marx 1960a, p. 120; Marx 1979a, p. 109.

whether the Revolution constitutes such a rupture or not.[83] The problem is to identify the revolution within the Revolution as a discontinuity with that history and that process. Marx paints us a picture of revolutionary history in terms of progressive stages of the process of the centralisation of state-power: the French Revolution 'had necessarily to develop fully that which the Absolute Monarchy had begun: centralization'; Napoleon perfected this state-mechanism [*Staatsmachinerie*]; the July Monarchy did not add anything, except, perhaps, a greater division of labour in state-administration; the parliamentary Republic, in the end, reinforced 'the resources and centralization of governmental power'.[84] What is missing in this history-as-process, however, is the discontinuity that discloses itself to the historian capable of grasping the revolution within the Revolution. The reinforcement of state-power and centralisation do not fall from the sky, but are the result of the 'struggle against the revolution' and of the repressive measures against revolutionaries.[85] The struggle against the class-struggle has resulted in the reinforcement of the executive power of the state and its centralisation; these are now read by Marx in terms of a reaction to an insurgent proletariat. With this overturning of perspective, Marx shows the proletariat as the active side of the fight and presents it from the point of view of the working class in struggle.

> But the revolution is thoroughgoing. It is still travelling through purgatory. It does its work methodically. By December 2, 1851, it had completed half of its preparatory work; now it is completing the other half. It first completed the parliamentary power in order to be able to overthrow it. Now that it has achieved this, it completes the executive power, reduces it to its purest expression, isolates it, sets it up against itself as the sole target, in order to concentrate all its forces of destruction against it. And when it has accomplished this second half of its preliminary work, Europe will leap from its seat and exult: Well worked, old mole!'.[86]

The method of the Revolution is welded to the class-struggle. If it produces, as a reaction, the centralisation of state-power, then this situation needs to be understood as revolutionary. Marx does not delineate centralisation, either in terms of an imminent destiny in the concept of the state, or in Tocquevillian

---

83. According to Kouvelakis, in his writings on the Commune, Marx rehabilitated the Revolution as a moment of rupture, abandoning the Tocquevillian scheme of *The Eighteenth Brumaire*: Kouvelakis 2007. I disagree on this point, because, in my view, *The Eighteenth Brumaire* exhibits a combination of both the linear scheme and the idea of historical rupture.
84. Marx 1960a, p. 197; Marx 1979a, p. 186.
85. Ibid.
86. Marx 1960a, p. 196; Marx 1979a, p. 185.

terms as a historical process that must be contained. If the revolution at work in the Revolution has led to centralisation and the reinforcement of state-power, this reinforcement of state-power must be understood as an opportunity for its destruction. Here, materialist historiography sets itself a double task. On the one hand, after having represented the history of the centralisation of state-power from the point of view of the working class, it shows it to have been the working class's own activity that produced this reinforcement; therefore, it already possesses the destructive force necessary to be able to break up this state-machine. On the other hand, as against the historiography of continuity that sees only the growth of centralisation, Marx poses the true problem of the rupture of the state-machine: 'All political upheavals perfected this machine, instead of smashing it [zu brechen]'.[87] If power, up until now, has been considered the spoils that go to the winner, Marx intends, instead, to interrupt this statist logic of revolution and, therefore, the continuum of centralisation. The materialist historiographer investigates the other temporality of the revolution within the Revolution: what is needed, without delay, is to distinguish between bourgeois revolutions and proletarian revolutions.[88] The former

> storm quickly from success to success. They outdo each other in dramatic effects; men and things seem set in sparkling diamonds and each day's spirit is ecstatic. But they are short-lived; they soon reach their apogee and society has to undergo a long period of regret until it has learned to assimilate soberly the achievements of its period of Storm and Stress [Drang- und Sturmperiode].[89]

Marx has no intention of expounding further on the law of bourgeois revolutions, but rather on the historiographical genre of bourgeois revolutions with all their Promethean romanticism. For proletarian revolutions, a different historiography is needed, sensitive to the different temporalities of this revolution.[90]

---

87. Marx 1960a, p. 197; Marx 1979a, p. 186. In a letter to Ludwig Kugelmann of 12 April 1871, Marx confirmed this same idea with regard to the events of the Commune, recalling the Eighteenth Brumaire: 'If you look at the last chapter of my Eighteenth Brumaire you will find that I say that the next attempt of the French revolution will be no longer, as before, to transfer the bureaucratic-military machine from one hand to another, but to smash it, and this is essential for every real people's revolution on the Continent': from Padover 1979, p. 280.

88. Marx 1960a, p. 118; Marx 1979a, p. 106.

89. Ibid.

90. On the different temporal registers of the bourgeois revolution (temporality of hoarding) and proletarian revolution (temporality of distillation), see Wendling 2003.

Proletarian revolutions, however, such as those of the nineteenth century, constantly engage in self-criticism, and in repeated interruptions of their own course. They return to what has apparently already been accomplished in order to begin the task again; with merciless thoroughness they mock the inadequate, weak, and wretched aspects of their first attempts; they seem to throw their opponent to the ground only to see him draw new strength from the earth and rise again before them more colossal than ever; they shrink back again and again before the indeterminate immensity of their own goals, until the situation is created in which any retreat is impossible, and the conditions themselves cry out: *Hic Rhodus, hic salta!* Here is the rose! Dance here!'

The materialist historiographer pays attention to the temporality of proletarian revolution, which consists of advances, interruptions and regressions. It is as far from faith in progress as the 'inert exaltation of the future' that makes democrats lose 'all understanding of the present'.[91] Such faith in progress impedes us from grasping the present situation, namely, the revolutionary temporality of ruptures. The job of the materialist historian is to work toward representing a situation as one of no return, because a situation may be called revolutionary inasmuch as the proletariat, free from the phantasms of the past, can make the leap into the *novum*.

With Napoleon III, 'society seems now to have retreated to behind its starting point'. It is, in reality, only now, replies Marx, that 'it must first create the revolutionary starting-point, i.e. the situation, relations, and conditions necessary for the modern revolution to become serious'.[92] But the revolutionary force of the present situation does not come out of nowhere. It is necessary to follow the subterranean course of the revolution within the Revolution, showing how it was the class-struggle that forced the bourgeoisie to engage in an increasing reinforcement of state-power, leading to the exhaustion of parliamentary power and its democratic appearance. Here, there was a chance for an overthrow: the classes that supported Napoleon III were represented by him only inasmuch as the power of the middle-class was daily fragmented and the peasants, who did not even constitute a class, continued not to count at all. The stratification of class presented by Marx in order to explain the power of Napoleon III was extremely complicated.[93] There was a class

---

91. Marx 1960a, p. 119; Marx 1979a, pp. 106–7.
92. Marx 1960a, p. 118; Marx 1979a, p. 106.
93. Lefort 1986. Some, like Peter Hayes, propose reading Marx's writings on the class struggle in France as a revision of the polarising perspective of the *Manifesto*, which tends toward a circular paradigm of class-structure. Hayes's analysis has interesting

condemned to impotence, due as much to its own immaturity as to the weight of its recent defeat: the proletariat. There was the class opposed to it, a class that ran from the image of its own identity and that was united only by the common fear of its adversary: the bourgeoisie. There was an intermediate class in which the sharp interests of the opposing classes were dulled: the petty bourgeoisie. There was a non-class class, made up of discrete sums of an identical size, like a sack of potatoes constitutes a sack of potatoes: the peasants. And there was also a reject-class: the lumpenproletariat. Marx connected this complex stratification of social classes with the analysis of the social imaginary that made possible the phantasmagoric character of history from 1848 to 1851. Napoleonic ideas were, for Marx, 'hallucinations' of the agony of the small proprietor that survives on his own, 'words made into phrases, spirits [Geister] made into ghosts [Gespenster]'.[94] This marked his intersection between analysis of socio-economic conditions and the analysis of social imaginary, an intersection grasping the performative character of Napoleonic phraseology, able to transform hallucination into reality.[95] The work of Marx was, indeed, to show the reality of reality. The phantasms vanish when the shadows of the Second Empire are filled with the hard reality of class-struggle. The state of the second Bonaparte is presented as a 'parody of the Empire' in order to 'to free the mass of the French nation from the burden of tradition and to bring out the antagonism between the state power and society in pure form'.[96] By making it into a parody, Marx intended to destroy a representation of reality, so that a new social imaginary can open up the possibility of destroying the existing state of things. Only at this point does the parallel between the two eighteenth Brumaires end, and history opens to the true revolution. 'The social revolution of the nineteenth century can only create its poetry from the future, not from the past'.[97] Marx concludes: 'It cannot begin its own work until it has sloughed off all its superstitious regard for the past'.[98] The poésie of the future is not an evocation of a utopian image, but rather, a totally new political imaginary. It is not the past as such that must be liquidated, but superstition in an imaginary of the past that blocks revolutionary action. The

---

aspects, especially in relation to the declining classes and their composition in the dynamic of the class struggle with the proletariat or the bourgeoisie, but it ends up, in turn, falling into a schematicism for which the flexibility of the circular structure of class cannot compensate. See Hayes 1993.

94. Marx 1960a, p. 203; Marx 1979a, p. 192.
95. Petry 1988, p. 460: 'Words successfully transformed into phrases can produce the world they articulate'.
96. Marx 1960a, p. 203; Marx 1979a, p. 192.
97. Marx 1960a, p. 117; Marx 1979a, p. 106.
98. Ibid.

new imaginary, the imaginary that Marx tried to construct by rewriting the history of the failed Revolution of 1848 from the workers' point of view, liberates the possibilities of the present so that they can produce a real rupture in tradition of the victors. In this laboratory of materialist history, the event is not absorbed into an historical causal chain, but is investigated in the synchronistic intersection of the imaginary of a tradition and real class-conflict. The force of the past on the present can be employed to unhinge the present.*

---

* Translated by Steven Collatrella.

Chapter Two
A New Phenotype

Haben Sie schon einmal darüber nachgedacht,
daß das, was die Menschheit heutigentags noch
denkt,
noch denken nennt, bereits von Maschinen gedacht
werden kann, und diese Maschinen übertrumpfen
sogar schon den Menschen...
(G. Benn, *Probleme der Lyrik*)

In the *Grundrisse*, Marx presented capital as a continual revolution.[1] Capital destroys nature and space.
It 'strives...to annihilate space by means of time',[2]
destroying the limits of human nature by expanding
the sphere of needs and the variety of production.

Value excludes no use value, i.e. includes no
specific kind of consumption, etc., intercourse,
etc., as absolute condition, and likewise every
degree of the development of the social productive forces, of intercourse, of knowledge,
etc., appears to it as a barrier which it strives
to overcome.[3]

Nature, as well as human nature, becomes an artifice, a work of art. The capitalist mode of production leads to the creation of an artificial nature that
plays on the need to have needs. It satisfies and creates new needs, filling the world with commodities.

---

1. Marx's definition is *'beständige Revolution'*: Marx 1983b, p. 447; Marx 1986a,
p. 465. See also Marx 1983b, p. 323; Marx 1986, p. 337.
2. Marx 1983b, p. 445; Marx 1986, p. 463; translation modified.
3. Marx 1983b, p. 447; Marx 1986, p. 465; translation modified.

Needs are met even before they arise, so that the commodities themselves create the need, relieving the individual of the burden of having new needs. Human imagination has thus become the imagination of capital. Advertising is our contemporary poetry, speaking directly to the most intimate of our desires. The sing-song chanting of the auctioneers in the 1976 film *How Much Wood Would a Woodchuck Chuck* represents, as Werner Herzog reminded us, the last form of the poetry of capital.

The dissolutive power of capital was described in the *Manifesto of the Communist Party*. Within the capitalist mode of production,

> all fixed, fast-frozen relations, with their train of ancient and venerable prejudices and opinions, are swept away, all new-formed ones become antiquated before they can ossify. All that is solid melts into air, all that is holy is profaned, and man is at last compelled to face with sober senses, his real conditions of life, and his relations with his kind.[4]

It is difficult to imagine a cruder apology for the revolutionary bourgeoisie. However, the apology itself reveals the problem: the bourgeoisie

> has drowned the most heavenly ecstasies of religious fervour, of chivalrous enthusiasm, of philistine sentimentalism, in the icy water of egotistical calculation. It has resolved personal worth into exchange value....The bourgeoisie has stripped of its halo every occupation hitherto honoured and looked up to with reverent awe. It has converted the physician, the lawyer, the priest, the poet, the man of science, into its paid wage-labourers. The bourgeoisie has torn away from the family its sentimental veil, and has reduced the family relation to a mere money relation.[5]

This expansion of the sphere of needs, which comes as the consequence of the production of a superabundance of commodities, is called by the name of consumerism. It enhances and transforms human nature, finally resulting in an unprecedented animalisation of the human in Calypso's timeless garden.

From the moment it came into existence, the capitalist mode of production has produced a new type of human. With the early image of the Robinsonades, the hostile behaviours of individual atoms were hurled into a meta-historical state of nature, thus creating a logical-historical circularity capable of immobilising transformation and producing the elements of economic and political modernity: individuals. This image has acted beyond all expectations, bringing about the complete animalisation of the human, who lives in a world without history. Value has supplanted use-value, such that the

---

4. Marx and Engels 1959, p. 465, Marx and Engels 1976, p. 487.
5. Marx and Engels 1959, pp. 464–5; Marx and Engels 1976, p. 487.

individual no longer experiences use-value, but rather value and the status that value confers. More than the product itself, it is the advertising that is consumed. Use-value ceases to be a simple object of utility at the moment in which advertising reinvents the symbolic context within which a useful object is, in our eyes, a useful object. This inversion affects forms of experience and becomes perversion. A commodity's exchange-value itself becomes a quality to be enjoyed, as Adorno observed in relation to the fetish-character in music.[6] The exchange-value of a commodity, in subsuming its use-value and becoming its *raison d'être*, takes its place. The capitalist mode of production is characterised by the dominion of the abstract, of value, over the concrete.[7] This inversion changes the very nature of use-value. It is a mournful imaginary, for the use-values so pyrotechnically launched into the collective imagination are marked by an utter indifference that derives from their nature as bearers of value and nothing more. This is the indifference that characterises modern experience. The mournful character of modern art, that character that Walter Benjamin showed in Baudelaire, is the poetic reaction to the death of use-value and, at the same time, to the atrophying of the ability to appreciate experience when that experience deals solely with the use-value of an exchange-value.

The result is a repressive totality, where needs are satisfied only insofar as we abstract from them. Inner worldly asceticism and hyper-consumerism are the two faces of capitalist modernity. The modern individual, torn between his or her own will and the general will, just like the Rousseauean subject, schizophrenically contains these two sides within him- or herself. It is in this contradiction that we find the malaise of society. Contemporary experience appears to be fragmentary, yet each fragment reflects the same image, for the multiplicity of the phenomenal has become a multiplicity of equivalents. Postmodernism's attempt to sell us a fragmentary image of the world is false. The only truth it holds is the fact that it is, itself, an indifferent perspective. The historical materialist disassociates him- or herself from this indifference, in the same way that the surrealists removed the object from the domination of value. However, this is only possible by assuming the non-indifference of points of view, and not through the creation of a new *Weltanschauung*. Marx's true legacy is a shift in our point of view, a shift that moves the entire issue from the objective to the true.

---

6. See Adorno 1991, p. 29.
7. On capitalist abstraction and the hollowing out, by abstraction, of the concrete in postmodernity, see Finelli 2005. See also Finelli 1987.

Crisis and history

In the *1844 Manuscripts*, while searching for elements capable of prefiguring socialism, Marx examined the relationship between the *'new mode of production'* and the *'wealth* of human needs'. '[A] new manifestation of the forces of *human nature'*, he wrote, 'and a new enrichment of human nature',[8] should characterise socialism. In the context of private property, however, the significance of all these things is reversed. The creation of new needs demands fresh sacrifices; 'every new product represents a new potentiality of mutual swindling and mutual plundering'.[9] The increasing number of products goes hand in hand with the extension of 'inhuman, sophisticated, unnatural and *imaginary* appetites'.[10] Within the realm of private property, the strengthening of individual needs is inverted into individual misery. The concept of the individual is the lens through which the development of the relations of production must be viewed.

'Man', Marx writes, 'becomes individualised [*vereinzelt sich*] only through the process of history'.[11] The gradual exposition of historical formations in the *Grundrisse* deals with the individualisation of man through the progressive disintegration of the original unity of man and community. Stages of development are marked according to matrices common to many post-Hegelian theories of history. In some cases, the exposition is explicitly triadic in nature:

> Relations of personal dependence (entirely spontaneous at the outset) are the first social forms, in which human productive capacity develops only to a slight extent and at isolated points. Personal independence founded on *material [sachlicher]* dependence is the second great form, in which a system of general social metabolism, of universal relations, of all-round needs and universal capacities is formed for the first time. Free individuality, based on the universal development of individuals and on their subordination of their communal, social productivity as their social wealth, is the third stage. The second stage creates the conditions for the third.[12]

---

8. Marx 1973, p. 546; Marx 1975f, p. 306.
9. Marx 1973, p. 547; Marx 1975f, p. 306.
10. Marx 1973, p. 547; Marx 1975f, p. 307.
11. Marx 1973, p. 404; Marx 1975f, p. 420. Translation modified. Hobsbawm contradictorily affirms, on the one hand, that Marx's presentation of precapitalist formations should be understood 'not as referring to chronological succession', but, on the other hand, still speaks of these formations as different forms of a 'gradual individualisation of man, which means the break-up of the original unity', going on to state that they 'correspond to the different stages of history': Hobsbawm 1971, p. 36.
12. Marx 1983b, p. 91; Marx 1986, p. 95; translation modified.

The philosophy of history organises and imposes order on the development of individuality, thus giving a progressive meaning to history: personal dependence, material dependence, free individuality.

Marx attempted to reconstruct the historical process leading from the original condition of *Gattungswesen* through various levels of dissolution,[13] including the distortions of the *homo economicus* described in the *1844 Manuscripts*, finally reaching the state of the *social* individual, reconciled once more with the *Gattung*.[14] It is a pattern derived from the philosophy of history: transcending the natural limits of the capitalist mode of production constitutes progress towards the 'free and full development' of the individual, and is a necessary element for its achievement.[15] However, this development represents both the ruin and the decadence of the previous formations. Unlike reactionaries and progressives – who, complementarily, seek to identify an algebraic sign that they can assign to the tendency of a particular process – Marx attempts to think development within decadence.

While the gaze of the reactionary is romantically turned toward the past, and the ancient concept of man as the goal of production (and not 'wealth as an end unto itself') seems much loftier to him than the modern conception, the point of view of the historical materialist is the opposite. Although both the reactionary and the historical materialist perceive the crisis, one sees it as an inescapable destiny of decadence, while for the other it is the sign of a prophecy that must be disproven. The true reactionary, like the historical materialist, believes neither in progress nor in the transitory and conjunctural nature of the crisis. For both of them, this crisis is a constitutive element of modernity. The point where their views diverge and enter into mortal conflict is over the anti-prophetic nature of political intervention. Before being subsumed into the vortex of modernity and falling prey to the process of valuation, elements of novelty flash up for one last time, allowing one last glimpse of the full spectrum of colours. These are the colours that make up the palette of the historical materialist.

The *Grundrisse* emphasise the ambivalence of the denaturalisation of nature as well as that of human nature with regard to needs, with traces of Prometheanism. In Marx, this Prometheanism is an expression not of a naïve and misguided faith in progress, but rather of a conviction, interwoven with a political gamble, that capital, insofar as it constitutes a 'continual revolution', will also work toward the destruction of its own limits and, thence, its own downfall. These were the expectations of a revolutionary confronted by the

---

13. Marx 1983b, pp. 405–6; Marx 1986, pp. 421–2.
14. On this topic, see Basso 2008; Texier 1992, particularly p. 143 ff.
15. Marx 1983b; Marx 1986, p. 411.

crisis of the 1850s. In October 1857, Marx wrote to Engels that the 'American crisis – its outbreak in New York was forecast by us in the November 1850 *Revue* – is beautiful'.[16] In this spirit, and with the conviction that a great crisis was at the doorstep, Marx began to write the *Grundrisse*. Convinced that this crisis would be the catalyst that fired up the revolutionary machine, he worked on his project intensely. On 8 December 1857, he wrote to Engels: 'I am working like mad all night and every night collating my economic studies so that I at least get the outlines clear before the deluge'.[17] Things did not go as expected. Capitalism seemed to have come out of the crisis stronger than before. Revolution was no longer around the corner. In India, the 'Sepoy Rebellion', as the British called what the Indians term the 'War of Independence of 1857', was violently crushed. The power of the East India Company passed directly into the hands of the Crown, which, after having robbed the natives of their personal property, stripped them of their real estate as well. Marx wrote his comments on the event for publication in the *New York Daily Tribune*. India was providing new energy for the British engine of capital-accumulation. Indeed, by the 1860s, the cultivation of cotton and other export-products had replaced the cultivation of grains in the fertile lands of the south. By the close of the 1870s, the forests, which had, until then, been common property, 'were completely enclosed by armed agents of the state.[18] Indian poverty was a deliberate outcome of Indian economic policies, Smithian in their intent, Hobbesian in practice.[19]

The optimism of the previous months began to fade. In a letter dated 8 October 1858, Marx sketched out for Engels an initial assessment of the reorganisation of capital in the aftermath of the crisis:

> There is no denying that bourgeois society has for the second time experienced its 16th century, a 16th century which, I hope, will sound its death knell just as the first ushered it into the world. The proper task of bourgeois society is the creation of the world market, at least in outline,

---

16. Marx 1983c, p. 191. The crisis kindled Marx's optimism, as he writes to Engels on 13 November 1857, 'Though my own FINANCIAL DISTRESS may be dire indeed, never, since 1849, have I felt SO COSY as during this OUTBREAK' (Marx 1983c, p. 199). Actually, ever since the end of 1856, when Jenny had gone back to Trier to collect the inheritance left to her by her mother, Marx's financial situation had improved. The Marx family left the hovel in Dean Street for a furnished, four-room house at 9 Grafton Terrace. On 26 September 1856, he wrote to Engels, 'The very fact that I've at last got round to setting up house again and sending for my books seems to me to prove that the "mobilisation" of our persons is AT HAND' (Marx 1983d, p. 72). Private optimism and political enthusiasm were fuelling each other.
17. Marx 1983e, p. 217.
18. Davis 2002, p. 327 ff.
19. Davis 2002, p. 339.

and of the production based on that market. Since the world is round, the colonisation of California and Australia and the opening up of China and Japan would seem to have completed this process. For us, the difficult question is this: on the Continent revolution is imminent and will, moreover, instantly assume a socialist character. Will it not necessarily be crushed in this little corner of the earth, since the *movement* of bourgeois society is still in the *ascendant* over a far greater area?[20]

This letter set the course for Marx's theoretical and political work across the course of the 1860s. When read carefully, and bearing in mind later developments, it is possible to identify, here, material that was discarded before the elaboration of the *Grundrisse*. Marx raised three crucial issues. The 'second sixteenth century' of capitalism forces us to think of accumulation as a long-term process. Capitalist accumulation cannot, therefore, be limited to the protohistory of the capitalist mode of production. Second, not only theoretical analysis, but also political analysis, has to be thought in terms of the world-market. The world is round, and the world-market creates connections between different geographic areas and different forms of exploitation. Capitalism cannot be analysed simply by looking at the nations where it is most highly developed. One should not imagine that these nations are the locomotive that tows the other cars of the train. Finally, and, indeed, as a result of these reflections, Marx asked himself, as well as his friend, what possibilities of success a revolution – and *not* only in one single country, but *even* a European revolution – might have in the face of the globalisation of the market. Without international prospects, the revolution would necessarily be crushed. These three points, which made up the palette for Marx's work over the following years, were to be ignored in much of twentieth-century Marxism. The struggles of the European working class need to be observed from a perspective that also takes into consideration uprisings worldwide, which are only apparently not located on the same level of capitalist development. During and following the writing of the *Grundrisse*, Marx not only studied political economy, but was also interested in following the independence-movements and struggles occurring in many different parts of the world. His gaze was increasingly fixed on world-dynamics, in order to make that larger stage the point of view from which he could observe that 'little corner of the Earth' that is Europe, and not the other way around.

---

20. Marx 1983f, pp. 346–7.

Research into precapitalist forms

When he had finished writing the *Grundrisse*, in which the crisis is used to create a critical consciousness attentive to the chinks and gaps that capital exhibits in the face of the world-market,[21] Marx began to rethink the entire categorial framework of his analysis. In particular, he began to deal with the concept of value,[22] rethinking the law of the falling rate of profit in such a way as to no longer apply it to 'capital in general' – a term that he eventually abandoned – but to competition between capitals. These analyses, and the comparison of different forms of production and different forms of uprising, are what opened new perspectives for Marx, even if he did not always explore all of them fully. It became possible for him to imagine the capitalist mode of production not according to a pattern defined by origin, development and crisis, but rather as a constantly concurrent combination of those three moments and of their temporalities. Original accumulation was to be imagined not as an initial form, but, rather, as an always-present method of extortion of surplus-labour.[23] Some Marxian reflections that measure up to the standards of *Capital* develop in this direction. However, Marx did not always develop these intuitions to their fullest extent. Herein lay the possibility of a non-historicist interpretation of different modes of production.[24]

Already in the *Grundrisse*, Marx focused his attention not only on continuity, but also, and above all, on the discontinuity between different forms of production. This discontinuity was explored in terms of transformation of

21. Gidwani 2008, p. 869.

22. Tuchscheerer 1968 observes that, in the *Grundrisse*, Marx passes from the phenomenal form to the essence of value, and not the other way around (from work to value and from value to exchange-value) as in the *Critique of Political Economy* and in *Capital*. See also Hecker 1987; Fineschi 2003. On categorial transformations between the *Grundrisse* and *Capital*, see Pennavaja 1975, p. xlvi. Karatani observes that, between the *Grundrisse* and *Capital* there appears to be a 'Marxian turn' provided by Marx's reflection on 'value-form' that recalls Samuel Bailey's criticism of Ricardo: Karatani 2003 pp. 193–6. Dussel observes that Marx dedicates twenty-five pages of Notebook XIV of the 1861–3 *Manuscripts* to a commentary of Bailey's 1825 *A Critical Dissertation on the Nature, Measures and Causes of Value*, and that it was thanks to having read this text that he was able to rethink the question of value: Dussel 1998, p. 219.

23. Sacchetto and Tomba (eds.) 1998.

24. These themes have been taken up again today in the context of postcolonial studies. According to Chakrabarty, to speak of a residue or 'survival of an earlier mode of production' means to think in historicist terms. Challenging the theory of *uneven development*, he holds that it is historicist to consider the distinction between formal and real subsumption of labour 'as a question of historical transition': see Chakrabarty 2007, pp. 14, 261, 28–30. On the same issue, see also Smith 1990, p. 140. For further discussion of these aspects, see Tomba 2009b.

individuality and of humanity itself.[25] Weaving together a double interpretative framework, and combining evolutionary and repetitive histories, Marx
represented an unprecedented type of social development.[26] The problem
lies in understanding the historical break that the establishment of capitalist
production represents. On this basis, it is possible to investigate precapitalist
modes of production as *something else*. In the anatomy of man lies the key to
the anatomy of the ape,[27] in the sense that the synchronous existence of man
and ape become a key for the diachronic explanation that reveals not *evolution*, but rather, the *distinction* between man and ape.

The *Urtext*, written in August and September of 1858, immediately following the writing of the *Grundrisse*, makes it possible, on the one hand, to highlight retrospectively the precapitalist forms developed in the *Grundrisse*; and,
on the other hand, prospectively, to cast an illuminating beam of light on
the reflections on fetishism which, developing through the *Contribution to the
Critique of Political Economy*,[28] would finally arrive in *Capital*. The two aspects
are interwoven. At the moment that Marx analysed the historical origin of
the capitalist mode of production, he also had to deal with the tendency of
modern economic categories to assert themselves as ahistorical and universal.
Marx had, therefore, to prove the historical nature of this mode of production
as distinct from other historical forms of production. Both of these steps are
crucial in order to be able to imagine its other: communism.

In the capitalist mode of production, individuals relate to each other as
'abstract social persons, merely representing exchange value as such before
each other'.[29] In this way, all political and patriarchal bonds stemming from
the particularity of the relation are dissolved. This is a passage that Marx took
from Carlyle, who, in his book on Chartism, observed that

> in feudal times *cash payment* had not grown to be the sole *nexus* of man
> to man. Not as buyer and seller alone, but in many senses still as soldier
> and captain, as loyal subject and guiding king, etc. was the low related to
> the high. With the supreme triumph of cash, a changed time has entered.[30]

---

25. Lefort pointed out that in Marxian analysis, '[i]t is not the continuity of the
historical process, a change of forms governed by a fundamental contradiction, that
he brings to light, but rather a radical discontinuity, a mutation of humanity': Lefort
1986, pp. 141–2.

26. Lefort 1986, pp. 149–51.

27. Marx 1961a, p. 636; Marx 1986, p. 42. See Rosdolsky 1968, p. 273.

28. 'But since in bourgeois production, wealth as a fetish must be crystallised in
a particular substance gold and silver are its appropriate embodiment'. Marx 1961b,
p. 130; Marx 1987a, p. 387.

29. Marx 1987b, p. 430.

30. Carlyle 1840, p. 58, as cited by Marx 1980, p. 20; Marx 1987b, p. 431.

Carlyle's analysis is, however, insufficient. In the act of dissolving previous communal relationships, money establishes a new *social nexus*; one which, while spreading universally, destroying communal boundaries, on the one hand, also bears the mark of the most absolute indifference, on the other.[31] This new social nexus, which is expressed in exchange-value and is visible in money, endows money with a universal social power that the individual can carry in the pocket in order to wield it over the activities of others.

Money, in this sense, forms the 'social substance':[32] the 'social nexus…itself appears in money as something entirely external'.[33] Fetishism, while not mentioned as such, is, here, the symptom of a lack. As social relations are dominated by money, taking the form of an unconscious relationship, they become 'a social relation between things', as though individuals only come into contact with each other as private property owners exchanging commodities. Social relations take on a mythic form, within which individual destinies are dominated by an external force.

Confronted by a new social nexus of individuals, each indifferent to the other insofar as they are ruled by exchange-value, it is just as incongruous to look back towards the 'original fullness' of relationships found in 'earlier stages of development' of the individual as it is to believe that it is necessary to stand still at the stage of 'complete emptiness' of today's indifferent relationships.[34] Marx offers a third option that rejects the alternative between original fullness and modern emptiness. It is precisely production based on exchange-value that is proposed as the possibility for 'universally developed individuals' to subject their social relationships to their own communal control [*gemeinschaftliche Kontrolle*].[35] Indeed, production based on exchange-value would appear to produce, 'along with the universality of the estrangement of individuals from themselves and from others…also to produce the universality and generality of all their relations and abilities'.[36] The historical reconstruction of precapitalist formations serves to reveal the capitalist production of a new individuality.

In order better to direct that beam of light capable of illuminating the future, one's gaze must turn towards the past, to precapitalist historical formations, in search of a historiography that is able to interweave the dual registers of

31. Marx 1983b, p. 97; Marx 1986, p. 431.
32. In comparison with the corresponding passage in the *Grundrisse* (Marx 1983b, p. 90; Marx 1986, p. 94), Marx develops this idea in the *Urtext*: Marx 1980, p. 20; Marx 1987b, p. 431.
33. Marx 1980, p. 20; Marx 1987b, p. 432.
34. Marx 1983b, p. 96; Marx 1986, p. 99.
35. Marx 1983b, p. 95; Marx 1986, p. 99.
36. Ibid.

evolutionary and repetitive histories. The analysis of precapitalist formations, differentiated according to a historical-geographical model (Asia-Rome-Germany),[37] represents an attempt to fit historical presuppositions into a logical mould.[38] The point of departure is the 'naturally evolved community',[39] in which each single individual behaves as a member of this community, which pre-dates him or her as something divine or natural. *This is 'oriental despotism'*. The basis of the 'oriental community' is communal property, and any reference to other members is a reference to 'co-proprietors'. Labour is, therefore, not separate from the objective conditions of its realisation.

The second formation also assumes the community as its first presupposition, but in this formation individuals are no longer accidental factors or naturally evolved parts of the community. The earth becomes the 'inorganic nature of the living individual',[40] and communities go to war to occupy it. The foundation of this new social organisation is the city, and the purely spontaneous nature of the tribe is broken down through new migratory movements. *This is Roman antiquity*. It was here that the ancient world entered into a stage of dynamism. In these new conditions, the individual became the private proprietor of the land. To be a member of the community remains, as in the first formation, a precondition for appropriation. Now, however, as a member of the community, the individual is a private proprietor. The development from the first to the second formation is represented by the dissolution of the naturalness of the communal relationship. This is the necessary prerequisite for an individual to become private proprietor. Only now can the community be recognised as an artifice, as a historical product. With the denaturalisation of communal relations, new founding myths of political relations arise. The transition to the second formation is, therefore, progress in the denaturalisation of relations and the opening up of new possibilities for individual liberation. The emergence of the individual is one of these possibilities, but it is not the only one.

Continuing this comparative history and evaluating *Germanic property as the third formation*, Marx did not intend to delineate a unilinear historical process of the forms of property,[41] but rather to show the possible different forms of production within which the union of man and land is not put in question. Here, the individual is only a possessor. He is not endowed with

---

37. Wainwright 2008, p. 883. For Marx's geohistorical framework and the location in Asia of the most primitive formation, see Sereni 2007, pp. 134–5.
38. Spivak 1999, p. 81.
39. Marx 1983b, p. 384; Marx 1986, p. 400.
40. Marx 1983b, p. 386; Marx 1986, p. 402.
41. For more on this, see also Hobsbawm 1971, p. 34.

the *jus utendi et abutendi*, and property remains the property of the community. There are extremely diverse forms of property-relations between the individual and land, and of communal relations between individual and individual – but in none of these formations is there yet found a separation of the community from the conditions of its existence. From this point of view – from the point of view of the breakdown brought about by the capitalist mode of production – these formations represent more the aspect of invariance than of progress. Marx tried to highlight the element of invariance within their differences. He explored the analogous elements and differences between the Germanic community and the Roman *ager publicus*. He observed that if, for the Germans, the home represents the economic totality, not the city as for the Romans, or the whole community as in the Asian formations,[42] the element that characterises all these formations is the fact that, within them, the economic object is the production of use-values, the reproduction of the individual in his or her particular relationships to the community.[43] Appropriation does not occur by means of labour, but has the prerequisite of labour as its naturally given condition – labour is provided in objective conditions that are not the product of labour, but are already its given nature. The ownership of land depends upon the activity of the individual, who, for his or her part, is constantly presupposed as a member of the community and can be a proprietor only in this form.

In all three of these precapitalist formations,

> [T]he basis of development is the reproduction of *presupposed* relationships between the individual and his commune – relationships more or less naturally evolved or else historically developed, but become traditional – and a *specific objective* existence, *predetermined* for the individual, both as regards his relation to the conditions of labour and his relation to his co-workers, fellow-tribesmen, etc. The development therefore is from the outset a *limited* one, but once the limit is transcended [*Aufhebung*], decay and ruin ensue.[44]

A gaze focused upon the past from the perspective of the present crisis is reflected back onto the present to reveal *its* tendency. There is, however, a double reflection, which is typical of a Eurocentric approach. The establishment of the capitalist mode of production in Europe, following the dissolution of precapitalist communal formations, is generalised within the 'ontopogenic division' of the world into ideal forms.[45] Their dissolution and destruction

---

42. Marx 1983b, p. 392; Marx 1986, p. 407.
43. Marx 1983b, p. 393; Marx 1986, pp. 408–9.
44. Marx 1983b, p. 395; Marx 1986, pp. 410–1.
45. Wainwright 2008 pp. 883–5.

are projected onto the capitalist present. If 'all previous forms of society were destroyed by the development...of the social productive forces', the 'development of the material productive forces, which is at the same time the development of the forces of the working class, *at a certain point transcends capital itself*'.[46]

Two variables prevent this framework from falling into a mechanistic ideological schema. First, the destruction is shown as being in relation with the 'development of the forces of the working class'; therefore, the battle could also be lost. Morever, because Marx's attention is always focused on that which distinguishes the capitalist mode of production from any other mode of production, the model of dissolution and destruction cannot simply be duplicated, since the 'propagandistic (civilising) tendency is unique to capital – it distinguishes it from all earlier conditions of production'.[47] The denotation of the expansive movement of capital as 'civilising' is the fruit of a historicist and Eurocentric conception of history.[48] It led Marx, in the 1850s, to express an ambiguous view on colonialism. This conception of history can be found in the analysis of the *Grundrisse*,[49] and in the outline for the 1859 'Introduction', in which the progressive process of universal history is delineated in stages or, in other words, according to the Asiatic, ancient, feudal and modern bourgeois modes of production, defined as 'epochs marking progress [*progressive*

---

46. Marx 1983b, pp. 445–6, 449; Marx 1986, pp. 464, 467.

47. Marx 1983b, p. 448; Marx 1986, p. 466.

48. On the Eurocentrism of the Marxian model of the genesis of capitalism displayed in the *Grundrisse*, see Wainwright 2008, p. 885. At the time when he wrote the *Grundrisse*, Marx's historical knowledge concerning the history of primitive communal societies was not very well-developed. He knew next to nothing about Africa, had mediocre knowledge regarding the ancient and medieval Middle-East, had more in-depth knowledge about some parts of Asia, mostly India, and quite thorough knowledge of classical antiquity and the middle-ages in Europe. His knowledge, especially concerning Eastern Europe and primitive societies, grew appreciably during the 1870s, after the publication of the first book of *Capital* and in the context of dialogue with Russian socialists. On this topic, see Hobsbawm 1971, pp. 24–5. Goody 2006, p. 211, argues that not only is the sequence of modes of production culminating in capitalism Eurocentric, but that the very concept of capitalism pushes any analysis in a Eurocentric direction.

49. See Mohri 1979, p. 35. Mohri writes: 'In the 1840s and 1850s Marx emphasised the "revolutionary" role of British free trade, basing himself upon a general expectation that it would destroy the framework of the old society which was an obstacle to the growth of productive forces, and would generate in its place the kind of development that would lay the basis for a new society. However, this view was discarded by Marx himself from the 1860s onward, as he became well aware that the destruction of the old society would not necessarily give rise to the material conditions for a new society' (p. 40).

Epochen]'.[50] This progress involves the dissolution of limits, and is observed from a present-day perspective or, rather, from the point of view of the bourgeois epoch, which is defined as 'the last antagonistic form of the...process of production.'[51] 'Last', because all natural and communal limits are destroyed under a mode of production the objective of which is value and not use-value. There emerges at this point a theoretico-political alternative that is decisive for understanding the historicist ambiguities of Marx's discourse: either the absence of limits of the capitalist mode of production is driven forward towards the creation of new needs, of a new human nature and the 'progressive' and 'civilising' destruction of precapitalistic formations, or limits can be placed on a mode of production that appears as a nexus of destruction and self-destruction. The limiting of that which cannot be limited, the struggle between limitation and the limitless – this is the clash between two forms of production: communism and capitalism. At different times, Marx would follow both of these paths.

The individual as a modern phenotype

Capitalist modernity, 'if the narrow bourgeois form is peeled off', can become a 'universality of the individual's needs, capacities, enjoyments, productive forces...'[52] Marx searched for a trace of this development in man's emancipation from nature, insofar as nature is a limit to the development of the

---

50. Marx 1961b, p. 9; Marx 1987a, p. 263. As is well-known, Balibar argued that Marx's concept of the 'mode of production' was an 'epistemological break with respect to the whole tradition of the philosophy of history': Balibar 1970, p. 201. Hindess and Hirst agreed, considering the task of constructing a general theory of modes of production to be 'scientifically unfounded, as the effect of a teleological and idealist philosophy of history' (Hindess and Hirst 1975, p. 5). Going beyond the ensuing controversies, Hindess and Hirst called into question the concept of structural causality and of the correspondence between the thought-object and the real-object. In their opinion, 'history is not a real object, an object prior to and independent of thought, it is an object constituted within definite ideologies and discourses' (p. 318). General concepts are not concepts of a science of history that can be applied to the past and to the stages of a teleological process. 'The idea that the concepts of pre-capitalist modes, the ancient or the slave modes, for example, relate to the past is an effect of the teleological histories which have dominated Marxist theory' (p. 320). Korsch had already observed that in the 'Marxian concept of development, there is another fundamental difference between the materialistic theory of the historical process and that metaphysical concept of "evolution"...Marx recognized from the outset the delusive character of that so-called "historical evolution", according to which "the last stage regards the preceding stages as only preliminary to itself and, therefore, can only look at them one-sidedly" [Marx 1956–90d, p. 636]': Korsch 1963, pp. 50–1.
51. Marx 1961b, p. 9; Marx 1987a, pp. 263–4.
52. Marx 1983b, p. 395; Marx 1986, p. 411.

individual. The universal unfolding of needs and enjoyments corresponds to the unfolding of a new human nature and the 'absolute unfolding of man's creative abilities'.[53] In light of the historical caesura of capitalist modernity, precapitalistic formations appear to have invariant aspects: they are all characterised by relationships of servitude binding the worker to the land or to a lord, and by relationships where production for immediate use and, therefore, use-value, is predominant.[54] Modernity can be seen as a 'historical process...of dissolution',[55] which transforms and produces individuals who are free wage-workers, who exchange their own capacity to labour, and who are no longer subject to the personal authority of a lord, but rather to the objective powers of social conditions.[56]

This process of the production of abstract wealth triggers not only the denaturalisation of nature, but the transition to a *third* human nature, following on from the Hegelian second nature whose relationships are determined in the system of needs. An unprecedented field of anthropological potential hangs on the equally concrete possibility of the loss of the human. Marx lists these open possibilities of capitalist modernity: the exploration of nature in its entirety in order to discover new useful properties of things; the exploration of the entire planet in order to discover new useful objects; the development of the natural sciences to the point they are at today – that of being able to directly manipulate nature; the universal exchange of products and, therefore, the creation and infinite multiplication of new social relations; 'new (artificial) modes of processing natural objects'; the discovery, creation and satisfaction of new needs arising from society itself; a new human nature of limitless needs; *Kultur* of all the qualities of social man, 'producing him in a form as rich as possible in needs because rich in qualities and relations'.[57]

'Social man [*gesellschaftlicher Mensch*]' is the term Marx temporarily employs to denote the anthropology of a man without nature, capable of creating his own artificial nature. It is a new phenotype that is not only emancipated from all 'idolatry of nature', but also able to set his own development on a social plane, now possible thanks to the multiplication of relations, needs, and possibilities for enjoyment. *Kultur* as the negation of human naturalness is its creation as artifice. Nature becomes a work of art.

---

53. Marx 1983b, p. 396; Marx 1986, p. 411.
54. Marx 1983b, pp. 409–10; Marx 1986, pp. 424–5.
55. Marx 1983b, p. 409; Marx 1986, p. 426.
56. Marx 1983b, p. 551; Marx 1987c, p. 40.
57. Marx 1983b, p. 322; Marx 1986, p. 336.

In prefiguring an automated future, the *Grundrisse* identify the fuse that can blow up the capitalist encasing [*involucro*]. The development of technological science and of machines makes possible, for the first time in human history, the freeing up of an immense amount of time. This topic is considered afresh, on the dual levels of the development of productive forces and of a new human nature. The increase in free time as leisure-time to dedicate to higher activities is, as time for the 'full development of the individual', and of the development of his capacity for enjoyment, the transformation of the subject into 'a different subject [*ein andres Subjekt*]'. It is a development that as 'the greatest productivity, in turn reacts upon the productive power of labour'.[58] The *social man* is cultivated to a high degree, and in order to be able to enjoy the many different kinds of things that are available to be enjoyed, he must also have a greater capacity for enjoyment – a new capacity for enjoyment.[59]

Economic forms of production, be they capitalist or otherwise, are, at the same time, forms of a '*reproduction process...of the individual* as a member of a community'.[60] In exploring the nexus between the production of individuality and forms of production, Marx searches within the capitalist mode of production for signs of that which appears to go beyond it. He writes: '[T]he producers...transform themselves in that they evolve new qualities within themselves, develop through production new powers and new ideas, new modes of intercourse, new needs, and new speech'.[61]

We must search within these signs – signs so deep as to be capable of changing human nature – to find the ways in which this new individual nature might, in turn, act upon the productive forces. We glimpse the possibility that there could be a new *type* of human, one who would have to re-learn the ways of using his time that were destroyed by the capitalist disciplining of the Industrial Revolution.[62] He will have to re-learn how to fill his day with enriched and more pleasurable social relations. If a measure of human progress exists, it is, on the one hand, the increase in the amount of free individual and social time and, on the other, the qualitative and quantitative decrease in the elements of physical and psychological harm related to work. The daily

---

58. Marx 1983b, p. 607; Marx 1987c, p. 97.
59. Marx 1983b, p. 322; Marx 1986, p. 336. Marx 1983b, p. 607; Marx 1987c, p. 97. Kemple observes how Marx attempts to transform the nightmare of technological possession of the mind and body by capital into a new social body: Kemple 1995, pp. 41–2.
60. Marx 1983b, p. 393; Marx 1986, p. 409.
61. Marx 1983b, p. 402; Marx 1986, p. 418.
62. On this topic, see E.P. Thompson's concluding observations in Thompson 1967.

growth of the sphere of work, if compared to the concrete possibilities of liberation from work that exist today in mature capitalist countries, marks a point of regression which can only be maintained through violence.

The famous 'Fragment on Machines'

Enhancing productive forces through the use of machines is, for the Marx of the *Grundrisse*, the fulcrum upon which pressure must be applied in order to rupture the capitalist encasing and free immediate communist elements. Marx does this on two levels simultaneously. In the growth of the sphere of needs and the potential for more free time, he shows us a new type of human that goes beyond modern individuality. In the substitution of human labour by the machine, he tries to pinpoint the self-destructive tendency of capital. The development of the machine, which should dissolve the capitalist mode of production from the inside out, is observed according to an objective and subjective dynamic. On the one hand, there is the overthrow [*Zusammenbrechen*],[63] and on the other, there is the 'development of the social individual'.[64] At this point, the possibility of a new individual existence opens up, that of 'being a social entity [*Gesellschaftskörper*]'.[65] In a last, desperate attempt to work with the ambivalences of capitalist modernity, Marx gets sucked into a historical dialectic of objective forces. His famous *Fragment on Machines* closely integrates these reflections. This *Fragment* should not be given excessive weight,[66] but rather should be re-read in the light of its problems, which become most visible if seen in hindsight, from the perspective of *Capital*.[67]

As is known, these pages examine the consequences that automation has for the hypothesis that value is labour objectified. This contradiction is exploded within capital itself, in such a way that, following the mechanisation of production, production based on exchange-value would supposedly collapse. It is no coincidence that not only in *Capital*, but in all his reflections of the 1860s, as he rethought the law of value and his analysis of competition between capitals, Marx abandoned the view that automation will lead to collapse. This is not due to a lack of radicalism in his mature writings, but rather to a rethinking of these paradoxical conclusions. In the *Grundrisse*, in an attempt to keep mechanical automation and the centrality of the relationship between labour

---

63. Marx 1983b, pp. 601, 643; Marx 1987c, pp. 92, 134.
64. Marx 1983b, pp. 601, 641; Marx 1987c, pp. 92, 133.
65. Marx 1983b, p. 601; Marx 1987c, p. 92.
66. For interpretations of Marx's *Fragment on Machines*, see Bellofiore and Tomba 2009.
67. For an interpretation along these lines, see Bellofiore 2008a.

and value together, Marx was forced to draw the conclusion that if human labour is reduced to a meagre amount, then the value that it generates must also be reduced. The resulting tension is discharged in a *geschichtsphiloso-phisch* horizon: 'Thus capital works to dissolve itself'.[68] Automation leads to a drastic reduction in 'labour in its immediate form', which ceases to 'be the great source of wealth', so that '...labour time ceases and must cease to be its measure, and therefore exchange value [must cease to be the measure] of use value.... As a result, production based upon exchange-value collapses'.[69] These words appear in Notebook VII of the *Grundrisse*. Marx returns to the same theme 14 pages later, where it is interwoven with the question of the crises that arise from the falling rate of profit. It represents an index with which to measure the degree of maturity of capital. The falling rate of profit provides the measure of the obsolescence of capital in terms of an increase in the constant part of capital. If, indeed, the falling rate of profit is given by the ratio of surplus-value as the numerator, and the sum of variable capital (wages) and constant capital (machines and raw materials) as the denominator, by increasing investments (and, at the same time, assuming that labourers are being paid the bare minimum necessary for survival, so that almost all labour-time is surplus-labour), the denominator tends to increase, leading to a decline in the rate of profit. Marx thus identified one of the dynamics that produces crises within the capitalist mode of production. Capital responds to these crises by destroying a part of capital itself, in order to be able to 'go on fully employing its productive powers without committing suicide'.[70]

Two different directions are possible. On the one hand, there is the hypothesis of collapse, where 'these regularly recurring catastrophes lead to their repetition on a higher scale, and finally to its [capital's] violent overthrow'.[71] On the other hand, we find the countertendencies, according to which '[t]he fall may also be checked by the creation of new branches of production in which more immediate labour is needed in proportion to capital, or in which the productive power of labour, i.e. the productive power of capital, is not yet developed'.[72]

---

68. Marx 1983b, p. 596; Marx 1987c, p. 86.
69. Marx 1983b, p. 601; Marx 1987c, p. 91.
70. Marx 1983b, p. 643; Marx 1987c, p. 134.
71. *Grundrisse*, in Marx 1983b, p. 643; Marx 1987c, p. 134. This conception of the final overthrow of capital is only found in the *Grundrisse*. The end of the 1858 economic crisis led Marx to rethink the concept of crisis at a new categorial level, complicating the analysis of 'capital in general' (a phrase which he did not use after the *Grundrisse*) and the competition between different capitals. On this topic, see also Heinrich 2009, pp. 80–1.
72. Marx 1983b, p. 643; Marx 1987c, p. 135.

It was on this second aspect that Marx later focused his attention, concentrating on the countertendencies brought into being through the creation of new branches of production. From the *Manuscripts* of 1861–3 onward, Marx began to examine the question of competition between capitals, significantly complicating the schema of 'capital in general [*Kapital im Allgemeinen*]' as outlined in the *Grundrisse*, where economic laws could still be analysed by abstracting from the existence of a plurality of capitals in competition with each other.

From 1863 onward, this expression *Kapital im Allgemeinen* disappeared from the Marxian lexicon. An analysis of the competition between single capitals allowed for new analyses of the outcomes of the growth of the productive forces as a method of producing relative surplus-value.[73] He introduced the concept of 'extra surplus-value' and reconsidered the law of falling rates of profit in terms of 'tendency', while dropping the theory of collapse set forth in the *Grundrisse*. These increasingly more extended crises cease to be the precursor of a 'violent overthrow' of capital, instead being presented as a corrective measure, capable of re-establishing a decent rate of profit and beginning capitalist accumulation afresh.[74]

In the *Grundrisse*, however, Marx sought to turn the crisis into revolution. The categorial framework itself was turned to this purpose. Marx thought that large-scale industry, by enhancing its productivity through the use of machines, would reduce human labour-time to a minimum, and thus also the value contained in the commodities.[75] Having identified the way in which 'capital works to dissolve itself',[76] eroding the law according to which labour is the measure of value, we must conclude that, 'as a result, production based upon exchange-value collapses'.[77] Revolutionary expectations were thus channelled into a theory of collapse. Marx rethought many aspects of this framework in the 1860s. There had to be an ever-greater amount of concrete history in his analysis. It was not enough to demonstrate tendencies on a suitably abstract level: it was necessary to see how the countertendencies work. Every page of history recounted and every factory-report transcribed in *Capital* measures up to the standard of this analysis. If, in the *Grundrisse*, Marx thought that he could explain competition by starting from the concept of 'capital in general', by the 1860s it was the competition between capitals that could explain the way capital behaves: 'capital becomes conscious of itself as a

---

73. Heinrich 1999; 2002.
74. Reuten and Thomas 2011 calls attention to these aspects.
75. See Marx 1983b, p. 601; Marx 1987c, pp. 91–2.
76. Marx 1983b, p. 596; Marx 1987c, p. 86.
77. Marx 1983b, p. 601; Marx 1987c, p. 91.

social power in which every capitalist participates proportionally to his share in the total social capital'.[78] The analysis found in the *Grundrisse* takes place at a decidedly more abstract level.

The social individual

The pages on precapitalist and future formations in the *Fragment on Machines* should be read together, holding Notebooks IV and V in one's left hand and Notebook VII in one's right hand. The reflections on the different subject and on the *social individual* represented the completion of the path begun with his analysis of precapitalist formations.[79] What the forms have in common, constrained within the social relations that serve as their *natural* limit, is the impossibility of producing the 'free and full development' of the individual or of society.[80] But '[Only]...capital forces labour beyond the limits of natural need and thus creates the material elements for the development of the rich individuality which is as varied and comprehensive in its production as it is in its consumption'.[81] Only the capitalist mode of production lays the foundations for *the social individual*, the expression of a productive form that has driven labour beyond the limits of natural necessity and which, therefore, constitutes the basis for the development of a new and richer individuality, and thus, also, of a new social formation. The concept of the social individual, abandoned after the *Grundrisse*, evokes a sort of zenith of capitalist development, the point at which this mode of production even produces a new human nature.

In the pages of the *Fragment on Machines*, Marx sought to create a lexicon for communism. The 'social individual' and 'social brain' are products of this mode of production, but at the same time they are extensions that go beyond it. With the expression 'social brain', Marx seeks to express the potential of the knowledge of the species in a way that reinforces the new anthropology brought about by capitalism. The brain is no longer the heritage of one skull alone. The myth of the genius, a romantic invention created in response to the crisis of individuality, finally succumbs, together with modern individuality, to be reborn as a collective labour of accumulating knowledge.

---

78. 'Das Capital kommt sich in dieser Form selbst zum Bewußtsein al seine *gesellschaftliche Macht*, an der jeder Capitalist pro rata of his share in the total capital of the society, participates': Marx 1992d, p. 269. These parts came together in the third volume of *Capital*, edited by Engels: Marx 1964, p. 205; Marx 1998, p. 194.

79. Marx 1983b, p. 607; Marx 1987c, p. 97. On the ambivalencies of the concept of the 'social individual', see Di Marco 2005, pp. 101–2; Basso 2008, pp. 210–11.

80. Marx 1983b, p. 395; Marx 1986, p. 411.

81. Marx 1983b, p. 244; Marx 1986, p. 251.

The current crisis of the branches of knowledge and of the entire educational system is a symptom of knowledge becoming social. Throughout the course of history, branches of knowledge that existed for much longer than current ones have been lost, because they became useless. Steering today's ships requires a different knowledge from that which was required to navigate a ship with sails. A large portion of that knowledge is objectified in electronic devices and marine forecasts that no individual would be able to produce or control on his or her own. However, no-one would dream of trading in this collective knowledge for the knowledge of a helmsman of the days of yore. Today, this objectification of knowledge is invading the fields of humanistic knowledge. The work of the philologist who counts the number of times a term recurs in a classical text has become completely useless; any machine today can do that job in a few seconds.

Sometimes, the single individual of today's relations of production may appear more ignorant than any individual of the last century with a university-degree. However, if we stop thinking in terms of individuals and individual minds, then the entire picture changes, at least as far as these questions are concerned. The quantity of objectified social knowledge is much higher than it was two centuries ago, as is the quality of the knowledge to which people have access, thanks to the Internet. From this perspective, there has been in increase in knowledge, not an impoverishment. The problem lies, rather, in the domination of this objectified knowledge and, therefore, of dead labour over living labour, particularly as it continues to generate poverty instead of social wealth. Furthermore, the end of humanistic knowledge and of *Bildung* appears to be dominated by the capitalist use-value of technological and scientific knowledge. The analysis of new forms of production and of knowledge cannot, therefore, ever be separated from the critique of science: 'Science, which compels the inanimate members of the machinery, by means of their design, to operate purposefully as an automaton [*Automat*], does not exist in the worker's consciousness, but acts upon him through the machine as an alien force, as the force of the machine itself'.[82] Machines are designed and built to enhance and intensify labour-power. This goal is set in opposition to the worker, given that, in the form of the machine, science itself acts upon the worker as an alien force. This is true of all of 'society's general... knowledge [*das allgemeine gesellschaftliche Wissen*]', all the more so to the extent that it becomes an 'immediate productive force'.[83] The accumulation of science

---

82. Marx 1983b, p. 593; Marx 1987c, p. 83.
83. Marx 1983b, p. 602; Marx 1987c, p. 92; translation modified.

and of the productive forces of the 'social brain [*gesellschaftliches Hirn*]', when absorbed into capital, are endowed with an intrinsically capitalist use-value.

Foreshadowing the future

If, in precapitalist formations, man proved to be the goal of production, to such an extent that these formations might be imagined to be superior to the modern world,[84] Marx replied to any such reactionary model with a series of inversions: '[I]f the narrow bourgeois form is peeled off', wealth will be based on 'the universality of the individual's needs, capacities, enjoyments, productive forces, etc.', and on the 'full development of human control over the forces of nature'; the unlimited development of productive forces makes the existence of a new individuality possible, since 'the absolute unfolding of [the individual's] creative abilities' is only possible within a mode of production that 'makes the totality of this development...an end-in-itself'.[85] It would be wrong to think that this post-individuality has already come to pass, when, within capitalist modernity, we find, instead, the traces of the destruction of the modern concept of the individual. One need only look to Hobbes to find the type of individuality produced by modernity: persons or, in other words, interchangeable masks. The historical materialist takes his cues from these *Charaktermaske*, and considers individuals to be 'categories personified' and shows how they are produced.

At this point, *Grundrisse* and *Capital* proceed in different ways. *Capital* takes as a given the idea of the *ab ovo* destruction of modern individuality, tracing epic bourgeois subjectivity back to mythic forms of the self-representation of the modern. Marx gave no credence to the idea of free individuals, since when he focused his gaze on the laboratories of production, he saw only twisted individualities and suffering. The *Grundrisse*, on the other hand, take as a given the modern self-representation of the individual, its consequence being his destruction, and the possibility of laying out new possibilities from the shards that remain. This was, still, a dialectical way of moving forward: '[The] complete unfolding of man's inner potentiality turns into his total emptying-out. His universal objectification becomes his total alienation'.[86] In looking for a possibility for development that could offer an alternative to this emptying-out and total alienation of human nature, however, one assumes that 'human nature' was originally whole but was progressively emptied out. There are different possible interpretations, here, based on how one contextualises this

---

84. Marx 1983b, p. 396; Marx 1986, pp. 411–12.
85. Ibid.
86. Marx 1983b, p. 396; Marx 1986, p. 412.

historical dialectic. If 'human nature' is the communal nature of primitive communism, the alternative development of the individual will stem from a return to that communal form, combined with the modern development of productive forces. If, on the other hand, we observe this 'emptying out' from the standpoint of a condition of full individuality, we postulate, and take as a given, the modern self-representation of the concept of the individual. Its crisis can be interpreted either as decadence or as the possibility for a new post-individuality. *Übermensch* is one of its possible names. What appears to be an emptying-out is only an emptying-out from the standpoint of the bourgeois concept of the individual, whereas it is already the 'complete unfolding of man's inner potentiality.' What appears to be crisis is only a crisis in relation to past formations. The elements of crisis are thus conceived from the standpoint of their revolutionary overthrow. Tensions are channelled along the lines of historical tendencies: 'Once this point has been reached, capital, i.e. wage labour, enters into the same relation to the development of social wealth and the productive forces as the guild-system, serfdom and slavery did, and is, as a fetter, necessarily cast off'.[87] By use of these historical parallels, Marx wants to sketch out a new prognosis: just as the guild-system was an obstacle to the development of capitalist relations, now capitalist relations are an obstacle to the development of productive forces and social wealth. The elimination of these obstacles in the past is a model for the elimination of this last obstacle in the present.

The 'rich development of the social individual' is once again correlated with the development of productive forces, and the resulting tension is once more channelled into the abolition of the 'self-valorisation of capital' and, finally, into its 'violent overthrow'.[88] The historical patterns of precapitalist formations, when projected onto the future, acquire a prognostic sense. These pages were penned in an attempt to provide an immediate solution for the crisis:

> The growing discordance between the productive development of society and the relations of production hitherto characteristic of it, is expressed in acute contradictions, crises, convulsions. The violent destruction of capital as the condition for its self-preservation, and not because of external circumstances, is the most striking form in which it is advised to be gone and to give room to a higher state of social production.[89]

---

87. Marx 1983b, p. 641; Marx 1987c, p. 133.
88. Marx 1983b, pp. 641–3; Marx 1987c, pp. 133–4.
89. Marx 1983b, p. 641; Marx 1987c, p. 134.

The acute convulsions of a capitalist crisis led Marx to believe in, and hope for, a collapse of the capitalist mode of production. His theory very rapidly turned to identify the objective and subjective conditions for overcoming the capitalist mode of production, building on the model of that which is historiographically available – the overcoming of previous modes of production. Marx referred back to these in order to delineate a dialectic between the development and the limit of productive forces within the capitalist mode of production, serving his effort to show how its *inherent limits* lead to its overcoming, exactly as happened in the past in the case of the corporations.[90] He applied this vision of historical stages politically:

> These indications, together with the correct grasp of the present [*richtige Fassung des Gegenwärtigen*], then also offer the key to the understanding of the past [*Verständnis der Vergangenheit*] – a work in its own right, which we hope to be able to undertake as well. This correct approach, moreover, leads to points which indicate the transcendence of the present form of production relations, the movement coming into being, thus foreshadowing the future.[91]

Verständnis der Vergangenheit, combined with a *richtige Fassung des Gegenwärtigen*, should shed some light on the future, which is not a utopia to be created, but 'the movement coming into being'. With the decline in the rate of profit, capital should become an obstacle [*Schranke*] to the very development of the productive forces. At this point, recreating the historical patterns developed within the historiography of precapitalist formations in a *geschichtsphilosophisch* form, the model for the dissolution of these forms is applied to the capitalist mode of production. Capital simultaneously obstructs the development of the productive forces, which capital itself liberated, and the development of the individuality and the new subjectivity, which capital itself made possible. The problem of the modernity of capital becomes that of how to contain and control the possibilities for liberation that the capitalist mode of production, as a 'continual revolution', continuously reveals.

Modernity as inversion

The end of the crisis, and the ability of capital to metabolise it, called for fresh analyses, as Marx told Engels in his aforementioned letter of 8 October 1858. Meanwhile, from August to November of that year, he was working on a

---

90. Marx 1983b, p. 328; Marx 1986, p. 342.
91. Marx 1983b, p. 373; Marx 1986, p. 389.

new piece of writing, now known as the *Fragment des Urtextes von "Zur Kritik der politischen Ökonomie"*. The *Urtext* began to address the problem of fetishism, bringing together, in establishing the historical character of the capitalist mode of production, two strategic plans: namely, the dissolution of ancient bonds of community and the becoming-independent of exchange-value. Once 'exchange value become independent' has been imposed, the peasant no longer appears before the landowner as a peasant with his agricultural product, but as a money-owner. A new form of community is established, in which money-relationships take the place of the previous personal 'motley ties'.[92]

The new form of community in which 'exchange value become independent' reigns is characterised by an inversion [*Verkehrung*], which is the mark of capitalist modernity.[93] The traditional form of exchange, where use-value is the aim of selling for the sake of buying (C-M-C), is inverted, becoming M-C-M. Value becomes the aim.[94] Aristotle, in order to save economics (C-M-C), attempted to relegate the form of exchange where people buy for the sake of selling (M-C-M) to chrematistics, a form of exchange in opposition to its objective.[95] In the capitalist inversion, chrematistics take the place of economics. This inversion appears as 'the perversion of money [*Verkehrung des Geldes*]', which 'from means [turns into] end'.[96]

Money does not always carry out its function in the same way. Although it always remains a 'means of exchange', money changes its function based on the historical-conceptual setting in which it is found. If, however, selling in order to buy 'is kept within bounds by the very object at which it aims', by consumption or the satisfaction of definite wants, by 'buy[ing] in order to sell', then the beginning and the end are the same thing. A movement begins that is endless [*endlos*] and boundless [*maßlos*].[97] Money – be it gold, silver, or anything else – possesses no inherent mystical characteristic that constitutes it as money. Any commodity can be the currency of all the other commodities [*Rechengeld der übrigen Waren*],[98] the thing against which their price is set. This is true in every social structure where exchange exists, even if only in the 'mediated form of barter'. In this case, the transformation of a commodity

---

92. Marx 1980, p. 19; Marx 1987b, p. 430.
93. Hatem 2006, p. 12. Hatem finds seven levels of inversion in Marx: intersubjectivity, intrasubjectivity, ontic, semiotic, economic, political, and ideological.
94. Marx 1980, p. 74; Marx 1987b, p. 488.
95. Ibid. The prehistory of modern economic science, which began to develop in the mid-eighteenth century, lies in chrematistics, and not in economics. See Brunner 1956.
96. Marx 1980, p. 34; Marx 1987b, p. 447.
97. Marx 1962a, pp. 166–7; Marx 1996, p. 162.
98. Marx 1980, p. 72; Marx 1987b, p. 486.

into money is an arbitrary and conventional [*konventionel*] act.[99] Such was coin [*nomisma*] for Plato, a *symbolon* of exchange, a kind of 'token' conventionally recognised within the *polis* that gave its holder the right to receive a product in exchange for it.[100] Etymologically speaking, the term *nomisma*, which first meant 'convention' and later 'currency', harks back to 'law', *nomos*.[101] Also according to Aristotle, money is conventionally introduced in order to make exchanges, to have 'something to...give and take' for the needs of life.[102]

Marx refers to Plato and Aristotle as critics of the degenerate use of money: 'In his *De Republica*, Plato wants forcibly to keep money as mere means of circulation and measure [of value], but not to allow it to become money as such. For the same reason, Aristotle regards the form of circulation C–M–C, in which money functions only as measure and coin – a movement which he calls economic – as natural and reasonable, and brands the form M–C–M, the chrematistic one, as unnatural and inappropriate'.[103] Marx's concern is to point out how both Plato and Aristotle attempted to bring exchange back within the confines of a mediated form of barter. Plato, in limiting money to the sole function of exchanges made for mutual need,[104] was attempting to neutralise the disruptive effects of the circulation and accumulation of money on the social and economic structure of the *polis*.[105] In a similar way, Aristotle attempted to limit the negative aspects of money, the creation of riches through trade and the transformation of money into 'the first principle and the end of trade'.[106]

The negative aspects of money have been denounced throughout its history. These denunciations could be made because the Greeks were still able to distinguish, also in the sense of terminology, between *oikonomia* and chrematistics, between that which has a limit and that which does not. Despite the fact that Aristotle drew a distinction between different forms of chrematistics, 'in the meaningful sense of the term', chrematistics has 'no limits, for the object of that is money and possessions'.[107] In this sense of the term, money

---

99. Ibid.

100. Plato, *Republic*, 371b; Schofield 1993; Howgego 1995, pp. 1–22; Kim 2001; Faraguna 2003.

101. Aristotle, *Nicomachean Ethics*, 1133a30–1: '...money has by general agreement come to represent need. That is why it has the name of 'currency' [*nomisma*]: it exists by current law [*nomos*] and not by nature...'

102. Aristotle, *Politics*, 1257a35–8. See Faraguna 2003, p. 128 ff.

103. Marx 1980, p. 74; Marx 1987b, p. 488. See Marx 1962a, p. 167; Marx 1996, p. 162.

104. Plato, *Republic*, 372a.

105. Maffi 1979, p. 166.

106. Aristotle, *Politics*, 1257b22–3.

107. Aristotle, *Politics*, 1257b40–1.

becomes both the 'element and purpose of exchange', giving rise to a 'strange kind of wealth', where abundance offers no salvation from starvation,[108] as in the legend of King Midas. Most of all, the accumulation of wealth as an end in itself conspires against living well; therefore, it is unjust.

Pliny the Elder argued that the 'greed for gold' and *permutatio* were direct threats to *traditio*: 'Heads of statues are interchangeable...As for likenesses of themselves, their concern for honour extends only as far as the price... and men leave portraits that represent not themselves, but their money'.[109] The ascendency of unregulated *permutatio* condemns memory and tradition to their deaths. For Pliny the Elder, it was a question of saving the *imago*, to be handed on from one generation to the next, as a way of limiting the corruption of traditions. These denunciations were directed against the degenerate use of money: thus Thomas Aquinas condemned the exchange of goods with the goal of their multiplication as contrary to the proper end according to which the useful should be measured. The problem was that of the limit – the measure – of money in the economy, since human needs are finite.

The difference between ancient and modern luxury [*Luxus*] should be examined in relation to the expansion of the sphere of needs, to the 'new (artificial) modes of processing natural objects',[110] and to [man's] new capacity for experience. There is a corresponding anthropological change, 'cultivating all the qualities of social man and producing him in a form as rich as possible in needs'.[111] *Luxury* is consonant with a new artificial nature and a new human nature. Luxury, though closely related to the *luxuria* of materials and of the body denounced by Pliny the Elder, was not, for him, a measure of decadence. For Seneca, it was.[112] New illnesses arise from *luxuria*, which is a mixture of various different elements:

---

108. Aristotle, *Politics* 1257b14–15.
109. Pliny the Elder, *Naturalis Historia*, XXXV, 4–5.
110. Marx 1983b, p. 322; Marx 1986, p. 336.
111. Ibid.
112. Seneca, *Epistulae morales ad Lucilium*, 95, 20–1: 'The illustrious founder of the guild and profession of medicine remarked that women never lost their hair or suffered from pain in the feet; and yet nowadays they run short of hair and are afflicted with gout. This does not mean that woman's physique has changed, but that it has been conquered; in rivaling male indulgences they have also rivaled the ills to which men are heirs. They keep just as late hours, and drink just as much liquor; they challenge men in wrestling and carousing; they are no less given to vomiting from distended stomachs and to thus discharging all their wine again; nor are they behind the men in gnawing ice, as a relief to their fevered digestions. And they even match the men in their passions, although they were created to feel love passively (may the gods and goddesses confound them!). They devise the most impossible varieties of unchastity, and in the company of men they play the part of men. What wonder, then, that we can trip up the statement of the greatest and most skilled physician, when so many

Mark the number of things – all to pass down a single throat – that luxury [*luxuria*] mixes together, after ravaging land and sea. So many different dishes must surely disagree; they are bolted with difficulty and are digested with difficulty, each jostling against the other. And no wonder, that diseases which result from ill-assorted food are variable and manifold; there must be an overflow when so many unnatural combinations are jumbled together. Hence there are as many ways of being ill as there are of living.[113]

Marx did not accept the vocabulary of decadence. It is only through an error of perspective that Seneca's observations could still appear relevant today. The luxury to which Seneca refers was not yet industrially produced. For the ancients, it still made sense to attempt to block the progress of *permutatio*. Modernity does not know such a block, for the simple reason that, since it does not produce goods in light of their use-value, it transforms the very nature of utility.

'*Luxury* is the opposite of natural necessities'.[114] If the individual, insofar as man is a natural subject, is bound to his basic needs, the development of modern industry goes beyond the limits of natural necessity, and thus also beyond the image of luxury set in direct contrast to natural necessities. The melting away of this contrast is deliberately ignored in conceptions of decadence. In the absence of natural necessity and a natural subject, not only can *Luxus* not be defined as being in contrast with nature, but it becomes an indefinite extension of the social individual's human needs.[115] In the *Grundrisse*, Marx examined the positive side of capitalist development. Where it is destructive, specifically of a form of individuality, Marx attempted to find signs of a new possible individuality. Unlike the reactionaries, he saw the socialisation and objectification of knowledge and skills that were formerly the province of certain individuals not as a loss, but as a new quality of the individual, who feeds his own knowledge and intelligence back into society.

Luxury should be considered in the context of the relation between use-value and individual consumption, where the changing nature of needs has repercussions on consumption and on the nature of the consumer. Luxury, as Sombart observes,[116] gives considerable encouragement to capitalist development, expanding the sphere of needs beyond its natural limits and

---

women are gouty and bald! Because of their vices, women have ceased to deserve the privileges of their sex; they have put off their womanly nature and are therefore condemned to suffer the diseases of men'.

113. Seneca, *Epistulae morales ad Lucilium*, 95, 19.
114. Marx 1983b, pp. 322, 434; Marx 1986, pp. 336, 452.
115. Marx 1983b, p. 607; Marx 1987c, p. 97.
116. Sombart 1967.

democratising the consumption of unnecessary goods. Sombart was pointing in the right direction, towards the link between this democratisation of
the sphere of needs and the increase in consumption of luxury-goods, the
development of capitalism and the disintegration of feudal society. Capital
also democratises luxury, such that, during the seventeenth and eighteenth
centuries, Parisian ladies could flaunt their elegance in the face of the sweat
of slaves in the Americas. Today, every Western child can enjoy the right to
play, as set forth in the *Convention on the Rights of the Child*, because his or her
toys are made at a low cost by children in other parts of the planet. Western
children's mothers and fathers, meanwhile, affirm their right to eternal youth
by erasing their wrinkles with serums that are the product of trafficking in
stem-cells stolen from newborn babies in Eastern Europe.[117]

Value, having become the objective of production, increases wealth and
produces new poverty, while at the same time expanding the natural limits
of human needs. The only limit this production knows is the conflict between
labour and capital. The criticisms of money made by the classic thinkers can
today find an echo only among reactionaries, since, in reality, they abstract
from the inversion that characterises the capitalist mode of production.

When inversion becomes dominant, money ceases to be a mere mediat-
ing form of commodity-exchange and becomes 'a form of exchange-value
growing out of the circulation process'.[118] As soon as a medium of exchange –
be it gold, silver, or any other commodity – becomes *Wertmaß* [measure of
value], it becomes money, 'without the society's aid or desire', and, therefore,
no longer out of convention. It is not the exchange of goods useful for the
fulfilment of needs that is mediated by money, but rather it is money, insofar
as it creates 'exchange-value as something independent', under which social
relations are subsumed. The 'domination of the accursed metal that appears
as sheer insanity [*Verrücktheit*]' is established.[119] The community in which
exchange-value has become something independent is now ruled by the
accursed and fateful violence of money, inverting and perverting relations.
Individuals are subsumed under monetary relationships, becoming 'equally

---

117. The 14 May 2007 *Corriere della sera* spoke of 'Children sold as replacement-parts.
Foetuses synthesised to instill vitality into the old and the sick.... Organ-trafficking,
disappearing newborns, clandestine surgeons and the new stem-cell business.... The
Ukraine could discover itself to be an underground supermarket for organs, body-
tissue and human cells. In a still-confidential report, the European Council inquires
into the disappearance of two hundred babies from delivery rooms in the former
Soviet republic'.
118. Marx 1980, p. 73; Marx 1987b, p. 487.
119. Marx 1980, p. 73; Marx 1987b, pp. 487–8.

worthy functionaries of the social process',[120] 'subjectivised exchange-values [*subjektivierte Tauschwerte*]'.[121] Social relations multiply hand-in-hand with the multiplication of exchanges, and assume the semblance of relations between things, while the individuals who made these exchanges become merely indifferent bearers of commodities. This is the domination of equality and of indifference.

Human nature and historical progress

In the *Manuscripts* of 1861–3, we read that the 'development of the capacities of the human species', though it must pass through the Gehenna of capital, 'coincides with the development of the individual',[122] even if this comes to pass 'at the cost of the majority of human individuals and whole human classes'.[123] This perspective leads us to place the 'development of the species' and of productive forces above the 'welfare of the individual'.[124] Marx considers Ricardo's point of view to be scientific, even when he places the proletariat on the same level as machines or beasts of burden, or when he displays his indifference to the slaughter of workers resulting from the development of productive forces.[125] His perspective is still the perspective of historical progress. He can grasp its ambivalences, but he cannot imagine its alterity. In order to do so, we require a critique of the capitalist use-value of science and modern technology, which is possible from the point of view of the use-value of the worker's living corporality. From this perspective, there is a divide between the species and the individual.

It was not enough to subject the objectified science of machinery to criticism. The same had to be done with the epistemological status of the critique of political economy, not in order to maintain the non-scientificity of Ricardo's viewpoint, but in order to develop another science. *Capital* was able to address this issue. In *Capital*, the terms 'species [*Gattung*]' and 'social individual' disappear, and Marx focused his attention on the destructive traits of the capitalist development of the productive forces. He imagined liberation in terms of a break with a mode of production indifferent to use-value, in which the capitalist, 'fanatically bent on making value expand itself...ruthlessly forces the human race to *produce for production's sake*'.[126] 'All methods for raising the

---

120. Marx 1980, p. 59; Marx 1987b, p. 474.
121. Marx 1980, p. 57; Marx 1987b, p. 471.
122. Marx 1967, p. 111; Marx 1989a, p. 348.
123. Ibid.
124. Marx 1967, p. 111; Marx 1989a, p. 347.
125. See Marx 1967, p. 111; Marx 1989a, pp. 347–8.
126. Marx 1962a, p. 618; Marx 1996, p. 588.

social productiveness of labour are brought about at the cost of the individual labourer; all means for the development of production transform themselves into means of domination over, and exploitation of, the producers'.[127] Such was the changed rhetorical register employed in *Capital*. The critique of capitalist development, as seen from the perspective of the living corporality of the labourer, not only attacked machines and technology, but also the modern justification of progress as such. The means for the development of production, Marx continued, 'mutilate the labourer into a fragment of a man, degrade him to the level of an appendage of a machine, destroy every remnant of charm in his work and turn it into a hated toil'. This is not all they produce. They also *'estrange from him the intellectual potentialities of the labour process in the same proportion as science is incorporated in it as an independent power*; they distort the conditions under which he works, subject him during the labour process to a despotism the more hateful for its meanness; *they transform his lifetime into working time*, and drag his wife and child beneath the wheels of the Juggernaut of capital'.[128] Modern manufacture now

> converts the labourer into a crippled monstrosity, by forcing his detail dexterity at the expense of a world of productive capabilities and instincts; just as in the States of La Plata they butcher a whole beast for the sake of his hide or tallow.... [T]he individual himself is made the automatic motor of a fractional operation...By nature unfitted to make anything independently, the manufacturing labourer develops productive activity as a mere *appendage* of the capitalist's workshop.... The knowledge, the judgement, and the will, which, though in ever so small a degree, are practised by the independent peasant or handicraftsman...are now required only for the workshop as a whole. Intellectual potencies [*geistige Potenzen*] in production expands in one direction, because it vanishes in many others. What is lost by the detail labourers, is *concentrated* in the capital that employs them. It is a result of the division of labour in manufactures, that the labourer is brought face to face with the *intellectual potencies* [*geistige Potenzen*] of the material process of production, *as the property of another*, and as a *ruling power*.[129]

As science develops, intellectual potencies grow, but they are incorporated into machines, into dead capital confronting living labour. The knowledge stolen from individuals and incorporated into machines sets itself against individual labourers, not only because it takes their place, but also because it cripples them, transforming them into its appendages. Machines and science

---

127. Marx 1962a, p. 674; Marx 1996, p. 639.
128. Ibid.
129. Marx 1962a, pp. 381–2; Marx 1996, pp. 365–6; translation modified.

are not of an ambivalent nature *per se*. They do not contain a single atom of liberation. It is their use that can bring about this ambivalence, when it is turned against capital. The historical materialist does not see, in machinery and technology, the fetishism of decadence; but nor does he see in them an immediate liberation from work. Instead, he sees a key that is capable of opening the lock only if held in the correct hand. Marx does not present us with the image of a mortified humanity in order to moralise, but rather in order to pose a new problem: the individualistic and capitalist outcome of modernity has proven to be self-destructive.

In the pages of *Capital*, the focus on the production-process that 'converts the labourer into a crippled monstrosity' is aimed at the body of labour, at that for which there is no compensation, that which cannot be measured in terms of wages.[130] This focus on the corporeal can be observed from the time of the 1844 *Manuscripts*, when Marx noted that 'the better formed his product, the more deformed becomes the worker'.[131] Now, in the suffering of a body, this focus becomes absolute. The worker does not have a body that he brings to work in order to provide labour-power; rather, the worker is a body that is forced to work. In the 1859 'Introduction' to *A Contribution to the Critique of Political Economy*, all of history, defined as the 'prehistory of human society',[132] is seen from the perspective of the most recent injustices, such that all the things occurring throughout history that have been presented in terms of progress and novelty are shown to be nothing more than the repetition of domination over nature and over the oppressed. It is a chain that binds history, allowing the reproduction of a mythical present.

---

130. It is for this reason that it is logically impossible to represent the capital-labour relationship in terms of equality. That which is formally correct and falls within the rights of the sphere of circulation, the buying and selling of labour-power, becomes an injustice when placed within the production-process, where the labour-power to be provided during the process of labour necessarily entails the wearing out and ruining of the body. Wages pay for the use of labour-power, but cannot pay for the wearing out of the worker. This should be the test-bed for disproving Rawls's theory of justice. Rawls 1971; 1993.

131. Marx 1973, p. 513; Marx 1975f, p. 273.

132. Marx 1961b, p. 9; 1987a, p. 264.

Chapter Three

The Phantasmagoria and the Temporalities of Capital

We think we have choice, but everything is compulsory.... This is a new kind of totalitarianism that operates at the checkout and the cash counter.... It's a new kind of democracy, where we vote at the cash counter, not the ballot box.... Sounds like hell...

(J.G. Ballard, *Kingdom Come*)

Inferno

Dante's hell provides a rhetorical and imaginative arsenal for modern labour, which, as Marx noted, already at the stage of manufacture had gone beyond the 'worst horrors of [Dante's] Inferno'.[1] The descent of Marxian science into the infernal laboratories of production signalled a change of register from that of political economy. Marx did not move towards the heavens of abstraction, but towards the materiality of acting and suffering bodies. If political economy is a phantasmagoria that transforms spirits

---

1. Marx 1962a, p. 261; Marx 1996, p. 254: 'The manufacture of lucifer matches...since 1845...has rapidly developed in England...With it has spread the form of lockjaw, which a Vienna physician in 1845 discovered to be a disease peculiar to lucifer-matchmakers. Half the workers are children under thirteen, and young persons under eighteen.... Of the witnesses that Commissioner White examined (1863), 270 were under 18, 40 under 10, 10 only 8, and 5 only 6 years old. A range of the working day from 12 to 14 or 15 hours, night labour, irregular meal times, meals for the most part taken in the very workrooms that are pestilent with phosphorus. Dante would have found the worst horrors of his Inferno surpassed in this manufacture'.

into bodies and bodies into spirits, Marxian science is the science of the extra-conceptual irreducibility of use-value. The limit of the scientificity of political economy consists not only in its eternalisation of the form of capitalist production. Political economy does not simply cede place to a superior Marxian science. On the contrary, Marx worked with another concept of science. We enter into the science of capital, 'as at the entrance to hell', above whose doors are placed the Dantescan warning: 'Qui si convien lasciare ogni sospetto / Ogni viltá convien che qui sia morta'.[2] This is the scenario of *Capital* – with gothic additions.[3]

Marx, at the age of 25, had been impressed by reading Mary Shelley's *Frankenstein* and Polidori's *Vampyre*. These works had been composed under the influence of *Fantasmagoriana, ou Recueil d'Histoires d'Apparitions de Spectres, Revenans, Fantômes, etc.*[4] Phantasmagorias are also the *fantômes artificiels* that Robertson[5] created by means of magic-lanterns in the middle of the French Revolution – images that dissipate. Evoked by Marx in the section in the first chapter of *Capital* Volume I on the fetish-character of the commodity,[6] phantasmagoria is also a category of the defeat of Enlightenment-rationalism. Spectres do not exist, as Robertson reiterated at the beginning of each of his spectacles. What is seen is only 'l'effet bizarre de l'imagination', real objective spectres that everybody sees. They are effects 'surnaturels dans les siècles de la crédulité':[7] phantasmagorias. The project of modern rationalism appears to be compromised: the spectres, driven into the world of the imagination, invade the image of the world. It was precisely the triumph of the Enlightenment and

---

2. 'Here all misgiving must thy mind reject / Here cowardice must die and be no more': Marx 1961b, p. 11; Marx 1987a, p. 265.

3. Roberts 2005. See also Wilson 2003, p. 308: 'Here all is cruel discomfort, rape, repression, mutilation and massacre, premature burial, the stalking of corpses, the vampire that lives on another's blood, life in death and death in life'.

4. The text, published in French in 1812, is the translation of a part of the five-volume anthology *Gespensterbuch* [Book of Ghosts], published in Leipzig between 1811 and 1815 under the editorship of F.A. Schulze (under the name of Friedrich Laun) and J.A. Apel. Five stories from the *Fantasmagoriana* were translated into English by Sarah Elizabeth Brown Utterson and published in 1813 together with her own story, 'The Storm', with the title *Tales of the Dead*. The progenitor of the romantic genre of vampire-stories, J.W. Polidori, participated together with Lord Byron, Mary Shelley, William Godwin and others in the soirée held at Villa Diodati in 1816, reading and telling horror-stories. Those readings gave birth, in 1818, to *Frankenstein* and, in 1819, to Polidori's *Vampyre*. Goethe, mistakenly attributing its authorship, called it one of the best works of Byron, and it was immediately translated into French and German.

5. It appears that it was Etienne-Gaspard Robert who invented the term 'fantasmagoria', from phantasma and *agoreuein* [to speak in public]: see Sauvage 2004; Castle 1988.

6. Marx 1962a, p. 86; Marx 1996, p. 81.

7. Robertson 1985, p. 165.

of rationalism that found its counter-melody in the spectacles of phantasma-goria and in the birth of spiritualism in Hydesville in 1848. The bourgeoisie, after having 'profaned every sacred thing', turned to spiritualism. Between 1852 and 1853, it became fashionable across Europe to make the tables dance, as Marx recalls in a note to his passage on the fetish-character of the com-modity. Yet in the same note, producing a combination seemingly as bizarre as the commodity itself, represented in its fetish-character,[8] Marx also evokes what really terrorised the European bourgeoisie: the anti-feudal revolution in China: 'One may recall that China and the tables began to dance when the rest of the world appeared to be standing still – *pour encourager les autres* [to encourage the others]'.[9] Breaking out in 1851 in the south of China, the Taiping Rebellion signalled the beginning of a decade of great agitation. It heralded the fall of the Manchu dynasty and extensive transformations on the political and ideological scene in China. Europeans, initially simple specta-tors not without sympathy for the rebels, then intervened to defend their own interests and ended up contributing in a significant manner to the triumph of the Imperial troops in 1862–3.[10] A distant revolution closely threatened the interests of European capital. Terrorised by the spectre of revolution, the bourgeoisie of the nineteenth century founded a parallel word of spirits.

The phantasmagoria constitutes the negative of modern rationality: not its negation, but its trace. The Cartesian project of the foundation of rational-ity on the certainty of the *ego cogito* is placed in check. In the phantasmag-oria, the senses 'deceive us' in an objective way;[11] equally objectively, 'waking can never be distinguished from sleep''.[12] Marx emphasises how the effect of fetishism is not simply illusory, but objective.[13] The phantasmagoria puts us in an inverted world of spells and spectres.[14] Marx does not propose an Enlightenment-style critique. He does not intend to deny the existence of monsters, but to demonstrate how real monsters really produce a monstrous

---

8. Marx speaks of the bizarre or 'absurd form [*verrückte Form*]' of the commodity in Marx 1962a, p. 90; Marx 1996, p. 87.

9. Marx 1962a, p. 85; Marx 1996, p. 82.

10. Much of that preached by the Taiping, such as forms of utopian socialism, dialogues with Christianity, equality of the sexes, universal Confucian harmony, and Western technology, formed the basis for later Chinese engagements with modernity. The Taping were defeated by Imperial and Western forces.

11. Descartes 2008, p. 17.

12. Descartes 2008, p. 18.

13. An overivew of the main interpretations of fetishism in Marx can be found in Dimoulis and Milios 2004, pp. 3–42. The authors emphasis how the Marxian concept of fetishism refers not only to the commodity, but to all the forms of capital (money, means of production) and capitalist relations (p. 27).

14. Marx 1962a, p. 90; Marx 1996, p. 87.

imaginary. Hence, the project of *Capital* announced in the 'Preface' of 1867: 'we have to remove the "magic cap" that we draw down over our eyes and ears as a make-believe that there are no monsters'.[15] Walter Benjamin was among the few to locate within Marx's critique of phantasmagoria an element for going beyond the Enlightenment-concept of critique.[16]

The phantasmagoria creates a 'framework in which its use value recedes into the background'.[17] The object of contemplation is not use-value, but exchange-value. The commodity really does have an absurd form [*verrückte Form*],[18] which can be comprehended by means of a shifting [*Verrückung*] of one's point of view in relation to the object of use. Use-value does not completely evaporate, but is reserved in exchange-value. The modern individual can enjoy products that are almost identical, because what counts most is the use-value of exchange-value: as the money spent in order to buy a ticket is worshipped, the consumers have the same enthusiasm whether it is a matter of filling the auditorium for a concert, for an art-exhibition or a literary festival, or a sports-stadium. What they have bought is, in the last instance, neither music, nor art, nor culture, nor sport, but a *lifestyle*. It is a lifestyle that they could not provide for themselves on their own: not due to some subjective incapacity, but because the social relations have become relations between commodities. The 'transfer of the use-value of consumption goods to their exchange-value', which disguises exchange-value itself in an object of enjoyment, today constitutes, as Adorno wrote already in 1938, 'the cement' that 'holds the world of commodities together'.[19] Individuals enter into contact with each other by means of monetary exchanges, paying a toll to capital. Atomised and isolated individuals pay for their own social relations: they pay for a subscription to the Internet in order to send each other emails, for a ticket in order to see a play, for the time of others in order to have their attention. Public squares as meeting places are replaced by shopping malls, in which it is possible to pass the entire day. It is the commodities that attract individuals and put them in relation. Human experience in its entirety becomes experience at a price: in this context, the commodity becomes a form of experience, and thus culture. What appears as the commodification of culture is nothing other than the image of the commodity that has become a culture itself. It is the production of commodity-images that produces the commodification of the imagination. The social form of capital destroys human community.

15. From Marx's 1867 'Preface', in Marx 1962a, p. 15; Marx 1996, p. 9.
16. See Cohen 1989, p. 105.
17. Benjamin 2002, p. 7. See Markus 2001.
18. Marx 1962a, p. 90; Marx 1996, p. 87.
19. Adorno 1991, p. 39.

It would be mistaken, however, to think that it does not reproduce new communities. Fascism fed and continues to feed upon this ambiguity.

From the point of view of circulation, a new anthropological type appears to be born, a *homo consumericus*, a type of turbo-consumer corresponding to the civilisation of desire.[20] However, the transition is not, as appears to be the case to a perspective dazzled by fetishism, a transition from 'economies of production' to the 'capitalism of consumption'. Rather, it is the result of a repositioned perspective on circulation. Oniomania expresses the difficulty of use-value satisfying needs insofar as the bought object is, above all else, an exchange-value. Satisfaction vanishes just as soon as the transaction is over. The experience becomes an experience of the indifferent commodity-form. Fetishism and fashion are united in an intimate complicity. As it is the commodity that, through exchange-value, creates difference, the ideal consumer is undifferentiated and androgynous.

The multicoloured appearance of circulation was shown for what it is – that is, a vast desert – by the critical theory of the Frankfurt school. It was right to construct this image, but it remains incomplete if we do not shift our perspective from circulation to production. The scenario of *Capital*, populated by vampires and omnivorous Molochs,[21] shows the destructive power of the capitalist mode of production, ready to expropriate 'all surplus labour which the human race can ever perform'.[22] Comprehending capital as a 'self-regulating automaton' increasing itself in a geometrical progression,[23] Dr. Price 'pouvait prouver par des calculs exacts qu'il faudrait annexer d'autres planètes à ce monde terrestre pour le mettre à même de rendre au capital ce qui est dû au capital'.[24]

The image of capital that does not consider the conditions of labour and of reproduction is precisely the image of fetishism.[25] It is shared both by apologists and romantics, supporters of a development without limits, and by critics of that development in the name of human nature or of a sustainable development. Capital can appear as an automaton only if it is represented as money that produces money, only if we remain within the perspective of circulation – only if the source of value is occluded: living labour.[26] With the change of perspective – the descent into the secret laboratories of production – neither the expansive force nor the destructive and self-destructive character

---

20. Lipovetsky 2006.
21. Hatem 2006, pp. 69–72.
22. Marx 1964, p. 410; Marx 1998, p. 394.
23. Marx 1964, p. 409; Marx 1998, p. 393.
24. Marx 1989f, p. 510.
25. Marx 1964, p. 409; Marx 1998, p. 393.
26. Dussel 1993, pp. 123–7.

of capital are negated. It is only that these aspects are represented in a new way, beginning from the relations of production, where labour is enhanced and intensified at the cost of the life of the living bodies of the workers. Marx's gothic scenario does not regard circulation, but the sites of labour. The image that capital produces of capitalist modernity is, therefore, that of crisis as a constitutive element of capitalist relations of production. The crisis is not a conjunctural event, but the normality of these relations of production. Naturally, this vision does not regard Mr. Moneybags,[27] but the worker. For the capitalist, the crisis begins when the possibility of realising profits is reduced. For the workers, the crisis begins when, in the productive process, the vampire sucks their blood, and continues with the expulsion of the mass of workers from the labour-process. It is in Chapter Eight of *Capital*, Volume I, on the working day, that the vampire and the werewolf make their appearance. It is here that we also encounter the image of Dante's Inferno. Marx's analysis is not a description of the world, coexisting alongside other descriptions in the way that different points of view coexist amongst the different perspectives looking at the same object. Rather, Marx calls into question the claimed objectivity and neutrality of perspective, though not in order to search for another point of view able to represent the object in its totality. Marx's shifting of perspective is not towards the totality, but towards a part: the workers' use-value, the living bodily nature of the worker. The perspective is that of living labour, labour effectively performed in the labour-process, where the living bodily nature of the worker is put to work and where, at the same time, it seeks to resist exploitation. There is nothing anthropologically natural in being constrained to work in a more or less repetitive way for eight or more hours per day. This violence is not visible from the perspective of circulation. Here, even though there can, indeed, be very violent conflicts, everything happens in a manner conforming with the law.[28] It is in production that absolute injustice is demonstrated. Materialism begins here. There is no wage that could compensate for the living corporeality of the worker constrained to work in a repetitive and injurious job. It is the assumption of the non-neutrality of the point of view of this part that is the perspective of *Capital* against capital.

Incipit capital

The capitalist mode of production signals the cutting of the umbilical cord that tied the human to nature. In the first half of the twentieth century, the Abbot

---

27. Marx 1996, p. 189. On the figure of Mr. Moneybags, see Wolff 1998.
28. See Tomba 2009c.

Breuil affirmed that with the exhaustion of peasant-civilisation, 'the cycle that began with the Neolithic age'[29] had also come to an end. Development without social and natural limits began. Towards the end of the 1860s, Marx toned down the Promethean notes about humans' potential to alter nature and came to a 'gloomy vision of the perpetual destruction of nature'.[30] He was impressed by reading Fraas,[31] and wrote to Engels that the first effect of cultivation [*Kultur*] in agriculture is to render fields barren, because when [cultivation] proceeds in natural growth and is not *consciously controlled* [it] leaves deserts behind it'.[32] Capitalist development, animated by profit, now appears as an immense process of desertification.[33] What we call today the 'ecological question' is not opposed to the question of labour. In Marx, they are two sides of the same problem: 'all progress in capitalistic agriculture is a progress in the art, not only of robbing the labourer, but of robbing the soil; all progress in increasing the fertility of the soil for a given time, is a progress towards ruining the lasting sources of that fertility'.[34] Technological progress linked to the capitalist mode of production is presented as a 'process of destruction' of 'the original sources of all wealth – the soil and the labourer'.[35]

The Promethean tones of the *Grundrisse* are abandoned. In the mid-1860s, though representing capitalist production as a squanderer of 'human lives, or living labour, and not only blood and flesh, but also nerve and brain',[36] Marx still suffered from a fascination for a sort of secular theodicy that allowed him to put in relation and, in part, to justify the most 'extravagant waste of individual development' with the 'development of humanity'. Marx's intention, here, was to represent the necessary transition through an 'epoch of

---

29. Cited in Camatte 1975, p. 103.

30. Elster observes that there is 'an interesting contrast to be made here between Marx's theory of perpetual progress of the productive forces and the more gloomy view of the perpetual destruction of nature': Elster 1991, p. 58.

31. Fraas 1847.

32. Marx 1987d, p. 559. Marx also read the 1840 book by the German chemist Justus von Liebig, *Die Chemie in ihrer Anwendung auf Agricultur und Physiologie*, whose seventh edition in 1862 contained a new introduction in which he declared the intensive, or 'high farming', methods of British agriculture to be a 'robbery-system', opposed to rational agriculture. Marx noted that to 'have developed from the point of view of natural science the negative, i.e., destructive side of modern agriculture, is one of Liebig's immortal merits': Marx 1962a, p. 529; Marx 1996, p. 507. See Foster 2002. On the regressive character of capitalism, see also Bordiga 1979.

33. According to Heinrich, Marx's still valid critique regards the destructive character of capital, the immanent destructive power that the process of valorisation demonstrates in relation to humanity and nature: Heinrich 2005, pp. 113–16, 129, 153.

34. Marx 1962a, p. 529; Marx 1996, p. 507.

35. Marx 1962a, p. 530; Marx 1996, p. 508.

36. Marx 1962a, p. 99; Marx 1996, p. 92.

history immediately preceding the conscious reorganisation of society'.[37] An idea of the progressive character of the capitalist mode of production, perhaps more emphatic in Engels than in Marx,[38] also left room for justifications of colonialism.[39] It was the encounter with the Russian populists and his analysis of the rural commune that allowed Marx to rethink this conception of historical progress.[40]

In order to indicate the epochal-historical character and thus the determinate caesura of the affirmation of the capitalist mode of production, the *incipit* of *Capital* shows the structural change that even 'wealth' undergoes in this mode of production. Insofar as it 'appears [*erscheint*]' as 'immense accumulation of commodities [*ungeheure Warensammlung*]', even scarcity assumes a meaning that is radically different from what it could have had in the past. The accumulation of commodities is *ungeheur*, immense and monstrous at the same time, because, with the capitalist mode of production, the purpose of wealth purpose is not, in the first place, that of satisfying needs. There can be scarcity amidst the greatest abundance. Marx uses the verb *erscheint* and not the indicative present of the verb 'to be': *ist*. Wealth *is not* exclusively an accumulation of commodities, but it *appears* in this way; that is, it is also possible that it is or becomes something else. The 'commodity is, in the first place, an object outside us, a thing that by its properties satisfies human wants of some sort or another'.[41] To begin from value and the commodity as bearer of value constitutes an abstraction. It is necessary, instead, to emphasise the use-character of the produced object, its utility in terms of satisfying needs: 'the utility of a thing makes it a use-value'.[42] The splitting of the product of labour into a useful thing [*nützliches Ding*] and a thing of value [*Wertding*] takes place when 'useful articles are produced for the purpose of being exchanged'[43] – not as a surplus that one community exchanges with another, but as rule; when, that is, 'their character as values has therefore to be taken into account, beforehand, during production'.[44] The first chapter of *Capital*, Volume I, presents a

---

37. Marx 1962a, p. 99; Marx 1996, p. 92.
38. Jaafe 2007.
39. Mohri argues that Marx's position on colonialism, ambivalent until the middle of the 1860s, began to change in relation to a different understanding of the Irish question and as a consequence of a deeper study of different social formations, particularly Russia: Mohri 1979, p. 34.
40. On the centre-periphery problematic, Dussel argues that Marx overcame his own Eurocentrism towards the end of the 1860s, as he engaged with the question of 'peripheral' Russia. See Dussel 1990a.
41. Marx 1962a, p. 49; Marx 1996, p. 45; translation modified.
42. Marx 1962a, p. 50; Marx 1996, p. 46.
43. Marx 1962a, p. 87; Marx 1996, p. 84.
44. Ibid.

double perspective corresponding to a double layer of meaning. Political economy works with a metahistorical concept of exchange; the critique of political economy, instead, shows how not even exchange can be a metahistorical category, because it has become something different in the inverted world of capital. When things are produced *for* exchange, when their production aims at their value rather than at their utility, there is an epochal change without precedent. It is comparable only to the Neolithic Revolution.

There is no need to seek in *Capital* the cell, the elementary form from which the system develops in its fullness.[45] The debate and post-debate on the categorial beginning [*Ausgangskategorie*] ended up reducing history to logic. However, this is an effect of an autofetishism produced by the categories in the capitalist mode of production themselves. It is a misunderstanding that the 'Preface' of 1873 tried to dispel: if the research has appropriated the material and its real movement has been presented in an adequate way, so that 'the life of the subject-matter is reflected [*sich widerspiegelt*] in the idea [*ideell*] as in a mirror, then it may appear [*aussehen*] as if we had before us a mere a priori construction'.[46] It is an appearance, because the ideal element, for Marx, is nothing other than 'the material [*das Materielle*] transferred and translated into the human mind'.[47] The point is that this translation occurs in the form of a mirror-image, inverted and without history.

However, it is not enough to overturn this inversion. If Marx's method was meant to be 'directly the opposite' of the Hegelian method, it had to take its cue from the *Materielle*. The first six chapters of *Capital*, which have given rise to very different (or even directly opposed) readings, present changes of perspective that continually dislocate and rearticulate his entire conceptual constellation. Here, we find fetishism and its critique, the ahistorical self-representation of the categories of the capitalist mode of production and analysis of their historically determined nature. If, in these pages, one sees only a deductive chain, one remains the prisoner of fetishism, seeing individuals as real only *qua* guardians of commodities. Such is capital's perspective – but it is not *Capital*'s perspective.

The *Konkretum* of the commodity

In his *Logic*, Hegel refuses to begin with something rather than with being. His *incipit* is being *qua* 'indeterminate immediacy [*das unbestimmte*

---

45. Jahn 1978. Aspects of this development are dealt with in Fineschi 2002.
46. Marx 1962a, p. 27; Marx 1996, p. 19; translation modified.
47. Ibid.

Unmittelbarkeit]'.[48] Logic, purified of its metalogical rudiment, cannot tolerate the non-identical, whose primacy is, instead, the ultimate meaning of materialism.[49] For this reason, there is an epistemological gap between Marx's exposition and the Hegelian dialectic. In his text directed against Wagner, who posited a deductive chain of all categories beginning with the concept of value, Marx replied:

> All this is 'drivel'. *De prime abord*, I do not proceed from 'concepts', hence neither from the 'concept of value', and am therefore in no way concerned to 'divide' it. What I proceed from is the simplest social form in which the product of labour presents itself [*sich darstellt*] in contemporary society, and this is the 'commodity'.[50]

Marx does not set out either from the *concept* of value or from the concept of the commodity, but from the commodity in its concreteness [*Konkretum der Ware*].[51] The materialist empirical dimension is linked to human needs and to the objects of use that satisfy them, whether they are materially sensuous or not. To begin with value, considering the commodity as mere *Träger* of value, is an abstraction. Instead, it is necessary to emphasise the use-character of the produced object, its utility in terms of satisfying needs.[52] It is the objects of use, in every epoch and in every social form, that constitute the 'substance of wealth'.[53] Use-value, the material content of wealth, is the element that allows us to consider historically the different social forms and the diverse forms that wealth has assumed in history.

The materialist constant of use-value allows us to comprehend the particular inversion that characterises this mode of production and in which the sensuous, use-value, counts only as a bearer of the abstract, of exchange-value:[54] capital produces not for the satisfaction of needs, but in order to valorise value, so that use-values becomes simple supports of exchange-value. Hans-Jürgen Krahl points out the particular character of Marx's concept of value:

---

48. Hegel 1986, p. 82; Hegel 2010, p. 59.
49. Adorno 1973, pp. 135, 192.
50. Marx 1962b, pp. 368–9; Marx 1989b, p. 544.
51. Marx 1962b, pp. 362; Marx 1989b, p. 538. On the commodity as 'conceptual beginning' of the analysis of the capitalist mode of production, see also Fineschi 2001, pp. 42 et sq.
52. Marx 1962a, p. 50; Marx 1996, p. 46.
53. Ibid.
54. 'This inversion [*Verkehrung*] by which the sensibly-concrete counts only as the form of appearance of the abstractly general and not, on the contrary, the abstractly general as property of the concrete, characterises the expression of value'. From the 1867 appendix to the first German edition – Marx 1983i, p. 634; Marx 1978a.

the abstraction of value that is not sensuous, but is neither positively supersensuous, needs, for its particular existence, sensuous and reified use-values; it is therefore mediated by them as well as subsuming them within itself.[55]

The relation between sensuous and supersensuous is an asymmetrical relation. The supersensuous is the *raison d'être* of the sensuous; but while the existence of the supersensuous is necessarily mediated by the sensuous, the sensuous can exist independently of the supersensuous. If, therefore, objects of use are produced simply as *Träger* of value, this relation mirrors only the objectivity of the point of view of capital. But it is not *true*. The existence of the supersensuous is necessarily mediated by the sensuous, which only in the capitalist relation of production is, in turn, subsumed in exchange-value. It follows that the supersensuous is something of indifference for the sensuous, insofar as the possibility of existence of the latter is in no way mediated by the former. The relation is not simply overturned, but is ruptured by the irreducible material excess of the object of use. Strictly speaking, we should say that the relation between the sensuous and supersensuous in the commodity is not, properly speaking, a single relation; it is, in fact, immediately diremped into a double relation: of the sensuous towards the supersensuous, on the one hand, and of the supersensuous towards the sensuous, on the other. Here, the logical categories are pushed beyond dualism. Sensuous and supersensuous constitute a particular unity called the 'commodity', in which the traditional philosophical categories are not adequate. Backhaus, seeking to dialecticise this relation, had to address this point when he wrote that 'the commodity, as something that has the properties of the sensuous and the supersensuous, of use-value and value, is not thinkable'.[56]

Criticism had never failed to emphasise the metaphysical character of Marx's concept of value.[57] What is, instead, often ignored is the fact that Marx was conscious of this when he sought to represent a thing that *is and is not* at the same time. 'The commodity is a use-value, wheat, linen, a diamond, machinery, etc., but as a commodity it is simultaneously not a use value'.[58] Marx did not present a dialectic of value. It is not a question of Hegelianising these passages in order to unearth a Marxian dialectic. We need, instead, to comprehend an asymmetry that is a conflict. In the first place, it is a conflict

---

55. Krahl 1971, p. 74. On Krahl, see Tomba 2011.
56. 'Die Ware als ein Etwas, dem Sinnliches und Übersinnliches, Gebrauchswert und Wert als Eigenschaft zukommen, ist nicht denkbar': see Backhaus 1970, p. 145. See also Arthur 2004, pp. 153 et sq.
57. On the critique of Marx's theory of value, see Backhaus 1974, pp. 52–4.
58. Marx 1961b, p. 28; Marx 1987a, p. 283.

of temporality.[59] The time of abstract labour objectivised in exchange-value does not exist without the time of concrete and particular labour. The time of labour that determines exchange-value also produces use-value, but these two times are not equal. The clock measures the labour-time concretely performed in production, while the time of abstract labour objectivised in the same commodity as socially-necessary labour – thus, as exchange-value – has a social measure, given by money. The first temporality is measured by the capitalist or by his overseers with the stopwatch in his right hand and the *Principles of Scientific Management* in the left; the second temporality is, instead, regulated on the global markets. The synchronisation of these two temporalities takes place in the competition between capitals through the capitalist exploitation of labour-power. This double temporality refers to the double nature of labour, and, on this basis, to that *specific* commodity that is labour-power. Here, we find a new, specific use-value relating to the concrete character of performed labour and to the body of the worker attached to that labour-power. The conflict between temporalities is presented on a new level: the labour-time and the free time of the worker, a time that is not only the empty time of non-work, but a time whose quality is intimately connected to the quality of the social relations of labour and to the time that is expended in them. Capitalist 'free time', on the other hand, tends to be the time of physical and psychological reproduction of the worker, with a view to the time of labour and of consumption. The picture is further complicated. *Capital* reveals a field of forces: the tension between exchange-value and use-value is, in turn, in tension with the ambivalent nature of living labour.[60]

The historical-epochal character of capital

Capital presents 'the categories of bourgeois economy', that is, the 'forms of thought expressing with social validity the conditions and relations of a definite, historically determined mode of production'.[61] It demonstrates, that is, the historical, rather than eternal character of this mode of production, as well as the conflictual nature of the categories by means of which it is represented. Marx explains exchangeability on the basis of historically-determinate categories: the exchange of commodities is not the same as the barter of objects of use. Because commodities are exchangeable, it is necessary

59. See Tombazos 1994, p. 27.
60. This excessive character of living labour and of its being in relation with the concreteness of the worker is emphasised also by Bellofiore, who demonstrates, from within economic analysis, its necessary political level. See Bellofiore 2007; 1996.
61. Marx 1983i, p. 47; Marx 1996, p. 87.

to determine a common substance that allows them to be made equivalent. Two different commodities are exchangeable because they have something in common, because they are things of 'a like substance, objective expressions of essentially identical labour'.[62] Value is the form of exchangeability of commodities: since it is required in order to explain exchange, to be its condition of possibility, it cannot derive from exchange. The equivalence of commodities is not the product of an equalisation that occurs within exchange: exchangeability has to be explained, and cannot be presupposed, otherwise it is elevated to a suprahistorical category, thus assuming that modern conceptuality that, finding itself in all previous historical forms, represents itself as eternal and insurpassable.[63] Viewed in terms of needs, however, production and exchange are one thing; viewed in terms of value, they are something else. Objects of use have always been exchanged, but not always in the same way. It is, certainly, possible to affirm that the 'commodity' and 'exchange' go through different forms of production, but their semantics have to be investigated in every single historical-conceptual configuration. If, as occurs in the case of the mass of products in small Indian communities, production occurs in view of the 'direct use by the community itself', they are not produced as commodities. 'It is the surplus alone that becomes a commodity', Marx argues.[64] A social form that produces with a view to direct use by the community and then exchanges the surplus is one thing, but a social formation that produces with a view to exchange, in order to valorise value, is something quite different. Only the second, strictly speaking, produces commodities. It is possible to extend the concept of commodity to non-capitalist formations, since it is in the nature of modern concepts to operate this type of subsumption, but we are dealing, here, with the same equivocal apologetics that are present when modern concepts of power, state and freedom are extended in order to comprehend premodern political forms.

62. Marx 1962a, p. 58; Marx 1996, p. 53.
63. This is what Korsch called the 'false idealistic concept of evolution as applied by bourgeois social theorists', which 'is closed on both sides, and in all past and future forms of society rediscovers only itself'. For Korsch, it was necessary to break up the 'magic spell of the metaphysical "law" of evolution', because if, for Marx, it is true that it is bourgeois society that gives the key to ancient society, 'it does not follow that such categories as commodity, money, State, law, etc., must have the same meaning for ancient society and its mode of production as they have for modern capitalist production and for the bourgeois society which is based upon it'. Korsch intended to counterpose the bourgeois concept of development, 'closed on both sides', to the new concept of development of historical materialism that is 'open on both sides': Korsch 1963, p. 51.
64. Marx 1962a, p. 378; Marx 1996, p. 362.

'Every product of labour is, in all states of society, an object of use [*Gebrauchs-gegenstand*]; but it is only at a definite historical epoch in a society's development that such a product becomes a commodity, viz., at the epoch when the labour spent on the production of a useful article becomes expressed as one of the objective qualities of that article, i.e., as its value'.[65] To consider the product without its production is what characterises fetishism and what triggers a process of eternalisation of concepts specific to the capitalist mode of production. Here, it is possible to introduce a further historical-conceptual distinction: every product of labour and every useful object existing in nature is an object of use [*Gebrauchsgegenstand*], while the use-value [*Gebrauchswert*] is, instead, the specifically capitalist form assumed by an object of use in the capitalist mode of production. The commodity, which is value and use-value, can also have a use-value without any utility, or a utility that is directly damaging. That is possible because the end of capitalist production is not the satisfaction of human needs, but rather the valorisation of value, and the commodity is not product *qua* object of use, but *qua* bearer of value. Capitalist use-value changes the nature of the object of use.

The survey of non-capitalist forms of production in the passage on fetishism does not have the same meaning as the exposition of precapitalist forms in the *Grundrisse*. In *Capital*, Marx shows not only that the surplus sold by a non-capitalist community cannot be assimilated to the commodity of capitalist production, but also why the inversion that occurs in capitalist modernity does not take place in non-capitalist relations; thus, fetishism does not occur either. The European middle-ages were characterised by personal relations of domination: 'the social relations between individuals in the performance of their labour...appear at all events as their own mutual personal relations'. Analogously, in the patriarchal home, the different acts of labour are functions of the family; individual labour-powers operate as organs of the common labour-power of the family.[66] Next to these two historical images, there are two fictional ones. The first is the island on which Robinson, after the shipwreck, starts to record the average labour-time required for the production of what he needs to guarantee his survival. The other image is made up of an association of free men. 'All the characteristics of Robinson's labour are here repeated, but with this difference, that they are social, instead of individual'.[67] The four cases illustrated are compared with the capitalist mode of production, in order to demonstrate how the categories of the latter can be extended to any form of production, real or imaginary, so as to generate the illusion

65. Marx 1962a, p. 76; Marx 1996, p. 72; translation modified.
66. Marx 1962a, p. 92; Marx 1996, pp. 88–9.
67. Marx 1962a, p. 92; Marx 1996, p. 89.

of the naturalness of the categories of the capitalist mode of production. It is the measure of labour-time, the common feature of any form of production, that determines the parallel with the production of commodities. The meta-historical and natural character of the production of the commodity derives from this.

But this is an error of perspective, arising from the lack of a distinction between labour 'as it appears in the value of a product' and how it is presented, instead, 'in the use-value of that product'.[68] The determination of the quantity of labour to be put into the production of use-values, with a view to the satisfaction of social needs, is one thing; the representation of the temporal duration of labour in the amount of value within the product of labour is another thing entirely. They are two different representations of time. The second is relative to a social formation 'in which the process of production has the mastery over man, instead of being controlled by him'.[69] Production with the aim of value dominates the time of human labour and thus also the life of individuals. Production scientifically oriented to the production of use-values, to their quality and quantity, occurs in an entirely different form. It is the distinction between value and use-value that allows us to see the inversion of the capitalist mode of production. If this distinction is occluded, not only does the inversion become invisible, but the categories of the capitalist mode of production are also expanded historically, to the point of subsuming within themselves every possible form of production.

It is for this reason that it is necessary to refer back to the labour that has produced the relevant object of use *qua* commodity. The commodity should be grasped as 'the concrete social form of the product of labour'.[70] It should not be viewed as a product of any labour in any social form, but as 'the product of labour in the current society'. 'The value of commodities has a purely social objectivity, and...they acquire this objectivity only in so far as they are expressions or embodiments of one identical social substance, viz., human labour'; thus, 'value can only manifest itself in the social relation of commodity to commodity'.[71] The objectivity of value is not produced by exchange between commodities. It is already given in the production of commodities, but is manifested in exchange. To affirm, instead, that this objectivity of value takes place only in the relation of exchange means to presuppose exchange as a historical invariant;[72] consequently, the objectivity of value can be found

---

68. Marx 1962a, p. 94; Marx 1996, p. 91.
69. Marx 1962a, p. 95; Marx 1996, p. 92.
70. Marx 1962b, p. 369; Marx 1989b, p. 545.
71. Marx 1962a, p. 62; Marx 1996, p. 57; translation modified.
72. Heinrich 2005, pp. 47–8. See also Heinrich 2008.

anywhere that there is exchange. If exchange is presupposed, if the abstract character of labour occurs in exchange,[73] given that objects of use have always been exchanged, then the category of value is eternalised, thus losing the historical discontinuity that characterises the mode of production of commodities. In the *Ergänzungen und Veränderungen* to the first book of *Capital*, written between December 1871 and January 1872, Marx observes that

> The general or abstract character of labour is, in the production of commodities, its *social* [*gesellschaftlich*] character, because it is the character of the *equality* [*Gleichheit*] of the labours incorporated in the different labour products. This determinate form of *social* labour [*Diese bestimmte Form der gesellschaftlichen Arbeit*] distinguishes commodity production from other modes of production.[74]

The production of commodities is distinguished from other modes of production, because here, and only here, is the social character of labour not given by the fact that the different labours are functions of a community, as could happen in the patriarchal family,[75] but, instead, by the fact that the different labours that produce commodities have the character of equality. Marx called this 'common element [*das Gemeinsame*]', demonstrated in the exchange of commodities, 'value'.[76] The true problem is the origin of this element common to all commodities, entailed within the historical rupture that transforms the product of labour into a commodity.[77] The question regards the transition to the production of commodities and its categories. In order to arrive at the correct determination of the universal value-form, Marx went by way of intermediate levels of abstraction, like the 'expanded relative value-form', in which the expression of value relative to another commodity leads to an infinite chain of references, where it is not possible to find any unitary character. In the 'general value-form', however, value is no longer determined

---

73. Heinrich argues that if we seek this objectivity outside exchange, then we no longer know where we have to comprehend it: Heinrich 2005, p. 52. Rubin had already explained the social character of abstract labour 'by means of the process of exchange', in which 'private labour assumes the supplementary determination of social labour'; if follows that 'if there were not the relation of exchange, there would not be abstract labour either': Rubin 1972; see also Jahn 1968, pp. 80–3. For Colletti also, 'the process by means of which we come to abstract labour' is not a mental abstraction, but an 'abstraction that occurs everyday in the reality itself of exchange': Colletti 1970, p. 113. For a critical reconstuction of the debate related to the abstraction of labour, see Bellofiore 2005, pp. 142 et sq.
74. Marx 1987e, pp. 28–9.
75. Ibid.
76. Marx 1987e, p. 72.
77. Marx 1962a, p. 76; Marx 1996, p. 72.

in relation to the exchange between use-values, but rather is the expression of what is common to all commodities.[78]

> In this manner the labour realised in the values of commodities is presented not only under its negative aspect, under which abstraction is made from every concrete form and useful property of actual work, but its own positive nature is made to reveal itself expressly. The general value form is the reduction of all kinds of actual labour to their common character of being human labour generally, of being the expenditure of human labour power. The general value-form, which represents all products of labour as mere congelations of undifferentiated human labour, shows by its very structure that it is the social expression of the value of commodities.[79]

This homogenisation of different labours to undifferentiated human labour occurs when labour-power is employed not for the production of determinate use-values, but for the end of valorising value.[80] When the inversion is given, the commodities are exchanged as portions of labour-time indifferent to the qualitative character of labour itself and of the objective bearer of that labour. The thing that is really exchanged is labour-time, without qualities,[81] indifferent to the use-value of the object and ontologised in value, which is the aim of the process of valorisation. Only the capitalist mode of production deploys this absolute equality that makes of labour something generally common: abstract labour. It is this character of labour that means that a commodity, 'by virtue of the form of its value, now stands in a social relation, no longer with only one other kind of commodity, but with the whole world of commodities'.[82] Time becomes the thing that is exchanged, and in this exchange of time, the law that presides over its measurement – what Marx calls the 'law of value' – becomes a universal law, internalised in the consciousness of time.[83] The time of abstract labour, positing itself as that which regulates the relations of exchange, constitutes a new form of the transcendental, conditioning the *a priori* structures of experience. The theory of knowledge as adequation of the concept to the object is overturned insofar as value is not only the

---

78. Marx 1962a, p. 80; Marx 1996, pp. 76–7.

79. Marx 1962a, p. 81; Marx 1996, pp. 77–8.

80. I agree with Finelli that it is necessary to enter into production in order to find the place of the genesis of the dualism of use-value and exchange-value: Finelli 1987, pp. 135–36. Value, Finelli emphasises, can exist only as valoristion, as a throwing off of limits, because, in its qualitative indeterminateness, 'it is conceivable only in a labour-process entirely organised according to the modalities of valorisation [or according to the principle of surplus-value]': Finelli 1987, p. 171; see also pp. 212–13.

81. See Krahl 1984, pp. 31–3.

82. Marx 1962a, p. 77; Marx 1996, pp. 73–4.

83. Krahl 1984, p. 29.

concept of the commodity, but directly and simultaneously the thing in itself and in appearance. The experience of a multiplicity of indifferent commodities, concretions of abstract labour, strikes at the very capacity of experience, which projects into the manifold a plurality of indifferent differences. With the loss of the possibility of thinking difference, the *novum* that irrupts in the always-identical, the present is elevated to an ahistorical present.

The Robinsonade

In the capitalist mode of production, the producer of commodities is presented as an 'independent private individual'. It is from this that his isolation from the community and the (modern) image of atomism derives. 'The epoch which produces this standpoint, that of the isolated individual, is precisely the epoch of the hitherto most highly developed social (according to this standpoint, general) relations'.[84] Given that – from the inverted perspective of fetishism – social relations are relations between commodities,[85] the density of the population must be measured on the basis of monetary exchanges. Marx was the pioneer of this new statistics: 'a relatively thinly populated country, with well-developed means of communication, has a denser population than a more numerously populated country, with badly-developed means of communication'.[86] For this reason, 'the Northern States of the American Union, for instance, are more thickly populated than India'.[87] Marx's problematic was to change the point of observation from that of a perspective reading the indifference of modern social relations of production as isolation, thus producing the Robinsonades of economics and of politics. If, in the *Grundrisse*, isolation is still interpreted in its ambivalence, emptying out and indifferent, on the one hand, and herald of expansive potentials, on the other,[88] in *Capital*, the 'isolated worker' is the 'free' seller of his labour-power,[89] the modern individual produced by the separation of objective conditions of his existence and by the hundred years' war against collective rights.[90]

---

84. Marx 1983b, p. 20; Marx 1986, p. 18.
85. 'In the capitalist process, every element, even the simplest, the commodity for example, is already an inversion and causes relations between people to appear as attributes of things and as relations of people to the social attributes of these things': Marx 1968, p. 498; Marx 1989c, p. 507.
86. Marx 1962a, p. 373; Marx 1996, p. 358.
87. Ibid.
88. Basso 2008, pp. 196–8.
89. Marx 1962a, p. 316; Marx 1996, p. 312; translation modified.
90. See De Certeau 1997b. On the attack on collective rights in France in the eighteenth century, an attack undertaken with 'enclosures' and 'cultivation', see Bloch 1930.

The discourse on the ambivalence of modern individuality, as an effect of the parallax with the point of view of circulation, is attentuated in *Capital*, where the individual is born already crippled amidst modern relations of production. The error would be to think that this deformation is the technical production of a repetitive and alienating labour, when, in fact, modern technology is nothing but the product of the autonomisation of value. The problem is not to humanise technology and to realise a full individuality, but, instead, to open up a path alternative to that which has produced the modern individual as something opposed to community. If, in the world of commodities, the relations between people appear as social properties of things, the same social relations appear even more as an expression of isolation the more they are developed. Both the concept of the 'individual and isolated hunter and fisherman, who serves Adam Smith and Ricardo as a starting point', and the atomistic individuals of the doctrines of the social contract, represent 'unimaginative fantasies'.[91] The atomised individual appears not as the product of the dissolution of pre-existing social relations, 'not as an historical result, but as the starting point of history'.[92] In this reflected image, not only is the outcome turned into a presupposition, but we are raised to the level of ahistorical universality. Modernity contorts the process of its own genesis into an ahistorical image.

Fetishism and phantasmagoria

The fetishistic vision can, indeed, explain the mechanisms of the market, but it destroys the experience involved in moving through production to the product. It thus produces the image of a world of commodities without production and without history: the phantasmagoria. Because the use-value of commodities – that is, the precipitate of concrete labour – becomes the indifferent body of the commodities, what is produced is always identical: exchange-value. The longing for new commodities increases, in direct proportion to the destruction of the sphere of experience of the objects of use,. Thus the compulsive search for novelty occludes the *novum*, the element that could change the current relations of production. If fetishism is the result of the autonomisation of exchange-value, then phantasmagoria expresses the destruction of historical experience: the image of an eternal present without history. The *facticius* not only designates that which is artificial, but also indicates, as substantive, magic: 'the magic and necromancy' that envelops

---

91. Marx 1983b, p. 19; Marx 1986, p. 17.
92. Marx 1983b, p. 19; Marx 1986, p. 18.

the products of labour like a fog.[93] The disenchanted modern world produces a new mythology and is filled with new fantasies. The reality of the unreal, which characterises the autonomisation of exchange-value, also produces the unreality of the real, which makes possible the postmodern deconstruction of the mythical present in mythologies, rhetorics and narrations.

The fetish-character of the commodity arises from the particular social character of labour that produces commodities, that is, when 'useful articles are produced for the purpose of being exchanged',[94] and are considered in their production not so much in terms of their utility but in terms of their value. The producers exchange their commodities, the products of their private labours, as value, containers of homogenous human labour. This inversion, which denotes the fetish-character of commodities, becomes the expression of a social form in which social relations are social relations between things: phantasmagorias. With the subsumption of use-value into exchange-value and of the labour-process into the process of valorisation, production tends to be rarefied; thus, the experience that moves through production to product also tends to evaporate. The commodities seem to be produced from nothing, and individuals are represented only as consumers. As the categories of capitalist production tend to extend to all the relations of production, eternalising capital and its social relations, the phantasmagoria is affirmed as an ahistorical present.

Fetishism[95] is produced not by a distortion of vision, but by the positioning of one's point of view on circulation.[96] Fetishism produces not only a determinate image of social phenomena, but also behaviours adequate to that image: atomistic behaviours. The objects of use are commodities insofar as they are 'products of private labour, which are carried on independently of each other'.[97] They are labours undertaken by autistic producers who 'come into social contact with each other' when 'they exchange their products'.[98] This is fetishism: the single capitalist producer produces with a view to his own profit, such

---

93. Marx 1962a, p. 90; Marx 1996, p. 87.
94. Marx 1962a, p. 87; Marx 1996, p. 84.
95. Fetishism, Kemple writes, is not an image for something else, but a figure of the process of figuration itself, a figure that allows us to reflect upon ourselves as creators of our images. Kemple 1995, p. 177.
96. From this point of view, free individuality, originally indifferent to the social dimension, affirms its primary indifference in the claimed sociality of exchange. 'The atomistic and abstract individual relates atomistically and abstractly to other, equally atomistic and abstract, individuals, who are characterised by their identical determination and, in this connection with their equal, do not contain within themselves any element of alteration'. Finelli 1987, p. 142.
97. Marx 1962a, p. 87; Marx 1996, p. 83.
98. Ibid.

that, from this perspective, social relations, taking place only in the exchange of commodities, are presented as 'social relations between things'.[99] Circulation gives rise to an indifferent sociality of individuals, apparently free and equal, but it is a society only in appearance. The modern social image of atomistic individuals derives from this:

> The behaviour of men in the social process of production is purely atomic. Hence their relations to each other in production assume a thingly form independent of their control and conscious individual action. These facts manifest themselves at first by products of labour as a general rule taking the form of commodities.[100]

If we adopt the point of view of the atomised producers, 'the relations connecting the labour of one individual with that of the rest appear, not as direct social relations between individuals at work, but as what they really are, material relations between persons and social relations between things [*sachliche Verhältnisse der Personen und gesellschaftliche Verhältnisse der Sachen*]'.[101] As the soul of circulation is individual interest, the relations instituted, here, are relations between people and things, and never between people in their real alterity. Due to this, alterity becomes a problem in modernity.

If capitalist relations are observed from the perspective of single private producers, we will see only their atomistic behaviour.[102] The social relation will occur only in exchange. It will be, precisely, a relation 'that assumes, in their eyes, the phantasmagorical form of a relation between things'.[103] This point of view is not only not illusory, but it is on this basis that the 'categories of bourgeois economy' are constituted: categories which, for this mode of production, 'are socially valid and therefore objective forms of thought'.[104] Fetishism is objective.[105] It cannot be corrected by a more objective image. Utilising Charles de Brosses's term,[106] Marx 'undertakes a critique *within* the context

---

99. Marx 1962a, p. 87; Marx 1996, p. 84.
100. Marx 1962a, pp. 107–8; Marx 1996, p. 103; translation modified.
101. Marx 1962a, p. 87; Marx 1996, p. 84.
102. Marx 1962a, p. 108; Marx 1996, p. 103.
103. Marx 1962a, p. 86; Marx 1996, p. 83.
104. Marx 1962a, p. 90; Marx 1996, p. 87; translation modified.
105. Two images, according to Finelli, characterise fetishism: on the one hand, the myth of subjective freedom of circulation is translated into the image and principle of production; on the other hand, the process of production is reduced to the labour-process alone, which is then further reduced to capital as means of production: see Finelli 1987, p. 178.
106. In 1842, Marx read and annotated C.B.H. Pistorius's German translation of Charles de Brosses's 1760 work *Du Culte des dieux fétiches*: see Marx 1976d, pp. 320–9. References to the fetish, as a 'dieu d'un homme isolé', are also found in his notes on

of observation, by means of a simulation of an *external* point of view'.[107] The 'fetishism', which, on the basis of the hypostasis of a 'primitive mind' formulated by De Brosses, had been understood as a common trait of every primitive form of religion, expressed the colonialist view of the other, subsumed into the colonialist *episteme* in the very moment in which it was projected onto some primitive period in the West. The difference with the 'savage' was annulled by means of the comparative possibility offered by the uniformity entailed by the presupposition of the 'primitive mind', and was then redefined by the diachronic location of the 'savage' within the temporal axis of Western progress. The 'other' could thus be domesticated into Western universalism, assimilated to our primitive period. Modern Western conceptuality thus represented itself as universal and insurpassable. The West imposed on the world its own universalism, together with its own image of a unidirectional linear time.

Overturning the image of fetishism onto capitalist modernity itself, it becomes possible to put into question not only modern conceptuality's mechanism of self-eternalisation, but the very categories of universalism and historical time. The externality of the observer with respect to the phenomenon, which, in the modern Western vision of fetishism, sets savages at a sort of zero-degree of symbolic and representational capacity, is reflected back upon itself. Thus, internal observation operates as if it were external. It is not a neutral point of view. On the contrary, it is an epistemological shifting of perspective. This overturning of De Brosses's fetishism is noticeable in two 'masters of suspicion'. For Freud, fetishism is characterised by the replacement of the normal sexual object by 'another which bears some relation to it, but is entirely unsuited to serve the normal sexual aim'.[108] Just as for Freud, for Marx, too, fetishism involves substitution and goal.[109] In the production of commodities, use-value is substituted by exchange-value; the goal of production is not use-value and the satisfaction of human needs, but value. This inversion ends up invading the sphere of consumption as well, such that the consumed object becomes exchange-value itself and the commodities produced have increasingly less connection with the social utility of use-value. The fetish-character of the commodity thus also pervades the use-value of the commodity. It was from this perspective, often obscured, that Marx delineated the characteristics of a communist society: 'In a future society, in which class antagonism will

---

Benjamin Constant's 1826 work *De la religion considérée dans sa source, ses formes et ses développements*: Marx 1976d, p. 350. See Iacono 1985, p. 186.

107. Iacono 2001a, p. 39; Iacono 2001b.
108. Freud 2000, p. 19.
109. Iacono proposes a different interpretation; see Iacono 1985, pp. 170–1.

have ceased, in which there will no longer be any classes, use will no longer be determined by the minimum time of production; but the time of production devoted to an article will be determined by the degree of its social utility'.[110]

Because 'the use of products is determined by the social conditions in which the consumers find themselves placed, and these conditions themselves are based on class antagonism',[111] different uses and use-values correspond to a non-capitalist mode of production. The determination of time of production on the basis not of value, but of social utility, posits not only a different distribution of the relation between time of labour and free time (the latter being a use-value of primary importance), but also a different production and a different technical-scientific rationality. From this point of view – that is, from the perspective of use-value and social utility – modern rationality turns out to be compromised. It is domination over nature, shaped by the exigencies of technical rationalisation of the entire productive process, and by the deformation of living labour.

From the perspective of circulation, namely, from the perspective of atomistic individuals, the horizon of production with its asymmetrical relations disappears. In its place, there appears a sphere of free subjects of law, free consumers. The relations appear symmetrical, and conflicts can always be resolved. The political problem is no longer the change of the social and political order, but the equitable regulation of the relations between atomistic individuals. In this world without history, delineated in the political projects of John Rawls, there can be progress, but not change. This image does not cancel out conflicts, but gives them a particular physiognomy. If they are not procedurally resolvable, they are shifted under the veil of ignorance of the fetishised world described by James Graham Ballard. It is a deluxe version of the *bellum omnium contra omnes*, where violence operates simultaneously as disaggregation and as social bond. *Super Cannes* is the unwritten appendix of *Political Liberalism*. The social relation between reciprocally indifferent individuals, mediated by things, is reflected in the indifference of any received historical content. Tradition and community are not eliminated: rather, they become artefacts that fascism resuscitates in the eschatological form of the immortal nation.[112] The stronger the destruction of the perspective of individual biography in a society that renders existence precarious and subject to supra-individual forces, the greater the possibility of fascism using a disaggregated individuality, without memory, to its own advantage.

---

110. Marx 1959a, p. 93; Marx 1976b, p. 134.
111. Marx 1959a, p. 93; Marx 1976b, p. 133.
112. Neocleous 2005, pp. 2–3.

The image of the commodification of social relations is false. It is itself internal to fetishism, because the real question is not about the loss of supposedly authentic human relations, but how the commodity constitutes the social relation. Equally internal to the point of view of fetishism is the idea of the commodification of culture and of spiritual value. The true problem is the spiritualisation of exchange-value, or rather, how exchange-value has become culture.

Displacement

In order to make this necessary change of perspective, we need new eyes, eyes that are able to comprehend the sensuously supersensuous nature of the commodity. This is what Marx tries to do by superseding the physics of ocular vision. When we see, the light is really projected by an object onto the eye; but this 'physical relation between physical things'[113] is inadequate because

> the existence of the things *qua* commodities, and the value relation between the products of labour which stamps them as commodities, have absolutely no connection with their physical properties and with the material relations arising therefrom. There it is a definite social relation between men, that assumes, in their eyes, the phantasmagorical form of a relation between things. In order, therefore, to find an analogy, we must have recourse to the fog-enveloped regions of the religious world.[114]

We need a new way of seeing, able to pierce through the fog. The first chapters of *Capital* prepare this change of perspective. It is enough only to look at them for what they are: parts.[115] 'Part One' examines fetishism. The first chapter shows how this inversion works, and concludes with fetishism. The second follows the commodity to the market and carries us up to the 'enigma of the fetish of money'.[116] Since commodities cannot go to market alone, their guardians are introduced: the possessors of commodities. This leads us to the juridical relation between equal subjects. The image produced by the point of view of circulation considers the behaviour of individuals 'purely atomistically in their social process of production. Hence, their relations to each

---

113. Marx 1962a, p. 86; Marx 1996, p. 83.
114. Ibid.; translation modified.
115. As is noted, in the table of contents of the first edition of *Capital*, there is only a subdivision in 'chapters', that become 'parts' or '*Abschnitte*' [sections] in the subsequent editions.
116. Marx 1962a, p. 108; Marx 1996, p. 103; translation modified.

other in production assume a thingly form'.[117] The third chapter, continuing to explore fetishistic relations of 'personification of objects and the representation of persons by things', shows how circulation breaks 'all restrictions as to time, place, and individuals, imposed by direct barter',[118] how the 'radical leveller' of money and its nature that knows 'no bounds' in the impulse to hoarding react upon communitarian relations.[119] Showing how the social power has become 'the private power of private persons',[120] Marx outlines the forms in which capital was historically established. 'Part Two' signals a changing of the point of view. It begins by affirming that 'the circulation of commodities is the starting-point of capital',[121] and concludes by abandoning the sphere of circulation in order to enter into the laboratories of production. The demystification of fetishism has begun. This shift of perspective undertaken by Marx allows him to show the falsity of the metatheoretical presuppositions of the point of view of circulation. Marx's new beginning occurs at the beginning of the sixth chapter, where value ceases to be a simple 'automatic subject'[122] and becomes, instead, something produced by a 'special commodity [*spezifische Ware*]'[123] that the capitalist finds on the market: labour-power. This, furthermore, exists only in the 'living corporeality [*lebendige Leiblichkeit*]' of the worker, who sells and makes available for a determinate time his or her own labour-power.[124]

With the descent into the laboratories of production, there is a change of perspective. It is the modern rewriting of the Platonic myth of the cave. Marx adopts the point of view of those who have sold their labour-power and realise that they have taken their own skin to the market. 'Part Two' concludes with the absolute wrong, which is the genuine object of *Capital*. Injustice is occluded by the lights of circulation. From the third section onwards, Marx shows the injustice suffered by those who are forced to sell their lives and health along with their labour-power. Here, the monsters are real: dead labour sucks the blood of the living; at the centre of the scene, there is a 'mechanical monster [*ein mechanisches Ungeheuer*]' whose 'demon power [*dämonische Kraft*]' explodes 'into the fast and furious whirl of his countless working organs'.[125] If equal legal subjects bargain in circulation, in production not only

---

117. Ibid.
118. Marx 1962a, p. 127; Marx 1996, p. 123.
119. Marx 1962a, pp. 146–7; Marx 1996, p. 143.
120. Marx 1962a, p. 146; Marx 1996, p. 143.
121. Marx 1962a, p. 161; Marx 1996, p. 157.
122. Marx 1962a, p. 169; Marx 1996, p. 165; translation modified.
123. Marx 1962a, p. 181; Marx 1996, p. 177.
124. Marx 1962a, p. 183; Marx 1996, p. 179; translation modified.
125. Marx 1962a, p. 402; Marx 1996, pp. 384–5.

are those subjects not equal and the relations not symmetrical, but attached to labour-power is a body, also put to work in the labour-process. The injustice of which *Capital* speaks is the injustice inflicted on the body by the domination of dead labour over living labour. It is injustice against the body. From this perspective, the so-called 'historical' parts of *Capital* are neither accessories nor mere examples. Marx's historiography aims to reveal capital's 'Medusa head'.[126] Primo Levi, whose writings can legitimately be regarded among the original documents of the factory-inquiry, wrote that 'those who saw the Gorgon, have not returned to tell about it or have returned mute'.[127] Marx's historiography is the historiography of one who has seen the Gorgon. Bourgeois historiography has struck the witness dumb: it really has been reduced to an *instrumentum vocale*.

The *Verkehrung* is, above all, the result of a perspective that assumes the presuppositions produced by modernity itself: individuals. These are constitutive elements of Leviathan in Hobbes, and the private producers in Marx. Inversion constitutes the mystery of the commodity-form, which, like a mirror, 'reflects [*zurückspiegelt*] the social character of men's labour to them as an objective character stamped upon the product of that labour; because the relation of the producers to the sum total of their own labour is presented to them as a social relation, existing not between themselves, but between the products of their labour'.[128] It is a game of images reflected in the mirror: the image of the social character of products is reflected as a 'natural social property of the thing'.[129] Historically-determinate social relations appear as natural properties of things, thus naturalising and eternalising those social relations. Like in a game of mirrors where the image is reprojected an infinite number of times, capital represents itself as an insurpassable totality. It is the inverted world of the consequential stupidity that Shakespeare represented with the figure of Dogberry, as cited by Marx at the end of his passage on the fetish-character of the commodity: 'To be a well-favoured man is the gift of fortune; but reading and writing comes by Nature'. If modernity is inversion, the image of the mirror – 'hieroglyphic of truth' and 'symbol of falsity' at the same time, according to the words of Rafael Mirami[130] – is the image most adequate to representing the 'social hieroglyphic' of the commodity.[131]

126. Marx 1962a, p. 15; Marx 1996, p. 9.
127. Levi 1989, pp. 83–4.
128. Marx 1962a, p. 86; Marx 1996, p. 83; translation modified.
129. Ibid.
130. Mirami 1582.
131. Marx 1962a, p. 88; Marx 1996, p. 85.

The inversion that attaches itself to the products of labour, as soon as they are produced as commodities, characterises the 'fetishism of the world of commodities', a real illusion, a mirage. In order to dissipate the mists of this religious world,[132] we need to investigate what the phantasmagoria obscures: the 'peculiar social character of the labour that produces' commodities.[133] If the historical critique of religion, which the young Marx also engaged in, had the task of showing 'the earthly core of the misty creations of religion', the more mature 'materialist method' has to develop from the given real relations of life their celestial forms.[134]

In order to deconstruct the phantasmagoria that eternalises the capitalist mode of production, it is important to determine its historical nature, by means of a self-critique of modern categories, because even 'economic categories...bear the stamp of history'.[135] Until the inversion accomplished by the process of valorisation has been demonstrated (Chapter Seven), the determination of the element capable of explaining what makes the product of labour a commodity remains unclear. These difficulties are outlined in 'Part Two'. In order to become a commodity, α) the product 'must not be produced as the immediate means of subsistence of the producer himself'.[136] However, this determination is still insufficient, because different communities can exchange their surplus. Marx adds, therefore: β) 'The appearance of products as commodities presupposes...a development of the social division of labour'; but, he immediately notes, 'such a degree of development is common to many forms of society, which in other respects present the most varying historical features'.[137] A non-capitalist division of labour is possible, as occurs in small Indian communities, in which labour is divided. However, this division, instead of being founded on exchange-value, presupposes communitarian production. He then goes on to consider γ) money, and contests the notion that the historical conditions of existence of capital are given by the circulation of commodities and of money. What opens the capitalist epoch and distinguishes the capitalist mode of production is the circumstance in which δ) 'the owner of the means of production and subsistence meets in the market with the free labourer selling his labour-power'.[138] This is the historical condition that comprises a universal history [*Weltgeschichte*].[139] The workers,

---

132. Marx 1962a, p. 86; Marx 1996, p. 83.
133. Marx 1962a, p. 87; Marx 1996, p. 83.
134. Marx 1962a, p. 392; Marx 1996, p. 375.
135. Marx 1962a, p. 183; Marx 1996, p. 179.
136. Ibid.
137. Marx 1962a, p. 184; Marx 1996, p. 180.
138. Ibid.
139. Ibid.

in order to be a sellers of labour-power, have to be formally free. They have to be equal legal subjects, and produced as such.

Categories and history

The rupture with a constellation foreign to capitalist relations of production has to be further demarcated. Beginning with the *Anhang* to the edition of 1867, Marx appeals once again to Aristotle. The problem regards what makes a commodity 'immediately exchangeable' with another. This common element is, for Marx, 'undifferentiated human labour', that is, 'labour in an immediately social form like any labour that produces commodities'.[140] Aristotle shows that there cannot be exchange without equality, and that there cannot be equality without commensurability.[141] For Aristotle as well, two commodities cannot relate to each other as commensurable sums if there is not an equality of essence, but he stops short of nominating this common essence. He says that things that are so heterogeneous cannot be commensurable among themselves. The concept that Aristotle lacked, Marx emphasises, was that of 'equal human labour', which he was not able to find because 'Greek society was founded upon slavery, and had, therefore, for its natural basis, the inequality of men and of their labour-powers'.[142] Aristotle could not comprehend the 'secret of the expression of value'; he could think of some common substance that made different objects commensurable, but could not think the concept of value. Marx writes that 'the secret of the expression of value, namely, that all kinds of labour are equal and equivalent, because, and so far as they are human labour in general, cannot be deciphered, until the notion of human equality has already acquired the fixity of a popular prejudice [*Volksvorurteil*]'.[143] This specification allows Marx to show the transition to the commodity-form and to value in terms of a historical discontinuity. The intelligibility of value, impossible for Aristotle, becomes possible only when the concept of equality possesses the *ténacité d'un préjugé populaire*, as Marx says in the French edition, which he closely checked. It is evident that, introducing this historical determination, resounding around the world alongside the cannonades of the American Civil War,[144] Marx wanted to explain categorial abstractions in their concrete historical content. Equality as popular prejudice does not fall from the sky. It is the

140. Marx 1962a, p. 73; Marx 1996, p. 69.
141. Aristotle, *Etica nicomachea*, 1133b.
142. Marx 1983i, p. 636; Marx 1996, p. 70.
143. Ibid.
144. Marx 1985a, p. 419 ff.

result of concrete struggles, in which the oppressed classes have shattered the old authoritarian relations of the estates and hierarchical orders, which claimed to be founded in nature. This process of dissolution occurs in the concrete practices of liberation of the working classes, who then enter into the labour-relation contractually as formally-free workers, wage-workers who sell their labour-power. In other modes of production, like in the 'patriarchal family' or in ancient 'Asiatic communities', the product of labour is not a commodity, but possesses a 'determinate social character', which it derives from the fact that it is produced for the consumption of that particular community.[145] But they were not idyllic times. There was also surplus-labour in slave and feudal societies, but this was visible spatially and temporally in forced labour, in the *corvée*, in the taxes in kind and in the tithe. *Jacqueries*, revolts and refusal of surplus-labour led to a reorganisation of the social form and of the mode of production: surplus-value must be produced in the time of labour. This is the innovation of the capitalist mode of production. There thus emerges a new impersonal form of command. In the production of commodities, the social form of labour is indifference: the commodities relate to each other as equals [*Ihresgleichen*], as 'expenditure of human labour-power'. The indifferent sociality of abstract labour destroys the previous communitarian relations and the multiplicity of differences between particular spheres of society, producing a new difference: the difference between capital and wage-labour. It is within and beginning with this difference that the previous differences are reinvented and rearticulated as ethnic, racial and cultural differences.

The profound historical-epochal break introduced by the capitalist mode of production is confirmed also by the change in the nature of consumption. While, in the first instance, the use-value of an object, its utility or its being a means for the satisfaction of needs is a characteristic trait of every epoch, as soon as 'use-value comes within that sphere [of political economy]... it is modified by the modern production relations or itself exerts a modifying influence on them'.[146] Objects of use have always been produced, just as there have always been exchanges of different objects of use in order to satisfy different social needs: the 'product of labour is, in all states of society, a use value; but it is only at a definite historical epoch in a society's development that such a product becomes a commodity, viz., at the epoch when the labour spent on the production of a useful article becomes expressed as one of the objective qualities of that article, i.e., as its value'.[147] While Marx could still

---

145. See Marx 1987e, pp. 29, 44.
146. Marx 1983b, p. 767; Marx 1987c, p. 252.
147. Marx 1962a, p. 76; Marx 1996, p. 72.

write that one does not know who has produced the oats on the basis of their taste, and that one does not see the conditions under which the labour-process takes place,[148] this is increasingly less true today. The hamburger eaten in a fast-food joint provides a photograph of the social and labour-conditions both of the consumer and of the worker who cooked it; behind a dollop of ketchup we can catch a glimpse of the industrial raising of animals for minced meat. Use-value has been modified to such an extent by the current mode of production that it has generated a new artificial nature.

However, it is not in individual consumption, but in productive consumption, that the specifically-capitalist nature of use-value becomes clearly apparent: when, that is, labour utilises products of labour as means of production for new products. In this sense, the means of labour are 'indicators of the social relations under which that labour is carried out'.[149] The pages that Marx dedicates to describing the machinery used in order to increase the productivity of labour are nothing but prolegomena to a critique of capitalist use-value, of technology and modern science and of their supposed neutrality. The new order of Arkwright corresponds to the infernal pressure of the machine on the bodies of workers.[150] Capital is not only able to subsume the different modes of production that it encounters, but, when it modifies them, it impresses on the means of production the stigmata of specifically-capitalist use-value. Marx spoke of it in terms of a mechanical monster animated by a demonic force. Only some parts of twentieth-century Marxism knew how to resist the fascination of a socialism that saw a possibility of liberation in workers' self-management of factories and capitalist machinery. What is urgently necessary, instead, is a critique of the capitalist use-value of science and of technology,[151] a critique that is able to combine the demands for liberation from labour with the demand for a safeguarding of nature before it is completely destroyed.

Bill's knife

The image of the modern system of machines as an 'animated monster that begins to work as if by love possessed' simultaneously condemns both modern technology and modern culture.[152] The comparison between the feverish dance of the organs of the machine and the passage from Goethe about the

148. Marx 1962a, p. 199; Marx 1996, p. 194.
149. Marx 1962a, p. 195; Marx 1996, p. 190; translation modified.
150. Marx 1962a, p. 390; Marx 1996, p. 385.
151. See Bahr 1970; Wendling 2009.
152. Marx 1962a, p. 209; Marx 1996, p. 305; translation modified.

song in Auerbach's tavern is intended as a condemnation.[153] Benjamin issued the same condemnation when he denounced every document of culture as a document of barbarism.[154] Marx did not cite the classics in order to show off his erudition.[155] While he certainly did want to make the working class speak the language of high culture, giving back to it the words that had been taken from it and smashing the class-enemy in the face with its own culture, his citations were always, at the same time, also condemnations. Western culture, which talks loudly of great humanitarian values, has not been and is not able to stop the 'great slaughter of the innocents'.[156] For Marx, as Brecht is supposed to have once said, the entire palace of culture is built on dog-shit.[157]

It is for this reason that Marx rewrites and invents passages of literature that are comparable to the pages of the classic works cited. He integrates Charles Dickens's *Oliver Twist* into his own text, inventing a monologue for the jury by the cutthroat Bill Sykes:

> Gentlemen of the jury, no doubt the throat of this commercial traveller has been cut. But that is not my fault, it is the fault of the knife. Must we, for such a temporary inconvenience, abolish the use of the knife? Only consider! Where would agriculture and trade be without the knife? Is it not as salutary in surgery, as it is knowing in anatomy? And in addition a willing help at the festive board? If you abolish the knife – you hurl us back into the depths of barbarism.[158]

The literary style of *Capital*, its metaphors and its sarcasm are functional to the change of perspective that is able to disorient; to render foreign what is familiar.

The 'critical history of technology'[159] for which Marx hoped, taking inspiration from the history of the productive organs of social man, was supposed to demonstrate the role to which the single individual was reduced when confronted by the inventions of the nineteenth century. In the *Grundrisse*, the social individual indicated a direction of anthropological transformation effected by the capitalist mode of production: the breaking of the umbilical cord with nature, growth in the capacity of enjoyment, the creation of new

---

153. Goethe 2001, vv. 2126 et sq.
154. Benjamin 2003, Thesis VII, p. 392.
155. Capital, as Wolff 1998 observes, throws us into an 'extraordinary literary world' (p. 13). The text 'is rich in literary and historical allusion to the entire corpus of Western culture' (p. 12). On Marx's literary references, see also Wheen 2006, p. 7.
156. Marx 1962a, p. 785; Marx 1996, p. 745.
157. Adorno 1973, p. 366.
158. Marx 1962a, p. 466; Marx 1996, p. 445.
159. Marx 1962a, p. 392; Marx 1996, p. 387.

needs and the composition of psycho-physical energies. *Capital* showed how this increase in the capacity of the individual appears only in the cornucopia of circulation, while in the laboratories of production the individual tends to be without its own qualities, to be substitutable by any other individual and, ultimately, by the knowledge objectivised in the machine. In circulation, the glory of the sovereign consumer is proclaimed. In production, we hear the cries of misery of a mortified individual. These two visions are not placed beside each other like inert opinions, but rather, are like acid added to a base. The world of circulation as a phantasmagoria is the garden of Calypso: the end of the human.

Modern labour is without its own qualities not because it is deskilled,[160] and not because it is unskilled. Rather, it can become unskilled because it is without its own qualities, because it counts only as labour-power that is capable of valorising value: the qualities of labour are subsumed into capital. It can, therefore, be labour that requires a high degree of specialisation and of knowledge: but this specialisation and knowledge are not properties of the worker. Rather, they are qualities that capital has already incorporated into itself and can transmit to any other worker. The secrets of the trade, of which the artisan was particularly proud, are no longer secrets, for capital. Labour no longer has the mysterious characteristics of trades, which still in the eighteenth century were called 'mysteries', due to their being taught by the corporations in a secretive manner. Capital undertakes a daily struggle with workers in order to appropriate their excess-knowledge from them; it uses every little trick in order to save time. Technology and science are conscripted into this battle.

Using as his source-material the *Reports of the Inspectors of Factories*, some of which, like Leonard Horner, were slandered and persecuted by the industrialists, Marx describes the young substitute-workers supplying their labour-power in London printing shops as 'utter savages and very extraordinary creatures'; when they were no longer suitable for the work, they became recruits of crime', who, due to 'their ignorance and brutality, and their mental and bodily degradation', were unable to find new occupations.[161] The crippling of these young workers on the job comes into conflict with the tendency of large industry to make labour-functions more fluid and to mobilise the different capacities of the worker:

> But if modern industry, by its very nature, therefore necessitates variation of
> labour, fluency of function, universal mobility of the labourer, on the other

---

160. See Bellofiore 1996, particularly points 5.4 and 5.5. See also Rieser 2004; Bellofiore 2004.

161. Marx 1962a, p. 509; Marx 1996, pp. 487–8.

hand, in its capitalistic form, it reproduces the old division of labour with its ossified particularisations. We have seen how this absolute contradiction between the technical necessities of modern industry, and the social character inherent in its capitalistic form, dispels all fixity and security in the situation of the labourer; how it constantly threatens, by taking away the instruments of labour, to snatch from his hands his means of subsistence, and, by suppressing his detail-function, to make him superfluous. We have seen, too, how this antagonism vents its rage in the creation of that monstrosity, an industrial reserve army, kept in misery in order to be always at the disposal of capital; in the incessant human sacrifices from among the working class, in the most reckless squandering of labour-power, and in the devastation caused by a social anarchy which turns every economic progress into a social calamity. This is the negative side. But if [*Wenn aber*]...[162]

The capitalist division of labour renders individual workers replaceable and expropriates their qualities, which are objectified in fixed capital and opposed to them. Whether it is a case of an automatic lathe or of a computer, in both cases the competences of the workers are objectified in the machine, to the point that the workers themselves are rendered superfluous. The fifth to the thirteenth chapters of *Capital* Volume I show us the process of the deindividualisation of labour,[163] a process that has now even invaded the spheres of spirit and of intellectual labour.

If this is the negative aspect, Marx's '*Wenn aber*' announces the second voice of the fugue:

But if, on the one hand, variation of work at present imposes itself after the manner of an overpowering natural law, and with the blindly destructive action of a natural law that meets with resistance at all points, modern industry, on the other hand, through its catastrophes imposes the necessity of recognising, as a fundamental law of production, variation of work, consequently fitness of the labourer for varied work, consequently the greatest possible development of his varied aptitudes. It becomes a question of life and death...to replace the detail-worker of to-day, crippled by life-long repetition of one and the same trivial operation, and thus reduced to the mere fragment of a man, by the fully developed individual, fit for a variety of labours, ready to face any change of production, and to whom the different social functions he performs, are but so many modes of giving free scope to his own natural and acquired powers. One step already spontaneously taken towards effecting this revolution is the establishment of technical and

---

162. Marx 1962a, p. 511; Marx 1996, pp. 489–90.
163. Finelli 1987, p. 158.

agricultural schools, and of 'écoles d'enseignement professionnel', in which the children of the workingmen receive some little instruction in technology and in the practical handling of the various implements of labour. Though the Factory Act, that first and meagre concession wrung from capital, is limited to combining elementary education with work in the factory, there can be no doubt that when the working class comes into power, as inevitably it must, technical instruction, both theoretical and practical, will take its proper place in the working-class schools.[164]

The multiplication of the variation of labour in the division of labour demands of workers the greatest versatility, insofar as it is distorted within the capitalist division of labour. This, together with a potent mechanism for the appropriation of individual qualities and the production of a unilateralist model of workers, without qualities of their own, demands a new type of versatility. This is not the originary omnilateral orientation towards the world of a hypothetical initial stage of humanity, but a new versatility produced by means of a new education-system. At the time of the Industrial Revolution, Marx thought of the polytechnic-schools as elements of a subversive process that could and would need to change the direction of a destiny composed of unilaterality and obtuseness. 'But if...'. It was not only a case of containing the infernal effects that capitalist production had on those condemned to work, but to find between the folds of this mode of production the possibilities for developing the human beyond the limits of the 'partial individual'. The nature of this mode of production has been transformed, reproducing itself by means of the continual creation of its constitutive elements: intrinsically capitalist technical-scientific rationality and partial and isolated individuals. In order to break with the mythical character of the present, one needs to go beyond these two false paths, and avoid engaging in a rash exaltation of technological innovation and the cyborg, which has now become the postmodern form of apology for the existing order. The capitalist mode of production has incorporated, from its birth, one of the possible results of modern science and rationality, picking out among them the capacity to intensify the exploitation of humanity and of nature and to cripple living labour.

The juridical as concealment

Marx's change of perspective in *Capital* allows him to comprehend the non-neutrality of law and science. Turning his view to production allows him to

---

164. Marx 1962a, pp. 511–12; Marx 1996, pp. 490–1.

comprehend the use-value of constant capital in machines and the asymmetry of the relation in the labour-process occluded by the juridical. What he delineates is the counterposition of truth and *doxa*: this new point of view comprehends the falsity of the image of the free and equal juridical subjects that is the preserve of circulation.

From the point of view of circulation and of law, no injustice occurs. As Hegel also knew, and as Marx repeated in a note, what distinguishes the slave from the formally free worker is the fact that, as the latter, I alienate from myself only 'the use, for a limited time, of my particular bodily and mental aptitudes and capabilities'; on the other hand, 'by the alienation of all my labour time and the whole of my work, I should be converting the substance itself, in other words, my general activity and reality, my person, into the property of another'.[165] That is, it would make me a slave. But the commodity of labour-power is precisely a 'peculiar' commodity, as Marx continues to repeat.[166] With the contract completed, use-value has not yet really passed into the hands of the buyer, and the worker has not yet, in general, been paid. The use-value of labour-power is demonstrated only in real consumption, in the process of the consumption of labour-power [*Konsumtionsprozeß der Arbeitskraft*].[167] This process of consumption, from the Latin *consumptio*, is the process that uses labour-power, that consumes it and destroys it. This destruction regards especially a very particular use-value: the living corporeality to which that labour-power is inevitably attached. If, from the 'point of view of the labour process' the worker treats the means of production as the equipment for his productive activity, from the 'point of view of the process of valorisation' it is 'now no longer the labourer that employs the means of production, but the means of production that employ the labourer'.[168] The material elements of productive activity, overwhelmed in the process of the valorisation of value, instead of being simply consumed, 'consume [*verzehren*]' the worker as the ferment of their own vital process.[169] The dead dominate the living. It is here that the inversion really takes place, the inversion of the relation between dead labour and living labour that is reflected 'in the consciousness of capitalists'.[170]

Labour not only consumes products – the means of production – in order to create new products, but also consumes labour-power and its *Träger*: the

165. Hegel 2001, § 67; translation modified. Marx 1962a, p. 182; Marx 1996, p. 178.
166. Marx 1962a, p. 188; Marx 1996, p. 184.
167. Marx 1962a, p. 189; Marx 1996, p. 185.
168. Marx 1962a, pp. 328–9; Marx 1996, p. 314.
169. Marx 1962a, pp. 329; Marx 1996, p. 315.
170. Ibid.

worker in flesh and blood. If the wage seems to pay for a determinate number of hours of performance of human psychical-physical energy, it does not, however, pay for the total consumption of the bodies of the workers, including their minds and spirits, just as it does not pay the knowledge endogenous to the class, which is expropriated from the workers, incorporated into fixed capital and counterposed to the workers. The knowledge necessary for making a piece of pottery has been incorporated first into digitally controlled lathes, and then into automatic machines. If it is true that knowledge has an increasingly important role, it is equally true that this is immediately incorporated into fixed capital, such that workers have an increasingly smaller knowledge of the labour-process that could be counterposed to capital, which, instead, tends to appropriate for itself the worker's entire lifetime. Capital consumes the entire *Gemeinwesen* of the worker, including family-relations, domestic work, the growth of his knowledge and of the sphere of social relations, insofar as these can be used to increase his capacity to work. This is the case for many jobs that require not only talent in the field of public relations, but where the sphere of parental and friendship-relations are immediately exploited, when, for example, one tries to sell an insurance-policy or a domestic appliance to acquaintances. It is also the case, however, in many so-called creative jobs, in which any external suggestion or casual intuition is immediately put to work, thus rendering substantially indistinct the time of labour and free time.

Putting competencies, social relations and knowledge to work is not, in itself, immediately production, but can increase the productivity of labour. If, for example, an insurance-agent sells a policy to family-members and close friends, she has simply profited from her personal relations and her knowledge in order to increase the productivity of her own labour-time: she can, in fact, sell a greater number of policies in a shorter time. Once her circle of friends and family-members has been exhausted, her work will suffer a sudden slowdown. After the initial glory, she will probably seek a new job and will be substituted by another young worker, who is also ready to make profitable use of his own circle of personal relations. The know-how that is required in order to rip off relatives ready to help the young guy who has just gone into the world of work is so low that workers end up being easily replaced. A few days of education are enough to explain the business to those who have to sell insurance-policies. The capacity required by the young precarious labourers is increasingly less a form of specialised knowledge and ever-more the versatility, the capacity to change and to react to the change in a timely fashion. What is important is not what one learns, but the capacity to learn.

The division of labour is also reorganised according to time. The entry of women into the world of work and into university-studies has meant a partial upsetting of the gender-division of labour, but has also put enormous amounts of reproductive labour onto the market. New workers, male and female, now undertake the work that once was given to women in the richest Western countries: domestic cleaning, cooking, care of children and the elderly. These jobs, if they are also to be performed in the service of wage-workers' families, have to be low-paid. Beyond defining a new ethnic division of labour, some of these workers, like the so-called 'badanti [carers]',[171] are asked to work what is, in effect, a 24-hour day. They are asked not only for total availability in terms of time, but also that their affections should be made available. No matter how formally free it is, this typology of labour shows the trace of continuity between slave-labour and wage-labour.

The element of proximity between wage-labour and slave-labour is not visible from the perspective of circulation: here, the legal subjects are in a symmetrical relation, and the sale of the commodity of labour-power takes place, in however conflictual a way, without injustice.

> The capitalist maintains his rights as a purchaser [behauptet sein Recht als Käufer] when he tries to make the working day as long as possible, and to make, whenever possible, two working days out of one. On the other hand, the peculiar nature of the commodity sold implies a limit to its consumption by the purchaser, and the labourer maintains his right as seller [behauptet sein Recht als Verkäufer] when he wishes to reduce the working day to one of definite normal duration. There is here, therefore, an antinomy, right against right, both equally bearing the seal of the law of exchanges. Between equal rights force decides [Recht wider Recht, beide gleichmäßig durch das Gesetz des Warenaustausches besiegelt. Zwischen gleichen Rechten entscheidet die Gewalt]. Hence is it that in the history of capitalist production, the determination of what is a working day, presents itself as the result of a struggle, a struggle between collective capital, i.e., the class of capitalists, and collective labour, i.e., the working class.[172]

The tenth chapter reproduces in its structure Marx's usual change of perspective. After an incipit where the struggle for the working day is observed from the legal point of view, we descend into the laboratories of production. Here, the claimed neutrality of the law is replaced by the neutrality of the Reports of the Inspectors of Factories, which occupy almost two-thirds of the chapter. Marx limits himself to producing a montage of citations, inserting some comments within them, such as when he writes that the descriptions of work

---

171. See Ehrenreich 2004.
172. Marx 1962a, p. 249; Marx 1996, p. 243.

in manufacturing have superseded 'the worst horrors of [Dante's] Inferno'. The gothic arsenal is populated with vampires and werewolves. The descent into the laboratories of production shows that the struggle between classes is not only about a few more coins, but is the struggle for life and death itself. It is not only a struggle for physical survival, but for a true life. Capitalists can also guarantee survival, if they are willing to run the risk of being left without workers. Or they can generously toss down a few more coins, just as they sometimes scatter fertiliser on the fields they have rendered barren, exhausted through overexploitation. Looked at from the perspective of production, the juridical sphere appears as the battlefield where the 'civil war'[173] between the *Kapitalistenklasse* and the *Arbeiterklasse* occurs, each having their own rights and reasons, in a symmetrical relation. These rights are confirmed as equal by the law of the exchange of commodities, such that these equal rights are completely inscribed in the history of capitalist production. There is no 'just wage'; what is 'just' is the struggle for the wage and the reduction of the working day. 'Just' is the interruption of the wage-relation and thus the continuum of the 'civil war' between classes.

The point of observation has now decisively changed. It is not enough to look at production: it is necessary to put oneself at the particular point of view of a specific commodity, the worker. Marx represents this change in a theatrical fashion: if the sphere of circulation is the 'Eden of the rights of man' and the buyer and seller of labour-power are equal subjects of law, as soon as the contract is completed and they proceed towards the laboratories of production,

> we can perceive a change in the physiognomy of our dramatis personae. He, who before was the money owner, now strides in front as capitalist; the possessor of labour power follows as his labourer. The one with an air of importance, smirking, intent on business; the other, timid and holding back, like one who is bringing his own hide to market and has nothing to expect but – a hiding.[174]

Thus Marx closes the sixth chapter, which concludes the second part. Here, we see the change of perspective, the only point of view from which it is possible to penetrate into the third section: 'the production of absolute surplus value'. The juridical level of the selling of commodities, including labour-power, makes us see symmetrical relations between free and equal juridical

---

173. 'The creation of a normal working day is, therefore, the product of a protracted civil war, more or less dissembled, between the capitalist class and the working class': Marx 1962a, p. 316; Marx 1996, p. 303.
174. Marx 1962a, p. 191; Marx 1996, p. 186.

subjects, occluding the real asymmetry between the personification of capital and workers. The phenomenal form of the wage 'makes the actual relation invisible, and, indeed, shows the direct opposite of that relation'. It 'forms the basis of all the juridical notions of both labourer and capitalist, of all the mystifications of the capitalistic mode of production, of all its illusions as to liberty, of all the apologetic shifts of the vulgar economists'.[175] The exchange between capital and labour appears [*sich darstellt*] to perception [*Wahrnehmung*] like the buying and selling of any other commodity.[176] This perception is objective from the point of view of circulation, but, abstracting from the real asymmetry of the relation, gives rise to an ideologically marked abstract theory. Its falsity is demonstrated only in the change of perspective, that is, by looking at that same relation from the point of view of production and the relation of class, where those two subjects are not symmetrically free and equal, as contractualist theories like to think, but rather are situated in a real asymmetrical relation that cannot be mediated juridically.

Unavoidable guerrilla-warfare

In the process of valorisation, the capitalist is interested in the specific use-value of the commodity labour-power, which consists in being the source of value and of more value that it has itself.[177] The capitalist is interested in the living labour that labour-power provides. But these subjects are not juridical abstractions. The concreteness of the body of the worker is counterposed to the capitalist use-value of machinery. It is this *Konkretum* that constitutes the true framing structure of *Capital*. The whole work is constructed around this asymmetry, which relates to the dialectic as the fuse relates to dynamite. When Marx deprives the question of the 'just wage' of any meaning, his intention is not to cancel out the question of what is just, but to save it by showing the oxymoron of its being combined with wages. The question of the just is referred, instead, to the new field of possibility not comprehended in the doctrine of the wage: the field that begins with the abolition of the wage-system. The true problem is not the 'regulation of the working day', which is entirely within the 'history of capitalist production', but the end of this history; the end of that more or less latent civil war between the class of capitalists and the class of workers. As such, Marx concludes his 1865 text by saying that instead of the conservative slogan of 'A fair day's wage for a

---

175. Marx 1962a, p. 562; Marx 1996, p. 540.
176. See Marx 1962a, p. 563; Marx 1996, p. 540.
177. See Marx 1962a, p. 208; Marx 1996, p. 204.

fair day's work!', 'they ought to inscribe on their banner the revolutionary watchword, "Abolition of the wages system!"'[178] This is what the workers of the IWW did in the twentieth century.[179]

The struggle for life or death is also composed of battles for the wage or for the determination of the working day. In *Value, Price and Profit*, written by Marx in English for the General Council of the International in 1865, the economic analyses of the 1860s were grafted onto the experience of workers' struggles. Marx wanted to refute the hypothesis, maintained by Weston, according to which a general increase in wages would not have an advantageous effect for workers, because there would follow an increase in the price of commodities. In tandem with what he had done the previous year in the 'Inaugural Address of the International Workingmen's Association', Marx here praised not only the battle for legislation for a 10-hour day, but also the struggle for increased wages. At the end of the 1840s, in *Wage Labour and Capital*, Marx had, instead, affirmed that 'the same general laws that regulate the price of commodities in general of course also regulate wages, the price of labour'.[180] With the minimum-wage determined on the basis of the costs of existence and reproduction of the worker, the wage is thus linked to the laws of competition, as for any other commodity. The implication of this is a radical devaluation of the economic struggles of the working class. At the end of the 1840s, Marx seems to have shared the point of view of the economists against the workers' associations, and affirmed that 'the costs which [these struggles] cause the workers are mostly greater than the rise in the gains they want to get. In the long run they cannot withstand the laws of competition'.[181] This analysis was backward with respect to the level of workers' struggles. Still in 1850, Engels defined the laws for 10-hour working days to be a 'false step', 'a false step, an impolitic, and even reactionary measure'.[182] Not only were Marx and Engels mistaken in considering the 'price of labour', equal to other commodities, as subject only to the laws of the market, but they also thought that these economic struggles were obstacles to the unfolding of the immanent contradictions of the capitalist mode of production. They

---

178. Marx 1992e, p. 186; Marx 1985b, p. 149.

179. The IWW programmatic document of 1905 stated: 'The working class and the employing class have nothing in common.... Instead of the conservative motto, "A fair day's wage for a fair day's work", we must inscribe on our banner the revolutionary watchword, "Abolition of the wage system"'.

180. Marx 1959b, p . 406; Marx 1977b, p. 209.

181. Marx 1959c, p. 554; Marx 1976c, p. 435.

182. Engels 1960, p. 228; Engels 1978, p. 273. The orthodox-Communist publishers of this piece limited themselves to observing that 'in their later works Marx and Engels gave a more exact characterisation of the law of the 10-hour day': Engels 1960, p. 596.

were thus obstacles to the revolution itself.[183] In the 1860s, beginning with the notion of value as the objectivisation of socially necessary labour, Marx reconsidered the hypothesis according to which the wage determined the price of commodities, a hypothesis that led to considering wage-increases irrelevant, because there would necessarily follow an increase of the price of commodities. Instead, he maintained that the quantity of the individually paid wage, if it touches the profit of the capitalist, does not impact upon the quantity of the value of commodities. This consideration became particularly important in relation to the world-market and to wage-differentials in different countries.

The change of perspective was not provoked by some desire to adopt a reformist register in front of the workers of the International, but, on the contrary, was an attempt to take up a position at a high point of the 'infection of strikes...prevailing on the continent' at the time.[184] If the lights of circulation occluded the monsters of production, making them seem free and equal subjects, Marx needed an image that would show not only the autocracy of capital, but also the damage caused to life. In his 1865 *Value, Prices and Profit*, presented to the General Council of the International, Marx referred to *An Essay on Trade and Commerce*, which had been published anonymously in 1765. The author, J. Cunningham, proposed to institute workhouses, 'Houses of Terror' with 12 hours of work per day.[185] The science of the middle-class, with Doctor Ure and Professor Senior, argued that the limitation of the working day would ring 'the death knell of British industry'. Marx's response was that capital, 'vampire like, [can only] live by sucking blood, and children's blood'. He immediately adds another image to that of the vampire: 'In olden times, child murder was a mysterious rite of the religion of Moloch, but it was practised on some very solemn occasions only, once a year perhaps, and then Moloch had no exclusive bias for the children of the poor'.[186] In the next line, Marx again takes up the discourse he had left incomplete: 'This struggle about the legal restriction of the hours of labour...'. He has not inserted an *intermezzo*; he has inserted an image. The struggle for 10 hours is not only a struggle for the reduction of the time of labour. It is the struggle between life and death. Recalling the image of Moloch, he shows, on the one hand, that the modern Moloch is even more ferocious than that of ancient times, thus articulating a progress characterised by the intensification of destructive power; on

183. Vygodsky 1974, pp. 160–1.
184. Marx 1987f, p. 159. Regarding the hypothesis of the unimportance of a general increase in wages, Marx objects that if it were accepted, 'we should be in a terrible mess, both in respect of the trades unions here and the infection of strikes now prevailing on the Continent'.
185. Marx 1992e; Marx 1985b, p. 141.
186. Marx 1992f, p. 10; Marx 1985c, p. 330.

the other hand, the reference to ancient times serves to charge up the present with all the energy of the oppressed in the history of humanity. It is a tension that can be captured only in an image.

When the workers sell the use of their labour-power, they do so within 'certain rational limits': they do this in order to conserve it, not in order to destroy it.[187] Due to this, the rational is incarnated by the revolt [*rationelle Aufstand*] of the workers against the attempt to impose hourly wages.[188] If capital did not meet with any resistance, it would push the worker's salary down to its 'minimum limit' and the working class 'would be degraded to one level mass of broken wretches past salvation'.[189] The value of labour-power, unlike the value of all the other commodities, is constituted by a physical element, that is, the limit within which the working class is able to survive and to reproduce itself, and a historical element, that is, the limit of the '*traditional standard of life*' of a given country.[190] This historical or social element concerns the social conditions related to the satisfaction of the needs that the working class manages to gain from capital. It is a conflictual measure, that 'may be expanded, or contracted, or altogether extinguished, so that nothing remains but the *physical limit*'.[191] In different historical moments, capitalists are able to reduce the wages of workers even below this purely physical limit.

Here, *Capital* continues: 'In contradistinction therefore to the case of other commodities, there enters into the determination of the value of labour power a historical and moral element [*ein historisches und moralisches Element*]'.[192] There is a difference that marks labour-power apart from other commodities: Marx thus defines labour-power as a 'special commodity',[193] with a special use-value.[194] In the wage, all labour appears as paid labour. This phenomenal form, Marx affirms, as we have seen, 'forms the basis of all the juridical notions of both labourer and capitalist, of all the mystifications of the capitalistic mode of production, of all its illusions as to liberty, of all the apologetic shifts of the vulgar economists'.[195] Marx's critique of political economy did not consist of the superannuation of its limits and its contradictions; it was written in another register. Marx proposed another political economy: that of the working class. To bourgeois science and to its claimed objectivity and

---

187. Marx 1992e, p. 179; Marx 1985b, p. 141.
188. Marx 1962a, p. 568.
189. Marx 1992e, p. 185; Marx 1985b, p. 148.
190. Marx 1992e, p. 182; Marx 1985b, p. 145.
191. Ibid.
192. Marx 1962a, p. 185; Marx 1996, p. 181.
193. Marx 1962a, p. 181; Marx 1996, p. 177.
194. Marx 1962a, p. 188; Marx 1996, p. 184. Marx 1962a, p. 208; Marx 1996, p. 204.
195. Marx 1962a, p. 562; Marx 1996, p. 540.

neutrality, Marx counterposed the science of the partiality of the workers' point of view on use-value. Different temporalities of the capitalist mode of production and of class-conflict meet, here. There are two political economies: the determination of the wage and the length of the working day on the basis of the blind law of supply and demand constitutes the 'political economy of the middle class'; social production controlled according to social foresight forms the 'political economy of the working class'.[196] The political economy of the working class does not emerge from the theoretical and critical deduction of the immanent contradictions of political economy. It presents a reorienta-tion at the level of what the inversion that characterises capitalist modernity has produced. Its point of view is, from the first pages of *Capital*, that of the use-value of the commodity in tension with the use-value of the 'special com-modity' that is labour-power. This level runs over onto that of value and of the process of valorisation. The friction between these two layers gives rise to capitalist modernity.

The 'constant tendency of capital' is to extend the working day until its 'utmost physically possible length'.[197] That is why the 'working day, how-ever, has, by itself, no constant limit'.[198] The political economy of the work-ing class as critique of the political economy of the middle-class signals the pitch of the syncopated temporality of the counter-tendencies: the effort to put the working day back within 'certain rational limits'.[199] 'Yet, the whole history of modern industry shows, that capital, if not checked, will recklessly and restlessly work to cast down the whole working class to this utmost state of degradation'.[200] In order not to be reduced to beasts of burden, the work-ers have to pose limits to the 'tyrannical usurpations of capital'.[201] Once our glance is directed to the vampire, the image of *Monsieur le Capital* vanishes. The tendency of capital is purely abstract: it has to descend into the *'unavoid-able guerrilla'*[202] of the countertendencies, of workers' struggles to prevent the physical and spiritual degeneration of their class and in order to gain time for life. Because '[t]*ime is the room of human development'*.[203] Human development is not development mortified by the development of the productive forces.

---

196. Marx 1992f, p. 10. Cancelled out in Marx's manuscript is also the claim that 'social production is subjected to a foreseeing social control' which forms the 'political economy of the working class': Marx 1992f, p. 877.

197. Marx 1992e, p. 179; Marx 1985b, p. 140.

198. Ibid.

199. Marx 1992e, p. 179; Marx 1985b, p. 141.

200. Marx 1992e, p. 180. In the manuscript, there is also written: 'constant tendency of capital to degrade' the entire working class: Marx 1992e, p. 1151.

201. Marx 1992e, p. 180; Marx 1985b, p. 142.

202. Marx 1992e, p. 186; Marx 1985b, p. 148.

203. Marx 1992e, p. 180; Marx 1985b, p. 142

The space of human development exists in the time that the working class takes from capital in order to redefine it as non-capitalist time. The relation between the working class and capital is a struggle over time, for time. Every instant that the worker takes from capital is energy subtracted from valorisation. What *Capital* presents is not the tendency of the capitalist mode of production, but the clash between the different temporalities of tendency and countertendencies.

The establishment of the normal working day does not fall from the sky, but 'is the result of centuries of struggle between capitalist and labourer'.[204] Marx was interested in the counterposed currents [*entgegengesetzte Strömmungen*] in the history of this struggle. He wanted to understand how capitalists had attempted to impose the lengthening of the working day on workers by means of state-coercion, and how the workers had attained a state-imposed limitation of the working day. The state had oscillated, intervening according to the dynamics traced by the relations of force: neither neutral nor the executive committee of the bourgeoisie. It had intervened, in order to neutralise conflict, in the struggle against the class-struggle. In this struggle, it had exercised its own violence in order to impose a compromise and to put this into effect by means of legislation defining the limits of the working day.

The concept of time

It has been observed that the categories of the three volumes of *Capital* are differently situated in time.[205] The first volume obeys a linear and abstract time, homogeneous and measureable: it is the time of production. The determinations of the second volume are inscribed in a cyclical temporality, that of the time of circulation. The third volume deals with the organic time of capital, the unity of the time of production and circulation. Time is the central category of the capitalist mode of production:

> We have seen that the movement of capital through the sphere of production and the two phases of the sphere of circulation takes place in a series of periods of time [*Zeitliche Reihenfolge*]....The total time [*Gesamtzeit*] during which it describes its circuit [*Kreislauf*] is therefore equal to the sum of its time of production and its time of circulation [*Umlaufszeit*].[206]

---

204. Marx 1962a, p. 286; Marx 1996, p. 276.
205. Tombazos 1994, p. 9.
206. Marx 1963, p. 124; Marx 1997, p. 125.

The movement of capital occurs in time; it thus seeks to extend and to condense the time of valorisation and to diminish the negative times of interruption. It thus also tends to reduce, as much as possible, the time of storage of commodities and of circulation. It will tend, where possible, to work just-in-time. The distances and times are contracted by progressively increasing the speed of movement of commodities, including labour-power. The times of circulation of information, travelling electronically, have already reached their absolute limit.

Because circulation [*Zirkulieren*] is the effective roaming [*Umlaufen*] of the commodities in space and in time, the industry of transport constitutes 'a separate sphere of investment of productive capital',[207] but with the specificity of manifesting itself as the 'continuation of a process of production within the process of circulation and for the process of circulation'.[208] Transportation, changing its spatial position, changes the use-value of commodities. A commodity does not have the same use-value if it is found in the container of a warehouse or on the shelves of a supermarket. The process of valorisation is not finished until the produced commodities arrive on the market in order to be sold: the transport of commodities continues the process of valorisation and modifies the use-value of the commodity itself. Transport-workers extend the conveyor-belts and the production-line outside the factory. The speed of trains and of lorries is articulated by the world-market, which synchronises the multiplicity of temporalities to the abstract measure of the time of labour. Capital requires not only clocks, but also their synchronisation. If the diffusion of the telegraph enabled international communication, the presence of different times produced confusion and reduced profits. The circulation of humans and commodities in a growing number required a uniform measure, the destruction of the independence of the local hours regulated and calculated on the basis of the Sun. On 1 July 1913, at 10 o'clock in the morning, the Eiffel Tower sent the first hour-signal to the world. The clocks could be synchronised and the spaces crossed could be calculated in time. Now time, just like money, needed to be carried in the pocket. The diffusion of pocket-watches at the end of the nineteenth century was extraordinary. With the pocket-watch, individual life was made to conform to the time of economic transactions.[209]

Capital marks the rhythm of history in structural and tendential terms, but this temporality is abstract until it encounters the historical counter-temporalities of the class-struggle. The historical time that results from it is

---

207. Marx 1963, p. 153; Marx 1997, p. 155.
208. Ibid. See Harvey 2002; 2006; 2010.
209. See Simmel 1957.

flowing and contingent. It is not fate. To dissect the different temporalities means to be able to comprehend the political occasion of an intervention. *Capital* is a treatise on time, not only on stolen time, but also on its transformation and ontologisation. Because things are exchanged as objectivisations of labour and in relations that are proportional to the quantity of labour that they contain, the time of labour becomes everything. 'Time is everything, man is nothing', Marx wrote in his first studies on time.[210] Labour is levelled, such that it counts only as a quantitatively measureable expenditure of energy: 'therefore, we should not say that one man's hour is worth another man's hour, but rather that one man during an hour is worth just as much as another man during an hour'.[211] It is here that time gives the measure and the value of things and of men. But there are also superimpositions and conflicts between different historical temporalities.

In the first instance, there are at least two temporalities. The time of labour, which, for capital, is everything, and free time, which, for capital, is nothing and has to be reduced as much as possible. However, the time of labour is marked by a double temporality. Marx writes that the

> The working day is thus not a constant, but a variable quantity. One of its parts, certainly, is determined by the working time required for the reproduction of the labour power of the labourer himself. But its total amount varies with the duration of the surplus labour. The working day is, therefore, determinable, but is, per se, indeterminate.[212]

There is a conflict between the time of surplus-value and the time of the necessary labour that is required for the reproduction of the worker.[213] This must not be confused, however, with the time of socially-necessary labour, which is, instead, the labour objectivised in the value of the commodity. The latter does not depend on the quantity of time concretely employed in the production of a determinate commodity, but on the quantity of time that, in conditions of socially-average labour-productivity, is necessary for the production of that commodity. The labour that is necessary for the reproduction of labour-power is different: it also includes domestic labour, which does not, however, enter into the process of valorisation and does not, therefore, have a direct impact on the value of the commodity. This is, instead, determined by the quantity of socially-necessary labour. Analogously to the increase of the wage, the retribution of the labour of reproduction and of domestic labour has

---

210. Marx 1959a, p. 85; Marx 1976b, p. 127.
211. Ibid.
212. Marx 1962a, p. 178; Marx 1996, p. 240.
213. Ibid.

an impact on profits, not on the value produced. Certainly, a well-nourished worker, who always has something to eat, can work with a greater intensity than a starving or obese worker; a worker who is satisfied in mind and body can be more creative than a frustrated worker. All these elements, however, regard the productivity of the worker, for which capital does not pay anything extra. A muscular worker will be able to move more sacks of flour. But it is the capitalist's task to employ the muscular rather than the weak worker. Thus a beautiful and elegant worker will be able to sell more insurance-policies than a slovenly-looking worker. Also in this case, however, it will be up to the capitalist to take on the former and to free himself from the latter. The ox that turns the grindstone is not a productive worker, but, like a machine, enhances labour-productivity and thus needs to be subjugated. The physical power of someone who has to unload weight, the intelligence of somebody who designs software, the attractiveness of a worker who has to advertise a product and the eloquence of somebody who works in a call-centre are 'natural' gifts that capital seeks to procure for itself, but this does not impact immediately on the costs of production. These characteristics constitute the use-value of labour-power, not its value. They can increase the power of labour and can also be increased in power by labour: the physical force developed in body-building, the intelligence refined by a good education, the attractiveness enhanced by cosmetics and by those who iron the clothes, the eloquence developed from a wide reading of the classics. This labour, insofar as it has an impact on the use-value of labour-power, can play a role in the calculation of necessary labour, but not on socially-necessary labour.

Entanglement

Going beyond the infernal threshold, we enter into a new temporal dimension, where the 'vampiric nature' of capital dominates:[214] 'The prolongation of the working day beyond the limits of the natural day, into the night, only acts as a palliative. It quenches only in a slight degree the 'vampire thirst' for the living blood of labour'.[215] The vampire presses on, denying that it is impossible to make the workers work for more than 24 hours in a day, or intensify labour or increase productivity; thus, after having exceeded the limits of the natural day, it constrains them to night-work, it expands the day of 24 hours unnaturally, making it become thirty or forty hours of socially necessary labour. If 24 hours constitute the natural absolute limit of

214. Marx 1962a, p. 247; Marx 1996, p. 241.
215. Marx 1962a, p. 271; Marx 1996, p. 263.

the working day, different capitals, exploiting labour of different intensities and different productive powers, in the same time produce different masses of value and surplus-value.[216] Capital thus goes beyond any limit, presenting itself as the first mode of production without measure.[217]

The vampire is a creature that extends its life beyond the natural limits of death by sucking the blood of the living. Its life is, above all, a violation of nature at the cost of the living. What Marx critically represented in *Capital* was a political economy of the dead: a world of commodities soaked in blood. In order to describe this, Marx needed a new historiography. If, for the 'bourgeois historians', the process of transformation of producers into wage-workers is a process of liberation from servitude and from corporative coercion, the historical materialist writes the history of that expropriation of the workers from the point of view of their class.[218] It is a history that is 'is written in the annals of humanity in letters of blood and fire.[219] This history is not truer because it is more objective or conforms to historical facts. It is true because it is able to reveal new historical possibilities, putting an end to that infernal history. Materialist historiography does not follow the tendency of the sinusoidal curve of capitalist development, but cuts it vertically at a precise moment, corresponding to a political situation able to demonstrate not the 'tangent' of a tendency but the cusp, where either there is no tangent or there are infinite tangents. It is a new beginning. When Marx inserts pages of documentation on the 10-hour day, on the legislative interventions of the state, on factory-legislation and on laws regarding minors' labour, he is intersecting his conceptual exhibition with the fallout of the class-struggle. This marks the *contretemps* of capitalist development, reorienting and diverting it, forcing it to come to a compromise.[220]

The magnitude of value of a commodity, as we have already seen, is not given by the time employed for its production, but by the time of the socially necessary labour objectivised in it. However, this quantity is not definable *ex ante*. It is not possible to define in production what the quantity of the time

---

216. Marx 1962a, pp. 324–5; Marx 1996, p. 310–11.
217. Marx 1962a, pp. 328; Marx 1996, p. 314. The entire eleventh chapter is on the absolute limits and their overcoming. The difficulty relative to this contradiction is similar, Marx writes, to that required in algebra in order to understand that 0/0 represents a real magnitude: Marx 1962a, p. 325; Marx 1996, p. 311.
218. Marx 1962a, p. 743; Marx 1996, p. 706
219. Ibid.; translation modified.
220. I was pleased to note similarities between these reflections and those in Bensaïd 2002, pp. 69 et sq., which I had not had the opportunity to read before writing these lines.

of socially-necessary labour objectivised in a commodity is. This quantity can vary even when the process of production is complete.

If abstract labour explains the exchangeability of commodities in a world that materially makes an abstraction of needs and thus of the quality of use of commodities, exchange-value, the phenomenal form of value, instead expresses a 'quantitative relation, as the proportion in which values in use of one sort are exchanged for those of another sort'.[221] The quantity of labour objectified in a commodity, its exchange-value, 'is determined not by the quantity of labour actually realised in it, but by the quantity of living labour necessary for its production',[222] because 'that which determines the magnitude of the value of any article is the amount of labour socially necessary, or the labour time socially necessary for its production'.[223] Marx emphasised many times that only the time of socially-necessary labour counts as a creator of value,[224] such that it is only through relating the intensity of labour individually performed in the production of a given commodity to the 'usual degree of intensity in that given society' that it is possible to determine quantitatively the exchange-value and the surplus-value contained in a given commodity. This determination is possible only *ex post*, when the process of capitalist production has gone through circulation. We cannot, in fact, know beforehand the intensity and the productive power of socially-necessary labour.[225] The level of 'condensation of labour' can be superior or inferior to that which is socially necessary, just as the 'productive power [*Produktivkraft*]' – that is, the capacity to produce a greater or lesser quantity of commodities in the same time – can be different.[226] The productive power of socially-necessary labour is imposed as a national average of the productive power of the different working days and, on the global market, as 'the average unit of universal labour',[227] with respect to which the national differences constitute a scale of different productive powers.

Exchange-value and surplus-value cannot even be calculated within the boundaries of a single enterprise, as if surplus-value were determined by an excess of labour-time as compared to that necessary for the worker in order to produce their own wage. This conception supposes that surplus-labour – and, from this, surplus-value – is calculated in a linear way. If this were so,

221. Marx 1962a, p. 50; Marx 1996, p. 46.
222. Marx 1962a, pp. 558–9; Marx 1996, p. 536.
223. Marx 1962a, p. 54; Marx 1996, p. 49.
224. Marx 1962a, p. 204; Marx 1996, p. 200.
225. See, on this, Reuten 2004; Bellofiore and Finelli 1998. See also Fineschi 2001, pp. 58, 82.
226. Marx 1962a, p. 434; Marx 1996, p. 415.
227. Marx 1962a, p. 584; Marx 1996, p. 559.

the exchange-value of a commodity would be determined not by the time of socially-necessary labour, but by that individually employed in the production of that commodity. Rather, the productive power of socially-necessary labour is variable; its variability retroacts also on the determination of the value of an already produced commodity.[228] The notion of retroaction [*Rückwirkung*] allows Marx to explain a change of value that originates outside the process of production – specifically, following a change of the cost of primary materials or the introduction of a 'new invention'.[229] Marx's important acquisition, here, is possible only within a constellation that has clarified the social character of the labour that valorises value:

> The value of a commodity, it is true, is determined by the quantity of labour contained in it, but this quantity is itself limited by social conditions. If the time socially necessary for the production of any commodity alters...there is a retroactive effect [*Rückwirkung*] on all previously existing commodities of the same class...and their value at any given time is measured by the labour socially necessary, i.e., by the labour necessary for their production under the then existing social conditions.[230]

In other words, changes in the productivity of social labour retroact on the already produced commodities, changing the labour-time objectified in them. In fact, 'The real value of a commodity is, however, not its individual value, but its social value; that is to say, the real value is not measured by the labour time that the article in each individual case costs the producer, but by the labour time socially required for its production'.[231] Therefore, if the value of a commodity depends on the labour-time objectified in it, it should be remembered that this labour-time is not the labour-time effectively employed in the production of a given object of use, but can, instead, be inferior or superior to it. The labour-time objectified in the substance of value has to be referred to the time that social labour would employ in order to undertake that same labour. Thus, surplus-value is not a quantity that can be quantified within the accounts of a single enterprise. Marx's critique of Senior's last hour derives from this fact.[232]

Because surplus-value is not produced by the worker in the last part of the working day, that is, after having fulfilled his own wage in the former, it follows that a one-hour reduction in the working day does not mean the

228. See Marx 1965, p. 75.
229. Marx 1962a, pp. 224–5; Marx 1996, p. 220.
230. Ibid. See also Marx 1964, p. 122.
231. Marx 1962a, p. 336; Marx 1996, p. 322.
232. Marx 1962a, pp. 237 et sq.; Marx 1996, pp. 233 et sq.

subtraction of an hour of surplus-value. Rather, surplus-value is produced in each instant of the process of valorisation. It corresponds to the relation between the productivity of labour individually performed in a given enterprise and that of socially necessary labour. If the hours of labour were reduced but with salaries remaining the same, a circumstance that could occur only as a result of workers' struggles, then we would also have a diminution of the surplus-value produced, at least if labour were not intensified and enhanced by means of the employment of a new machine. It can, in fact, occur that an hour of labour of greater productive power corresponds to two hours of social labour, when society as a whole does not yet make use of technological innovation. This exchange, where one is equal to two, violates only the intellectual principles of those whose arithmetic skills are limited to the abacus. The value of the commodity in general, and thus also of that produced making use of some technological innovation, is its social value, that is, the quantity of social labour objectified in it. The fact that the labour-time effectively spent is inferior to the socially-necessary labour-time does not change anything in this relation, if not that the capitalist, selling the commodity at its value, appropriates social surplus-value, because he exchanges one hour of labour with two. 'If therefore, the capitalist who applies the new method, sells his commodity at its social value of one shilling, he sells it for three pence above its individual value, and thus realises an extra surplus-value [*Extramehrwert*] of three pence'.[233] Beyond the numbers, the *Extramehrwert* that the capitalist appropriates corresponds to the quantity of social surplus-value that he can obtain from society, to the extent that he exploits enhanced labour. In this way, a larger number of hours of labour concretely performed pass into the hands of that capitalist without violating the law of equivalence.

This is a theoretical acquisition that Marx made in the years 1861–3. If a capitalist uses a machine that allows him to exploit a greater productive power of labour, he can also 'sell his commodity at less than its social value, even though he sells it at more than its individual value'.[234] In fact, taking up Marx's example, if an hour of enhanced labour is equal to 5/4 'of labour hours of average labour', it follows that 10 hours of enhanced labour [*höhere Arbeit*] are equal to 12.5 hours of average labour. The capitalist can thus sell his commodities in the 'gap' given by 12.5 − 10 = 2.5. Even if it may seem that the surplus-value comes from the sale, and thus from circulation, it is determined by the differential between the labour-time used to produce a given commodity and the socially-necessary labour-time objectified in it. The

---

233. Marx 1962a, p. 336; Marx 1996, p. 322.
234. Marx 1990, p. 315; Marx 1988a, p. 319.

mirage of circulation vanishes as soon as we see that in it 'a smaller number of labour hours become...equal to a larger number of labour hours of average labour'. The capitalist 'pays for this labour as average labour and sells it as what it is, higher labour'.[235] The same question is presented in *Capital*, with different examples and figures.[236]

The immediate repercussion of a technological innovation is the lengthening of the time and an increase in the intensity of labour in those places where the innovation is not yet employed: 'One of the first effects of the introduction of new machinery, before it has become dominant in its branch of production, is to prolong the labour time of those workers who continue to work with the old, imperfect means of production'.[237] The sporadic introduction of new machinery allows the capitalists who use it to exploit labour whose productive power is greater than that of socially-necessary labour. It follows that the capitalists who still do not have the technological innovation can continue to compete on the global market only by extending and intensifying the time of labour of the workers they exploit. The capitalists who do not have the new machinery are forced to extend the working day and to intensify labour, increasing its degree of condensation [*Verdichtungsgrad*] by means of a 'closer filling up of the pores of the time of the working day'.[238] In fact, 'the denser hour [*die intensivere Stunde*] of the ten hours' working day contains more labour, i.e., expended labour power, than the more porous hour'.[239] Even abstracting from the quantity of relative surplus-value produced as a consequence of the increase of the productive power of labour, the machines

235. Marx 1990, p. 315; Marx 1988a, p. 320.
236. Marx 1962a, pp. 336–8; Marx 1996, p. 322: 'Suppose, that with the prevailing productiveness of labour, 12 articles are produced in these 12 hours. Let the value of the means of production used up in each article be sixpence. Under these circumstances, each article costs one shilling: sixpence for the value of the means of production, and sixpence for the value newly added in working with those means. Now let some one capitalist contrive to double the productiveness of labour, and to produce in the working day of 12 hours, 24 instead of 12 such articles. The value of the means of production remaining the same, the value of each article will fall to nine pence, made up of sixpence for the value of the means of production and three pence for the value newly added by the labour'. Thus, 'the individual value of these articles is now below their social value'; however, because its real value is its social value, and not its individual value, the capitalist that uses the new machinery can obtain three pence of extra surplus-value for each piece; or, he can decide to obtain less Extramehrwert, reduce the price of the commodity and beat his competitors. Riccardo Bellofiore, in a reading similar to that presented here, observes how Marx's notion of value contains from the beginning the dynamic 'competition of one capital in opposition to other capitals': see Bellofiore 1998, p. 223.
237. Marx 1990, p. 323; Marx 1988a, pp. 327–8.
238. See Marx 1962a, p. 431; Marx 1996, p. 413; translation modified.
239. Marx 1962a, pp. 432–3; Marx 1996, p. 413.

give rise to an intensification of labour, both due to the increased speed imposed by the machine, and due to the increase of the volume of machines: 'As soon as the new production method begins to spread...the capitalists working with the old methods of production must sell their product below its full price of production, because the value of this commodity has fallen, and because the labour time required by them to produce it is greater than the social average'.[240] Because the commodities produced by different capitalists have value according to the socially-necessary labour that they contain, there will be a transfer of suplus-value from capitals that exploit less productive labour to those that exploit enhanced labour. For the capitalists exploiting less productive labour not to lose out to those exploiting enhanced labour, in the period in which they cannot command the same productive power of labour, they have to increase the intensity and duration of the labour that they exploit. On the other hand, the benefits derived from the use of machines and enhanced labour are possible only by exploiting labour whose productive power is superior to that of socially-necessary labour. The latter has to be held back, therefore, in the global market, impeding the diffusion of the new technologies across all branches of production and across all countries. The advantages derived from the exploitation of high-tech labour, with a greater productive power, can be realised and preserved by capital only by maintaining and violently producing differentials of wages and of the productive power of labour, in such a way as to guarantee the extraction of that extra surplus-value that derives from the augmentation of productive power by means of the utilisation of new machines. Because these transfers of social surplus-value occur in the process of circulation, exploiting the differences between capitals of different organic composition, and specifically the differentials between productive powers,[241] it was possible to produce interpretative and political theories absolutising the sphere of circulation and denying the law of value.

Plural temporalities and synchronisation

Capitalist globalisation puts politics to work in order to defeat workers' resistance and to produce new wage-differentials in geographical areas where it

---

240. Marx 1964, p. 275; Marx 1998, p. 264.

241. Karatani 2003, pp. 11, 227, proposes a similar analysis. He explains surplus-value on the basis of a difference between value-systems. Less satisfying are Karatani's conclusions, which try to think politically the complementarity between production and circulation as an encounter between producers and consumers in LETS (Local Exchange Trading System) based upon non-mercantile exchange.

can reap fresh sums of absolute surplus-value. The simple registration of the co-presence of different forms of production and of subsumption remains linked to the point of view of circulation, if it does not articulate the relation between the different intensities and productive powers of labour in relation to socially-necessary labour. High-tech production is not only compatible with brutal forms of exploitation, but is based upon them: 'the computer requires the sweatshop and the existence of the cyborg is based on the slave'.[242] This relation is occluded in the fetishistic representation of capital, which constituted the perspective of the vulgar economy of Marx's time, of neoclassical economy and of the Negrian variant of postworkerism today.[243] Because the growth of value is manifested in circulation, from this point of view the process of valorisation can be reduced to the fetishistic formula M-M'. The process of valorisation, a 'synthesis of the processes of production and circulation',[244] when reduced to circulation alone, generates the illusion that value is produced in this sphere: the capitalist relation assumes the aspect of a 'fetish', such that it 'no longer bears the birthmarks of the origin of value',[245] which thus seems produced by any form and type of activity. Now, the entire society appears to be productive and, due to the negation of the path that goes from the origin of value to its manifestation, without history. This postmodernist vision occludes the core of the problem: how wealth produced capitalistically is possible only on the basis of exploitation of differentials of intensity and productive power, exploiting and continually generating labour of lesser productive power. But this does not mean that it is secondary or residual.

Relative surplus-value is relative because it has to be posited in relation to absolute surplus-value. The distinction between absolute and relative surplus-value is extremely fluid, or rather, Marx writes, from a certain point of view, it is 'illusory'.[246] What characterises the capitalist mode of production is the

---

242. Caffentzis 2003.
243. According to Negri, the Marx of the *Grundrisse* 'tells us that capitalist development leads to a society in which industrial labour (as immediate labour) is now only a secondary element in the organisation of capitalism', because capitalism has subsumed society, and productive labour becomes intellectual, cooperative, immaterial labour. 'In the final decades of the twentieth century, industrial labor lost its hegemony and in its stead emerged "immaterial labor"': Hardt and Negri 2004, p. 108. The 'General Intellect' becomes 'hegemonic in capitalist production', 'immaterial and cognitive labour becomes immediately productive' and the 'cognitariat' becomes 'the fundamental productive force that makes the system work': Negri 2007, pp. 169–70, 185. 'We live today in a society increasingly characterised by the hegemony of immaterial labour': Negri 1998, pp. 7–8.
244. Marx 1964, p 33; Marx 1998, p. 27.
245. Marx 1964, pp. 404–5; Marx 1998, p. 389.
246. Marx 1962a, p. 533; Marx 1996, p. 512.

combination of two forms of production of surplus-value. The increase of the productive power of labour by means of the use of machinery produces, at the same time, an intensification of labour, reducing its porosity and increasing its performance per unit of time.[247] Intensity of labour and productivity also increase, furthermore, following the increase in the speed of labour to which the machines constrain the workers. 'If machinery be the most powerful means for increasing the productiveness of labour – i.e., for shortening the working time required in the production of a commodity, it becomes in the hands of capital the most powerful means, in those industries first invaded by it, for lengthening the working day beyond all bounds set by human nature'.[248] In the battle for time, the machines destroy absolute, Newtonian time, whose flux cannot be changed. The machine, increasing the productivity of labour, shortens the time of necessary labour, at the same time extending the working day beyond its natural limit. Thus it is possible to have working days of thirty and more hours of (socially-necessary) labour within the 'natural' limits of the 24-hour day. The violence is double: it is violence done to the worker, constrained to work to rhythms of labour that are more intense and with a less porous time; and it is violence to human nature, because, if the machines have to be put to work for the greatest amount of time possible, it generates indifference between day and night.

Because machines 'create no new value',[249] their diffusion in a given branch of production also eliminates the possibility of obtaining extra surplus-value that their sporadic introduction permitted: 'As the use of machinery becomes more general in a particular industry, the social value of the product sinks down to its individual value, and the law that surplus value does not arise from the labour power that has been replaced by the machinery, but from the labour power actually employed in working with the machinery, asserts itself'.[250] When a technological innovation has been diffused, the growth of productive power of labour obtained through its use becomes socially dominant and the possibility of gaining sums of social surplus-value by means of the production of extra surplus-value is reduced. The production of this surplus-value ceases when the new level of productive power and labour-intensity is reached by the level of average social labour.

> If the intensity of labour were to increase simultaneously and equally in every branch of industry, then the new and higher degree of intensity

247. See Marx 1962a, p. 428; Marx 1996, p. 409.
248. Marx 1962a, p. 425; Marx 1996, p. 406.
249. Marx 1962a, p. 408; Marx 1996, p. 390.
250. Marx 1962a, p. 429; Marx 1996, pp. 409–10.

would become the normal degree for the society, and would therefore cease to be taken account of. But still, even then, the intensity of labour would be different in different countries, and would modify the international application of the law of value. The more intense working day of one nation would be represented by a greater sum of money than would the less intense day of another nation.[251]

The production of these differentials of surplus-value can occur either in the continuous revolutionising of the means of production, through the sporadic introduction of new machinery, or by encountering modes of production in which the productive power of labour is inferior. In its diffusion, capital does not need an exterior, something other than itself, but it does, instead, need a vast range of wage-differentials, of different productive powers and intensities of labour. Where it does not find these already pre-existing, it is able to generate them as a repercussion of its arrival. If a certain average intensity of labour is valid for a given country, such that the individual labour of an enterprise can be above or below that average, on the world-market the average intensity of labour changes from one country to the next. 'These national averages form a scale, whose unit of measure is the average unit of universal labour'.[252] In each country, a certain average intensity of labour prevails, below which level labour consumes more than the socially-necessary time in the production of a commodity, and thus does not count as labour of normal quality. On the world-market, the law of value is modified in its international application, since the more productive national labour prevails also as the more intense labour, so long as the more productive nation is not constrained by competition to lower the sales-price of its commodity to its value.[253] If this does not occur, the more productive nation will obtain the market social surplus-value of the less productive nations.[254] Marx's studies in the 1860s on competition between capitals and on average profit, which then went into what posthumously became the second and third volumes, allowed him to reconsider the entire question of the production of surplus-value at

---

251. Marx 1962a, p. 548; Marx 1996, p. 525.
252. Marx 1962a, p. 584; Marx 1996, p. 559.
253. Ibid.
254. Roy Mauro Marini has studied how, in relation to the inclusion of Latin America in the world-market, the *desfavorecidas* nations have to give, gratis, a part of the value produced to the nations that exploit more productive labour, and are furthermore forced to increase the intensity of labour and to exploit it more: Marini 1991, pp. 8–10; Dussel shows how the problem of the transfer of surplus-value remains invisible from the point of view of 'capital in general', which is the perspective of the *Grundrisse*, while it is thematised from the *Manuscripts* of 1861–3 onwards, where Marx studies competition between 1) individual capitals, 2) different branches of production and 3) nations: see Dussel 1990b, p. 76.

the level of the world-market. 'The competition between capitals thus seeks to treat each capital as a part of total capital, and thus also to regulate its share in surplus-value and therefore in profit'.[255] It was the study of competition between capitals, in the 1861–3 *Manuscripts*, that led Marx to reflect on the exploitation of labour of inferior productive power that occurs on the world-market.[256] His attention focused also on the transfer [*Übertragung*][257] of surplus-value from one sphere to another, or from one country to another. These transfers not only provoke oscillations in the rate of profit: what is even more important is that the different capitals participate *pro rata* in total surplus-value: 'Every individual capital should be regarded merely as a part of the total capital, and every capitalist [should be regarded] actually as a shareholder in the total enterprise, each sharing in the total profit pro rata to the magnitude of his share of capital'.[258]

The profit taken by the single capitalist is different from the surplus-value that he extorts. Thus, it appears to the capitalist that it is the market itself that creates profit and that this derives from the addition made to the price of the cost of commodities. But what is taken is a quota of total surplus-value, to which the individual capitalist has a right in a measure proportional to the productivity of labour that he exploits. Thus, a capitalist or a country that has advanced machines, and, consequently, has elevated the productive power of labour, will obtain extra surplus-value at the cost of those countries in which the productive power of labour is lower. It is a case of thinking the different forms of subsumption, both those formal and those real, not according to a stagist paradigm, but in their hybridisation. Formal subsumption is the basis of capitalist production insofar as the production of surplus-value is a process aiming at the production of commodities for sale; real subsumption is presented, instead, as specifically capitalist because it not longer tolerates the existence of previous social relations, but revolutionises the technical processes of production and social groupings.[259] To these two forms there is then a third,

255. Marx 1978b, p. 685.
256. Beginning with the *Manuscripts* of 1861–3, Marx abandoned the expression 'capital in general [*Kapital im allgemeinen*]', which was still used in the *Grundrisse*, allowing him, in these notebooks, to abstract from competition between different capitals. The decision to abandon this concept was not only a terminological decision, but was, rather, the indication of a new problem related to the relation between individual and social capital, and between individual labour and socially necessary labour.
257. See Marx 1964, p. 218; Marx 1998, p. 205.
258. Marx 1964, pp. 219–20, Marx 1998, p. 207.
259. Marx 1962a, p. 533; Marx 1996, p. 512.

little-studied in the literature:[260] the intermediate or 'hybrid-forms [*Zwitter-formen*]' of subsumption. Marx speaks of them for the first time in *Capital*.[261]

The hybrid-forms are forms in which surplus-labour is extorted by means of direct coercion [*direkter Zwang*], without there being formal subsumption of labour to capital. These forms can be understood as forms of transition, but can be also 'reproduced in the background of modern industry'.[262] The hybrid-forms, though not being formally subsumed to capital and though not being labour in the form of wage-labour, fall under the command of capital. They allow us to understand the contemporaneity of apparently anachronistic forms like slavery, forms that are produced and reproduced on the basis of the current capitalist mode of production.[263]

The productive power of socially-necessary labour is imposed in the world-market, and imposes its own temporality, synchronising the different forms of production: the patriarchal command and the whip of the slave-driver intervene continually in order to synchronise that particular labour to the universal chronometer marked by the temporality of socially-necessary labour. If it is true that 'the place of the slave-driver's lash is taken by the overlooker's book of penalties',[264] it is also true that these different forms of command exist alongside each other and constitute a single time when the law of value is imposed in the labour-market. Just as soon as apparently anachronistic forms of labour such as slavery or the *corvée* 'are drawn into the whirlpool of an international market dominated by the capitalistic mode of production...the civilised horrors of overwork are grafted on the barbaric horrors of slavery, serfdom, etc'.[265]

The subsumption of different social and productive forms occurs just as soon as they cease to produce use-values for their own needs and begin to produce for the world-market; in this same moment, they become phases of total capital. Command over labour, though remaining apparently the only brutal form of subjection, changes its own nature. The law of valorisation

---

260. One exception to this is Patrick Murray, who drew my attention to this passage. See Murray 2000; 2004.
261. Marx 1962a, p. 533; Marx 1996, p. 511; translation modified.
262. Ibid.
263. Marcel van der Linden, contrary to the Marxist thesis according to which slavery is an anomaly in the capitalist mode of production, argues that capitalism is compatible with different forms of labour, including slavery and non-free wage-labour: van der Linden 2005; 2007. Nimtz emphasises that if, for Tocqueville, racial oppression and slavery in the USA were marginal factors of the political system, for Marx they 'were key to understanding economic and political developments not only in America but worldwide': Nimtz 2003, p. viii, pp. 121 et sq.
264. Marx 1962a, p. 447; Marx 1996, p. 427.
265. Marx 1962a, p. 250; Marx 1996, p. 244.

obliges every single producer to put to work 'socially average labour' or, where the resistance is less, labour of an intensity superior to that of social labour. Thus slave-labour, anything but a residual form of labour, is presented as a possibility for augmenting the intensity of labour and guaranteeing to capital masses of absolute surplus-value. When the global domination of a system of calculation of labour-time based on socially-necessary labour puts the different forms of exploitation into relation, the emancipation of the workers has to affront the 'knot' of slave-labour; in its turn, slave-labour cannot emancipate itself without encountering the workers' movement and uniting with it in the struggle to limit the working day. Marx understood that the high level of exploitation of slave-labour on a racist basis poses a block to the emancipation of workers as such. In 1866, he wrote to his son-in-law Lafargue in relation to events in North America: 'The workers in the North have at last fully understood that white labour will never be emancipated so long as black labour is still stigmatised'.[266] He repeated this in *Capital*: 'In the United States of North America, every independent movement of the workers was paralysed so long as slavery disfigured a part of the Republic. Labour cannot emancipate itself in the white skin where in the black it is branded'.[267] Four years after the proclamation of emancipation of 1863, an entire series of racist gradations of exploitation continued to exist and to impede the emancipation of the workers. Absolute exploitation of a part of the population allows the extension of the sphere of needs of another, also working-class part of the population, with the added bonus of translating class-conflict into race-conflict. The whole history of modern colonialism, including colonialism today, is characterised by oscillations between class-conflict and race-conflict. Political violence also acts to stamp a racial stigma on new divisions of labour. It is political and economic modernity that has produced races, not nature.

Modernisation...of slavery

New forms of capitalist luxury stimulated the birth of large capitalist enterprises. The commodities suited to satisfy the new needs of this new industry (sugar, cocoa, cotton and coffee) were provided by the colonies, produced on large plantations that had clearly capitalist characteristics.[268] The capitalist

266. Marx 1987g, p. 334.
267. Marx 1962a, p. 318; Marx 1996, p. 305.
268. Forced labour in the colonies of the New World did not have an archaic form, but that of capitalist enterprises. The cycle of sugar-cane production, for example, was a genuine industrial cycle: the sugar-mill was a small factory. R.W. Fogel observed that 'The industrial discipline, so difficult to bring about in the factories of free England and

mode of production produced slavery and new forms of slavery, which were not residues of previous epochs, but a genuine product of capitalist modernity. Slave-labour was not backward or residual with respect to European capitalist development, but was increased precisely by that development. It was a form of labour absolutely adequate and complementary to the most developed capitalist production of the metropolises. The labour-time of slaves was and is marked by English and global industries. The whip of the slave-driver was and is moved by the global stock-markets. The capitalist mode of production does not spontaneously produce formally-free labour; rather, this is conquered on the terrain of the class-struggle. The capitalist mode of production, if it does not encounter sufficient resistance, is perfectly willing to use slave-labour even today. While, during the colonial period, black labour looked to the free labour of 'the free English', the English capitalist looked to the laboratory of the disciplining of slave-labour. The object of the rules of factory was not so much the promotion of a rational organisation of the productive process, as to force the workers into a total submission. The rules express the drive to exert the 'full domination over workers' bodies'.[269]

Historically, the extension of the use of machines in a branch of production has retroacted on other branches, augmenting the numbers condemned to the mines; the forced march of the cotton-spinning mill accelerated the extension of cotton-cultivation and increased the slave-trade and industry. According to the statistics available to Marx, there were 697,000 slaves in the United States in 1790; by 1861, their number had grown to 4 million.[270] With the slave-trade, the single slave became replaceable: 'the duration of his life becomes a matter of less moment than its productiveness while it lasts'.[271] The creation of the world-market, begun in the seventeenth century with the colonies and slavery, included ever-new forms of wage-labour, non-waged and slave-labour, giving rise, in the eighteenth century, to a second slavery: the 'archaic' forms

---

free New England, was achieved on sugar plantations more than a century earlier – partly because sugar production lent itself to a minute division of labor, partly because of the invention of the gang system, which provided a powerful instrument for the supervision and control of labor, and partly because of the extraordinary degree of force that planters were allowed to bring to bear on enslaved black labor': Fogel 1989, pp. 25–6. Analogously, Robin Blackburn has shown how the slave-labour of the plantations, negating individual control over a large part of the labour-process, anticipated many aspects of industrial capitalism: Blackburn 1997, p. 335.

269. Bauman 1982, p. 63.

270. Marx 1962a, p. 467; Marx 1996, p. 447. It has now been calculated that the total number of human-beings forced to leave the coasts of Africa, taking into account the high level of mortality connected to the middle-passage, was approximately 11 million. The number of slaves actually introduced into the Americas between 1519 and 1867 is thought to be roughly 9,599,000: Pétré-Grenouilleau 2004.

271. Marx 1962a, p. 282; Marx 1996, p. 272.

of organisation of labour were not destroyed, but were reorganised into a new constellation of political and economic powers.[272] To comprehend this inter-weaving of pluralities of temporal layers in this same historical dimension of modernity requires a historiography able to incorporate plural, spatial and temporal relations within new causal models.[273]

Capital was now completely internationalised, imposing its own temporali-ties on the different forms of exploitation, and the International Workingmen's Association, founded in London in 1864, represented the organisational form for intervening in these new international relations. We should read Marx's pages in *Capital* also holding in the other hand the programme and the stat-utes of the International, which Marx himself wrote. Marx certainly did this, inserting in *Capital* the resolution of the 1866 Congress of the International Workingmen's Association at Geneva: 'the limitation of the working day is a preliminary condition without which all further attempts at improvement and emancipation must prove abortive...the Congress proposes eight hours as the legal limit of the working day'.[274] In order to understand the theoreti-cal work of *Capital*, we need to put it back into the field of forces in which it is immersed; otherwise, we will not understand much more than what one could glean from a compass without a magnetic field. Negro labour, Marx noted, preserved 'something of a patriarchal character, so long as produc-tion was chiefly directed to immediate local consumption'. However, upon entering into the world-market – that is, when cotton was exported for the world-market – the overworking of negro labour in the American plantations became a factor in a 'calculated and calculating system'.[275] This was the transi-tion to modern slavery.[276] The labour of slaves was directed to the production of commodities for the world-market; from the moment that the productivity of labour had to be measured on the global stock-markets, labour-time had to be intensified and rendered as unporous as possible. The epoch of the dis-posable slave had begun. Marx cited John Elliot Cairnes:[277] 'It is accordingly a maxim of slave management, in slave-importing countries, that the most effective economy is that which takes out of the human chattel in the shortest

---

272. Tomich 2003, p. 61.

273. This is the task that Tomich takes on in his book, seeking to study these intersections by means of a model of cumulative causality that is able to explain the interaction between events and structures 'across plural times and differential spaces of the world economy': Tomich 2003, pp. 97, 118.

274. Marx 1962a, p. 319; Marx 1996, pp. 305–6.

275. Marx 1962a, p. 250; Marx 1996, p. 244.

276. See Benot 2003, pp. 123 et sq. According to Benot, slavery became a part of European capitalism at least from the middle of the eighteenth century (p. 162).

277. Cairnes 1862, pp. 110–11.

space of time the utmost amount of exertion it is capable of putting forth'.[278]
He continued with a citation from George M. Weston:[279]

> It is in tropical culture, where annual profits often equal the whole capital of
> plantations, that negro life is most recklessly sacrificed. It is the agriculture
> of the West Indies, which has been for centuries prolific of fabulous wealth,
> that has engulfed millions of the African race. It is in Cuba, at this day,
> whose revenues are reckoned by millions, and whose planters are princes,
> that we see in the servile class, the coarsest fare, the most exhausting and
> unremitting toil, and even the absolute destruction of a portion of its
> numbers every year.[280]

The popular edition of the *Werke* reproduced the above-cited passage, like
others, in a smaller font. In the Hamburg edition of 1867, this text was, instead,
presented as an integral part of Marx's text.[281] Marx took the passages cited
from Weston's work from Cairnes's book, which continues: 'The truth is, it is
the temptation of great, immediate profits, which, more than anything else,
causes slaves to be overworked, just as beasts of burden are overworked
under similar circumstances'.[282] Cairnes noted how the slave-trade incen-
tivises the use of slaves for intensive cultivation, leading to the infertility of
the soil (the 'tendency of slave labour to exhaust the soil'), even if the pro-
fessors of agricultural chemistry saw the hand of divine providence in the
combination of uncultivated lands in the South and the 'unemployed power
of human muscles in Africa'. At the end of the long citation, Marx speaks in
Latin: '*Mutato nomine de te fabula narratur!*' Modern slavery continues on the
labour-market. The long process of capitalist accumulation is not only fed
by modern forms of slavery, but also continues in the destruction of labour-
power. The absolute destruction of the servile class becomes the absolute
destruction of generations of workers of industry by means of what Weston,
citing Cairnes, called the 'slow torture of overwork'.[283] Marx then added further citations. A section of the William Busfield Ferrand's 27 April 1863 speech
to the House of Commons explained: 'The cotton trade has existed for ninety
years... It has existed for three generations of the English race, and I believe
I may safely say that during that period it has destroyed nine generations of
factory operatives'.[284] He continued by providing still-longer reports, to the

---

278. Marx 1962a, p. 282; Marx 1996, p. 272.
279. Weston 1857, pp. 131–3.
280. Marx 1962a, p. 282; Marx 1996, p. 272.
281. See Marx 1983i, p. 209.
282. Weston 1857, p. 133.
283. Weston 1857, p. 132; Marx 1962a, p. 282; Marx 1996, p. 272.
284. Marx 1962a, p. 282; Marx 1996, p. 273.

point of turning the conflict into theatre: 'Capital is reckless of the health or length of life of the labourer... to the outcry as to the physical and mental degradation, the premature death, the torture of overwork, it answers: Ought these to trouble us since they increase our pleasure [our profits]?'[285]

Marx was not making a moral judgement, but demonstrating the need to transfer the whole discourse onto a new level. Capital, in itself, precisely because it abstracts from use-value, can continue right up to the physical and spiritual annihilation of the worker. Many times in history, it has come close to this result, such that only the social imposition of a limit has saved the health of the worker. The machines are an 'instrument of torture' that 'beat the worker to death';[286] capitalist production is a 'greater spendthrift than any other mode of production of man, of living labour, spendthrift not only of flesh and blood and muscles, but of brains and nerves'.[287] Entering into the inferno makes visible what the phatasmagoria occluded: how commodities are produced and how the 'living corporeality'[288] of the worker is constrained to work. Capital becomes a vampire that 'will not lose its hold on [the worker] "so long as there is a muscle, a nerve, a drop of blood to be exploited"';[289] a 'werewolf'[290] whose hunger for surplus-value 'oversteps not only the moral, but even the merely physical maximum bounds of the working day'.[291] Death by 'overwork'[292] is not an exception, not a pathology of this mode of production, but its normality. The worker has sold her labour-power, but because labour-power is irremediably attached to her 'living corporeality', they are both worked together in the process of production. Her entire personality, including her body, is subsumed in the process of production. The contract of sale of labour-power can pay for the commodity labour-power, but cannot pay for the consumption of the body and the life of the worker. We can recognise, here, on the one hand, its proximity to slavery, and, on the other hand, a point of exteriority with respect to capital that marks the measure of an irresolvable conflict. There is no wage that could pay for the consumption of the life and the body of the worker.

There is an element of proximity between the slavery that we Europeans are accustomed to think of in terms of black skin, and 'wage-slavery'. Hegel

---

285. Marx 1962a, pp. 285–6; Marx 1996, pp. 275–6; translation modified.
286. Marx 1962a, pp. 446, 455.
287. Marx 1964, pp. 98–9; Marx 1998, p. 92; translation modified; cf. Marx 1988a, p. 168.
288. Marx 1962a, p. 183; Marx 1996, p. 179; translation modified.
289. Marx 1962a, p. 319; Marx 1996, p. 306.
290. Marx 1962a, pp. 258, 300; Marx 1996, pp. 251, 271.
291. Marx 1962a, p. 300; Marx 1996, p. 271.
292. Marx 1962a, pp. 486, 786; Marx 1996, pp. 466, 630.

could consider the modern principle of subjective liberty to be incompatible with slavery, for a good reason. The worker remains formally free if he alienates, freely, by means of a contract between equals, for a determinate period, the use of his own labour-power – and only this use, not his entire personality. It is not the particular physical and spiritual destitution of the modern worker that makes her comparable to the ancient slave. The slave-master had bought the entire person; it was certainly not in his interest to exhaust the slave early. He was thus forced to act in such a way that the slave's health was kept in a condition sufficient to allow continuing work. The capitalist does not have this scruple. He buys only labour-power, and it is in his interest to exploit it for the period of time for which he has paid for it. It is not the capitalist's business if the worker succumbs during the supply of labour-power, or if conditions of labour and a low salary weaken the worker's health to such an extent that inability to work or even mortal illness are the result. The production of dangerous labour's conditions is intrinsic to capitalist production. What Césaire wrote about slavery and reparations is also valid regarding the possibility of compensating for the consumption of the body and the life of the worker: 'There is no possible remedy for something irreparable and that is not quantifiable'.[293]

The exploitation of child-labour in Asian countries and working days of up to 18 hours should not be chalked up as cases of capitalist underdevelopment.[294] Rather, they express the current level of production of social surplus-value. The different forms of production existing contemporaneously in different geographical spaces are integrated in such a way as to frustrate any consideration in terms of developed or backward forms. Sergio Bagù correctly affirms that colonial society was not feudal, but of a type of 'colonial capitalism…Latin America emerged in order to augment early capitalism, not in order to prolong the agony of the feudal cycle'.[295] If we assume the full implications of the reciprocal co-penetration between absolute surplus-value and relative surplus-value, then the distinction between the North and South of the world, between First, Second and Third World, or, if we want, between centre, semi-periphery and periphery, and the concomitant

---

293. Cited in Benot 2003, p. 276.
294. According to the statistics of the ILO, there are around 218 million minors in the world who are forced to work, of whom more than 132 million are employed in agricultural work and are aged between five and ten years old. Of these, at least 400,000 are exploited in 'civilised' and 'modern' Italy (according to il manifesto, 12 June 2007). The ILO also claims that as of 2006, around six hundred million workers labour for more than 48 hours per week.
295. Bagù 1949, p. 260.

typology of advanced or backward capitalisms, loses any meaning.[296] It is no longer possible to reason in terms of tendency and residue: rather, the different forms of exploitation should be thought in a historical-temporal multiversum in which they are intertwined in the contemporaneity of the present. The history of capital, Bensaïd observes, is always subjected to the discontinuous times of relations of exchange, of exploitation and domination, showing 'a "process of rhythmical determination", constantly inventing new harmonies and disharmonies'.[297] The capitalist mode of production, left free to develop itself, to realise its own tendency, would present itself as an immense process of destruction that would not only lower wages to the absolute minimum necessary for workers' survival, but would also turn the entire planet into a desert. There are, however, countertendencies that continually reorient this tendency; so when Marx speaks of tendency, he does so in order to give body to those countertendencies, which are, in reality, what defines the tendency. In a letter to Kugelmann, written immediately after the publication of *Capital*, we read: 'Where science comes in is to show how the law of value asserts itself. So, if one wanted to "explain" from the outset all phenomena that apparently contradict the law, one would have to provide the science before the science'.[298] This is the way in which Marx reasons. He needs to fix the fundamental problem, that is, 'how the law of value asserts itself', in order to bring out the countertendencies, the 'apparently contradictory phenomena'. The countertendencies are only apparently contradictory, because the picture we see is made up of the figures that stand out in front of the background, which, once filled with subjects, assumes an entirely new meaning. Thus, when Marx reasons on the tendential fall of the rate of profit, his attention turns to 'the same influences which produce a tendency in the general rate of profit to fall, also call forth countereffects, which hamper, retard, and partly paralyse this fall'; thus, 'the law acts only as a tendency'.[299] For the same reason, he fills the first book with historical materials – the precipitates of the class-struggle – in order to show how the tendency of capital is in itself a pure abstraction, because this is, rather, the result of a clash with the laws on child-labour, with the laws for the 10-hour day and the syncopated rhythms of workers' revolts. The relation between history and logic in *Capital* is analogous to that between use-value

---

296. See Frank 2004.
297. Bensaïd 2002, p. 270.
298. Marx 1988b, pp. 68–9.
299. Marx 1964, p. 249; Marx 1998, p. 237. Bensaïd notes that 'those who claim to deduce a theory of the automatic and immanent collapse of capitalism from the tendency of the rate of profit to fall are mistaken about what the tendential involves according to Marx, and the transition from economic law to political strategy'. Bensaïd 2002, p. 283.

and exchange-value in the analysis of the capitalist mode of production; what counts is the parallax.[300]

Law, tendency, countertendencies

Marx tried to delineate tendencies in the same way that a painter begins to paint the background before painting the subjects of the picture. The historical tendencies are sketched out in order better to give evidence of the nature of the countertendencies. By the middle of the 1860s at the latest, Marx was decisively opposed to the 'idolatry of the rigidity of laws in history'.[301] Just as capitalism is not digging its own grave by itself, equally communism is not an ontological dimension already produced in capital. It is necessary, rather, to work in the space of the difference between law and tendency: there exists a law, which is the law of value, and there is a tendency that is the result of subjective countertendencies in relation to the law. The law of value is delineated as an abstraction from use-value and as a repetition of the identical: the valorisation of value. This tendency, which, were it to coincide with the law, would have already decreed the destruction of the planet and of humanity, is held open by the counter-times of the countertendencies: in this opening, there is also a passage for the new. Politics has to make this practical. This difference between law and tendency was clear for Marx: 'Under capitalist production, the general law acts as the prevailing tendency only in a very complicated and approximate manner, as a never ascertainable average of ceaseless fluctuations'.[302]

The law is always abstract. It becomes a tendency by intertwining itself in the contingent countertendencies of the competition between capitalists and the class-struggle. When Marx wrote to Kugelmann that it is not possible to 'provide the science before the science', that is, it is not possible to delineate the phenomena contrasting with the law before the law itself, he was sketching a double semantics of science. Science[II], which cannot exist before science[I], is the science of the different historical temporalities of tendencies and countertendencies. Science[I] is an abstract representation of the laws of capital. Much of Marxism has considered only this, while neglecting science[II] entirely. Science[I] does not yet break epistemologically with political economy. It shows its contradictions, but its way of proceeding is still that of immanent critique. The leap begins with the change of perspective. Political economy 'can remain

---

300. On this point, see Karatani 2003, p. 160.
301. Bloch 1975.
302. Marx 1964, p. 171; Marx 1998, p. 160.

a science only so long as the class-struggle is latent or manifests itself only in isolated and sporadic phenomena'.[303] Not when the class-struggle is extended quantitatively, but when the class-struggle becomes the perspective from which to observe the capital-labour relation, then political economy ceases to be scientific, and science[II] begins. The denunciation of the capitalist organisation of labour, of the use-value of constant capital and of the knowledge objectified in machines, requires the critique of the modern concept of science by means of another notion of science.

At the end of the 1850s, with the small amount of money in his pockets, Marx did not buy novels or books of philosophy, but the reports of the *Royal Commissioners on the Employment of Children and Young Persons in Trades and Manufacturers*, the *Reports of the Inspectors of Factories*, the *Reports from the Poor Law Inspectors on the Wages of Agricultural Labourers*, and the *Reports on the Adulteration of Food*. And he read them. The stories of the conditions of the workers in the factories enter into theory, marking its rhythm. The montage of these materials, to the point of making them an integral part of critical theory, presents the assumption of a supposedly neutral perspective, that of the inspectors, on the alleged neutrality of the process of production. Hence, the non-neutrality of the machine and of capitalist technology and the non-neutrality of those who let things follow their own course, translates into affirmations like the following: ' "Factory labour may be as pure and as excellent as domestic labour, and perhaps more so" ("Rep. Insp. of Fact., 31st October, 1865", p. 129)'.[304] Eleanor, Marx's daughter, later used the *Factory Reports* of 1884 in order to write, together with Edward Aveling, the pamphlet *The Factory Hell*.[305] Critics and interpreters have endlessly cited, to the point of boredom, the fact that Marx, 'by mere accident',[306] had again picked up Hegel's *Science of Logic*. They want to find correspondences and analogies. But they have not investigated the other side, namely, how history – of the conditions of the workers and of their struggles – entered into Marx's conceptual elaboration; how the structure of *Capital* is not deducible beginning from a presumed *Ausgangskategorie*, but has, rather, the discontinuity of strata in tension with each other; how the historical material is assembled in the text and enters into tension, but in the same constellation, with the conceptual exposition. A report on a workers' struggle is not, for Marx, only a fact of journalistic sensation that can be cited as an example, but the point of condensation in which the entire theoretical exposition is concentrated and exploded.

---

303. Marx 1962a, p. 20; Marx 1996, p. 14.
304. Marx 1962a, p. 514; Marx 1996, p. 493.
305. Aveling and Marx Aveling 1891.
306. Marx 1983g, p. 248.

Appendix

Layered Historiography.
Re-Reading the So-Called Primitive
Accumulation

Accumulation Street

Marx wrote to Mrs. Wollmann on 19 March 1877:

> Should you wish to leaf through some of *Capital*,
> it would be best to start with the last section,
> p. 314 [*Le procès d'accumulation du capital*]. In
> the scientific exposition the arrangement is
> prescribed for the author, although some other
> arrangement might often be more convenient
> and more appropriate for the reader.[1]

The capitalist mode of production does not produce
its own premises out of nothing. It is fed by external/
internal elements punctuated by historical temporalities that it tries to synchronise. It needs workers
who are formally free, shaped by the combination of
practical emancipation, the dissolution of the authority of intermediate bodies and the concentration
of force in the hands of the state. Struggles against
the estates, through which the servants freed themselves to become wage-workers, lost their emancipatory dimension as soon as the estate-structure was
destroyed. The aspect oriented to freedom, which
shone in the light of opposition to the estates and
inequalities of status, became opaque in the equality

---

1. Marx 1991a, p. 212.

of juridical subjects and the equality of the market. This was the beginning of
the epoch of synchronisation. The time of the church was replaced by abstract
time measured by clocks and merchants. Workers' lives are marked by the
'despotic bell', at the command of which they must eat, drink and sleep.[2]
The affirmation of this capitalist temporality is, however, syncopated by the
counter-times of 'workers' uprisings' that aim to silence the 'Werkglocke'.[3]

The structure of *Capital* is not that of a more or less Hegelian logical mono-
lith, but is rooted in conflicting temporalities that show how synchronisation
functions. The 'Preface' to the 1867 first edition of *Capital* shows the presence
of anachronistic [*zeitwidrigen*] social and political relations and their combination in the present.[4] These anachronistic relations, such as those found in
Germany, lead to working conditions worse than those existing in a more-
developed capitalist country like England, where the 'counterweight of the
factory legislation' puts a limit on exploitation; the consequence is that Germany is oppressed by modern miseries, and also by its anachronism:

> a whole series of inherited evils oppress us, arising from the passive survival
> of antiquated modes of production...We suffer not only from the living,
> but also from the dead. *Le mort saisit le vif!*.[5]

This is the problem: the interaction between non-contemporary levels of a historical *multiversum*.[6] If synchronisation is given by socially-necessary labour-
time, there still remains the question of anachronisms, which should be
understood both as times that are not synchronised by the capitalist machine,
and as workers' counter-times. Working conditions in England are less brutal
not because capital is more civilised, but because the English working class
has managed to impose factory-laws that put a limit on exploitation. The conquests of the class-struggle do not proceed in a linear and gradual fashion, but
according to a syncopated rhythm. These different temporalities constitute
the specific problem of Marx's analysis: how the different temporalities of the
class-struggle interact among themselves and with the time of capital.

Without state-violence, without the existence of proletarians, without the
dissolution of the authority of the *Hausvater* and of corporate bonds, without the disciplining of formally-free workers, without a new ethic, without

---

2. Engels 1975, pp. 467–8, quoted by Marx 1996, p. 427.
3. Le Goff 1980, p. 29 ff. On the new discipline imposed on time in the eighteenth
century, see Thompson 1967, p. 32.
4. Marx 1996, p. 9.
5. Ibid.
6. I refer frequently, in what follows, to Bloch 1985, pp. 104 et sq.; see also Bodei
1979.

enclosures and separation between the means of production and the living conditions of the workers, without these and other histories, without their synchronisation, the capitalist mode of production would not have arisen. Althusser spoke of a 'process of aleatory encounter':

> every mode of production comprises elements that are independent of each other, each resulting from its own specific history, in the absence of any organic, teleological relation between these diverse histories. This conception culminates in the theory of primitive accumulation, from which Marx, taking his inspiration from Engels, drew a magnificent chapter of *Capital*, the true heart of the book.[7]

Althusser argued that Marx and Engels often worked with a teleological history, in which the aleatory nature of the encounter of different elements gave way to a history oriented towards a specific end, such that the various historical elements became organically entrapped in that teleology. Their encounter was not aleatory, but somehow predetermined. For instance, this happens when the proletariat is presented as the product of capitalist expropriation, as if the capitalist mode of production could pre-exist before its essential element: 'expropriated labour-power'. In this kind of conception, 'the specific histories no longer float in history, like so many atoms in the void, at the mercy of an "encounter" that might not take place'. In this organic conception, everything happens beforehand, 'the structure precedes its elements and reproduces them in order to reproduce the structure'.[8]

If we were to follow Althusser's 'materialism of the encounter', however, we would run the risk of having as many modes of production as there are possibilities of encounter between distinct elements; or, at least, we would have to speak of different modes of capitalist production. The issue is that many of these elements are woven together and work only when combined, such that these distinct historical temporalities are catalysed toward one particular configuration, which, of course, could have not even taken place. In Italy, even with finance, technology and labour-power, capitalism did not manage to develop. What was lacking was what Machiavelli called for as soon as possible: a state. It is, in fact, the state that makes a first, violent synchronisation of the different historical temporalities, and that produces, as an effect of the concentration of *Gewalt* and as a reaction to the struggles for the emancipation of the serfs, workers who are formally free and a contract-system of labour-relations. Once individuals were created and once some of them had been

---

7. Althusser 2006, p. 199.
8. Althusser 2006, p. 200.

transformed into proletarians, it was necessary to discipline them to work:[9] to destroy the previous customary relations and impose an abstractly egalitarian law in what became the long hundred years' war against collective rights.[10]

State-intervention, which is not neutral but, as a part of the class-struggle, is also not always reducible to the interests of the ruling class, should be understood in its own relative autonomy. Marx was interested in its use by workers, for instance, in securing legislation on the working day. The state's laws on the working day, which are an expression of the victory of the working class in a sector of production or in a series of battles, become political victories of the entire working class. An entire paragraph of the fourth section of *Capital* is dedicated to the Factory Laws. The dynamic of this legislation, forced onto capital against its wishes, made it possible to consider the relative autonomy of the state, which can also come into conflict with capital or with other segments of the ruling classes, which, in turn, may be in conflict with each other. The Factory Act of 1864, by means of which the state imposed sanitary and hygienic measures for workplaces, had the effect, as a repercussion, of converting small workshops into factories.[11] Workers' struggles thus indirectly brought into being a greater concentration of workers and thus more class-power. In a different way, technological development can also facilitate the disintegration of large concentrations of workers, resulting in a financial and productive centralisation without a concentration of workers.[12] In this case, it is capital that is in a position of power, with the complicity of the ideology of progress and technical development.

When Marx showed the 'image of the future' that England presents, his intention was to sketch out a performative historiography written for other segments of the international working class.[13] The history of the workers' conquest of factory-legislation in England is told so that other workers can do the same: 'One nation can and should learn from others'.[14] This historiography is interested in the possible 'backlashes [*Rückschläge*]' of the lessons from England, in the ways in which class-struggles in one country can interact with those in another country: 'As in the 18th century, the American War of

---

9. 'The first generation of factory workers were taught by their masters the importance of time; the second generation formed their short-time committees in the ten-hour movement; the third generation struck for overtime or time-and-a half. They had accepted the categories of their employers and learned to fight back within them. They had learned their lesson, that time is money, only too well': Thompson 1967, p. 33.
10. De Certeau 1997a, p. 152.
11. Marx 1996, p. 485.
12. Bellofiore 2008b.
13. Marx 1996, p. 8.
14. Marx 1996, p. 10.

Independence sounded the tocsin for the European middle class, so in the 19th century, the American Civil War sounded it for the European working class'.[15] Marx tried to make different histories and *exempla* speak to each other. For 'this reason', Marx wrote in the 'Preface', 'as well as others, I have given so large a space in this volume to the history, the details, and the results of English factory legislation'.[16] Bourgeois historiography, which reads the transformation of producers into paid labourers in the radiant terms of freedom from servitude and corporative coercion, is counterposed to materialist historiography, which writes history with the blood and fire of the newly-freed workers who have became the salespeople of themselves.[17] On one side, the history of freedom's progress; on the other side, a discontinuous history, seen from its 'bad side'.[18]

Capitalist command, as command over the intensity and the productive power of labour, imposes itself by dissolving and re-articulating the forms of social relations. This process, which corresponds to the genesis of the capitalist mode of production, does reflect what happened in Western Europe, but it is not valid as a universal law. In the 'Preface' of the 1867 first edition of *Capital*, Marx wrote: 'The country that is more developed industrially only shows, to the less developed, the image of its own future'. In the 1872–5 French edition, revised by Marx, we read: 'The country that is more developed industrially only shows, to those who are behind it in the industrial ladder [*échelle*] the image of their own future'.[19] Marx's addition delimits the field: an industrially developed country shows the image of the future only to countries set along the same *échelle industrielle*.[20] Between the first and the third edition of the first volume of *Capital*, Marx revised his chapter on accumulation. In the first edition, the process of separation was described in the general terms of a 'series of historical processes' underlying the 'history of development [*Entwicklungsgeschichte*]' of modern bourgeois society.[21] In the third edition of 1883, the last one that Marx had the chance to review, the entire paragraph on this analysis was cut out.[22]

---

15. Marx 1996, p. 9.
16. Marx 1996, p. 9.
17. Marx 1996, p. 706.
18. Marx 1976b, pp. 170 et sq.
19. Respectively: Marx 1983i, p. 12: 'Das industriell entwickeltere Land zeigt dem minder entwickelten nur das Bild der eignen Zukunft'; and Marx 1989f, p. 12: 'Le pays le plus développé industriellement ne fait que montrer à ceux qui le suivent sur l'échelle industrielle l'image de leur propre avenir'.
20. On these passages, see Anderson 2002, pp. 87–8, according to which Marx's historical studies brought him, in the early 1870s, to consider 'alternative pathways' to those of capitalist industrialisation. See also Anderson 2010, pp. 162–3.
21. Marx 1983i, p. 576.
22. Marx 1989g, p. 669.

His analysis focuses more on the English case, where the different moments of original accumulation at first appear to be distributed in geographical and 'chronological order [*zeitliche Reihenfolge*]', from Spanish colonialism to the European trade-wars; then, from the seventeenth century, 'they arrive at a systematical combination, embracing the colonies, the national debt, the modern mode of taxation, and the protectionist system'.[23] All these systems use state-*Gewalt*. The transition to the capitalist mode of production is studied by paying attention to the 'forcible means' that have allowed it.[24] This is the same *Staatsgewalt* that powerfully effected the dissolution of the feudal system. The historical stages presented by Marx correspond to the chronicle of that birth: the 'breaking up of the bands of feudal retainers', in the fifteenth and sixteenth centuries, hurled a mass of free proletarians onto the labour-market;[25] the Reformation and theft of church-properties gave new impetus to the process of forced expropriation of the masses, impoverishing them;[26] the Stuart Restoration abolished the feudal tenure of land.[27] If a mass of proletarians had thus been produced by the dissolution of the feudal system, it was now necessary to discipline it and make it move to the chronometric rhythm of the market:

- at the end of the fifteenth century, across Europe there was the creation of 'a bloody legislation against vagabondage';[28]
- in 1530, Henry VIII prescribed whipping and imprisonment for 'sturdy vagabonds'. 'They are to be tied to the cart-tail and whipped until the blood streams from their bodies, then to swear an oath to go back to their birthplace or to where they have lived the last three years and to "put themselves to labour".... For the second arrest for vagabondage the whipping is to be repeated and half the ear sliced off; but for the third relapse the offender is to be executed as a hardened criminal and enemy of the common weal';[29]
- in 1547, Edward VI 'ordains that if anyone refuses to work, he shall be condemned as a slave to the person who has denounced him as an idler';[30]
- in 1572, Elizabeth I ordained that 'beggars above 14 years of age are to be severely flogged and branded on the left ear unless someone will take

---

23. Marx 1996, p. 739.
24. Marx 1996, p. 713.
25. Marx 1996, p. 723.
26. Marx 1996, p. 711.
27. Marx 1996, p. 713.
28. Marx 1996, p. 723.
29. Marx 1996, p. 724.
30. Ibid.

them into service for two years, and that at the third offence they are to be executed without mercy as felons';[31]

- James I (1603–25) then ordered branding with an 'R' on the left shoulder and forced labour for incorrigible and dangerous vagrants.

As shown by the case of the American colonies, the flight of workers constituted the fundamental problem of capital-accumulation from 1500 to 1800.[32] The aim of the English laws of the sixteenth and seventeenth centuries was the immobilisation and the disciplining of the workforce, even through slavery: 'far from representing an abnormal excrescence in the colonies...[it] constitutes an authoritarian, homogenous response of control of the mobility on the European and North-American labour-market, of which indenture is a particular declination'.[33] Capitalist slavery is a hyper-disciplined variation of wage-labour.[34] Original accumulation cannot be confined to a precise historical moment at the beginning of the capitalist mode of production.[35] Rather, it is constantly reproduced by the capitalist mode of production itself. The problem that Marx managed to pose at the end of the 1860s concerned the coexistence of different forms of exploitation and their intertwining, beginning from the relation between absolute surplus-value and relative surplus-value, and from the capitalist need to obtain increasing amounts of absolute surplus-value in order to support the labour enhanced by technological developments. Hence, the importance of extra-economic means that enable the establishment of differentials of wages and of surplus-value, such as the state-regulation of Chinese workers;[36] the new forms of forced labour in Brazil;[37] racism and the production of insecurity for migrant-workers in Western metropolises.[38] Rosa Luxemburg rightly stressed the involvement

---

31. Marx 1996, p. 725.
32. Boutang 1998, p. 25.
33. Boutang 1998, p. 175.
34. Boutang 1998, p. 244.
35. A similar perspective is found in the analysis of De Angelis 2001; 2007; Bonefeld 2001. See also the several papers published in Sacchetto and Tomba (eds.) 2008.
36. On working conditions in China, see Chan and Xiaoyang 2003. According to Rampini 2005, 'In April and May, the months in which Timberland increases its production, "the normal workshift lasts from 7 a.m. to 11 p.m., only one Sunday two is off; extra work-hours increase as well, and people work up to 105 hours a week inside the factory". Inside informants gave China Labor Watch four payslips. The monthly salary is 757 yuan (75 euros) "but 44 percent is withdrawn to cover food and lodging expenses"'. See also Ngai and Wanwei 2008; Ngai 2005.
37. On the non-residual character of forced labour and on the enslavement of the workforce, see Zanin 2002.
38. Globalisation makes the political command enforced along borders productive for capitalism in order to maintain the potential value of wage-differentials. See Sacchetto 2007; Gambino and Sacchetto 2009; Gambino 2003.

of non-economic factors as a characteristic of the accumulation-process.[39] An important difference from Luxemburg's argument is that accumulation does not need non-capitalist areas, but a world-market where what is traded also enters into competition by taking advantage of the differences between wages, intensity and productive labour-forces. These differences are also created through new ethnic divisions of labour or the total blackmailing of migrant-workers who are without residence-permits.[40] Capitalist accumulation is neither just separation, nor only dispossession;[41] these are only some of the extra-economic means of violence that characterise the entire history of capitalist accumulation.

Neue Welt Gasse

The capitalist mode of production has been globalised from its birth, because it finds in colonialism and slavery constitutive moments that are continuously re-combined.

> The discovery of gold and silver in America, the extirpation, enslavement and entombment in mines of the indigenous population of that continent, the beginnings of the conquest and plunder of India, and the conversion of Africa into a preserve for the commercial hunting of black-skins, are all things which characterize the dawn of the era of capitalist production. These idyllic proceedings are the chief moments of original accumulation. On their heel treads the commercial war of the European nations, with the globe for a theatre.[42]

The large amount of historical material employed by Marx in the chapter on accumulation is used to tell the counter-history of a development that was possible through 'the great slaughter of the innocents'.[43] It concerns colonial violence, the way in which Christian Europe treated colonised people, the Dutch colonial administration, and the stealing of the men of Celebes to get slaves for Java.[44] 'Wherever they [the Dutch] set foot, devastation and depopulation followed'.[45] This violence became extreme 'in plantation-colonies

---

39. Luxemburg 1951.

40. Walker calculates that in California, eighty percent of workers employed in agriculture are without legal documents: Walker 2004, pp. 73–4.

41. De Angelis 2007; Harvey 2003; for the debate on accumulation, see Glassman 2006.

42. Marx 1996, p. 739; translation modified.

43. Marx 1996, p. 745.

44. Marx here quotes historic materials, such as Howitt 1838 and Raffles 1817.

45. Marx 1996, p. 740.

destined for export trade only, such as the West Indies, and in rich and well-populated countries, such as Mexico and India, that were given over to plunder'.[46] These are the places where capital has to collect the labour-power to be employed in plantations where labour's pace and intensity are governed by the clocks of the world's stock-markets. Primitive accumulation is both capital-accumulation and state-*Gewalt*. Furthermore, the capitalist mode of production arises from fierce conflicts with the previously preponderant rela- 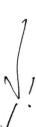 tions, and triggers even more ferocious struggles in terms of class-conflict. The state strengthens itself by directing its *Gewalt* firstly against common and customary rights,[47] and then by combating class-struggle.

It is necessary to pull apart the chapter on factory-legislation and put these pages next to those concerning so-called primitive accumulation. We could then note the attention that Marx pays to state-interventions in relation to class-struggle and the dissolution of pre-existing social forms.

> If the general extension of factory legislation to all trades for the purpose of protecting the working class both in mind and body has become inevitable, on the other hand, as we have already pointed out, that extension hastens on the general conversion of numerous isolated small industries into a few combined industries carried on upon a large scale; it therefore accelerates the concentration of capital and the exclusive predominance of the factory system. It destroys both the ancient and the transitional forms, behind which the dominion of capital is still in part concealed, and replaces them by the direct and open sway of capital; but thereby it also generalises the direct opposition to this sway.[48]

State-interventions in defence of workers' conditions, demanded by the workers themselves, produce, ultimately, a concentration of capital and the destruction of certain social forms, opening the possibility of a new social formation within the revolutionising elements of the old society.[49] The state's intervention in conflicts is an instrument that aims to monopolise violence and neutralise conflicts, not simply to look after the affairs of one class. Given the fact that, in some historical periods, there may be conflicts between different segments of the ruling classes, and between these and other non-proletarian and not fully synchronised sectors, like smallholders and declassed middle-class strata, what emerges is a conflict between political temporalities that may

---

46. Marx 1996, p. 741.
47. Bensaïd 2007.
48. Marx 1996, p. 504.
49. Ibid.

have different outcomes. The state-mechanism attempts to synchronise these temporalities, even by using asynchronous temporalities against each other.

The labour-times of the different forms of production are synchronised to the rhythm of socially-necessary labour-time through competition in the world-market. In the world-market, the capitalist mode of production encounters traditional and unwaged forms of production, which are not specifically capitalist, and are inserted into the capitalist market in hybrid-forms of subsumption.[50] In this way, patriarchal forms of exploitation and new forms of slavery not only coexist with high-tech production, but also combine with it.[51] Different temporalities are tied to each other, marking the rhythm of global production. Individual productive arrangements can exploit labour which has a higher or lower productivity than that of socially-necessary labour-time, which remains, however, the temporality that dictates the pace. What emerges is a scenario where global space is completely temporalised. Many Western products can, through new machines, exploit hyper-potentiated labour that is such only in relation to the productive force and intensity of a socially necessary labour-time; its average does not pass through the north-western latitudes and longitudes, but along non-European and non-US axes. Despite the transfer of surplus-value from the so-called 'backward' countries towards the hyper-technological ones, it is the former that determine the dominant temporality, while, in the world-market, the others have become their periphery.[52] It is this scenario that has made possible the cultural overthrowing of perspective, exemplified in the title of the book *Provincializing Europe* by the Indian historian Dipesh Chakrabarty.[53]

Since it is essential for capital to reduce its entropic tendency through generating geographical differentials of wages and surplus-value, the face of the planet is continuously striated by violent wars and controls on the flows

---

50. See Chapter 2.2 in the present work.

51. Tomich demonstrates how a research on modern slavery needs a historiography able to work with a 'plurality of temporal strata, of variable extension and duration that interact in the same historical dimension of modernity, and which can only be understood in relation to one another': Tomich 2003, p. 94.

52. 'The world economy has changed a lot over the past 50 years. Over the next 50, the changes could be at least as dramatic', state Wilson and Purushothaman 2003. According to the authors, who write for Goldman Sachs, one of the world's most important investment-banks, soon we will find ourselves facing a 'dramatically different world', a post-Western scenario dominated by Brazil, Russia, India and China. According to André Gunder Frank, after Western-European centrality, the world-economy is now becoming, once again, Asian-centred, recovering the hegemonic position that China managed to keep until 1800: see Frank 1998.

53. Chakrabarty 2007.

of migrant-workers.[54] In this sense, accumulation cannot be confined to the proto-history of the capitalist mode of production, as the English translation of *ursprüngliche Akkumulation* as 'primitive accumulation' would tend to suggest: rather, it accompanies the entire existence of this mode of production.[55] Thus, we could, instead, speak of 'primary accumulation'.[56] This is because, in a variety of contemporary processes of accumulation, what is primary is the accumulation that, by means of extra-economic violence, imposes the rhythm of socially-necessary labour-time on a global scale and works on the differentiation and synchronisation of different temporalities.

The chapter on *ursprüngliche Akkumulation*, presenting the 'series of violent methods' that mark the history of the capitalist system, aims to show how this system is developed at the international level, and how it produces 'the entanglement of all peoples in the net of the world market'.[57] This chapter is not at the beginning, but at the end of the first volume of *Capital*. The very last chapter is the starting point that follows Marx's analysis of accumulation: it focuses on 'the modern theory of colonisation'. The last pages of the chapter on accumulation are devoted to the 'historical trend of capitalist accumulation'. We know that the tendencies are only concrete in tension with and in opposition to the countertendencies. Thus, if there is a tendency towards a centralisation of capitals and the growth of exploitation, there is also an increase of the 'the revolt of the working class'.[58] In this sense, the capitalist tendency is not a straight line, but one broken by the counter-times of the workers' struggle.

The final part of the *Capital* is a political programme. The network of the world-market and the transnational chain of valorisation not only hold together various forms of exploitation, combining them synchronously, but also put in contact different working populations. This indicates the level that the workers' organisation must attain.

---

54. Sanyal 2007 shows how postcolonial capitalism continuously reproduces the dynamics of accumulation beyond the historical scheme of development and underdevelopment. In order to understand these new dynamics, which lead to the production of a mass of dispossessed people that exceed the needs of the capitalistic workforce, a new imaginary, able to make visible the 'obscure space of the "classless"' (Sanyal 2007 p. 259), is needed. In the postcolonial-capitalist narrative, the notion of exclusion, Sanyal argues, could replace the notion of 'class'.

55. On accumulation, see the essays that appear in the first part of Bonefeld (ed.) 2008.

56. Frank 1978 spoke about 'primary accumulation' in relation to the capitalist subsumption of non capitalist forms of productions. The same term, with a different meaning, was considered in discussions between Ferruccio Gambino and Devi Sacchetto during the editing of the volume Sacchetto and Tomba (eds.) 2008.

57. Marx 1996, p. 750.

58. Marx 1996, p. 750.

Russian Avenue

New analyses of the world-market and world-insurgencies, conducted from the 1860s onwards, together with studies on Asiatic modes of production and an engagement with the Russian populists,[59] forced Marx to re-examine accumulation. His analysis of capital and the processes of accumulation on the global scale pushed Marx into studying 'what capital could expect to confront in its global extension'.[60]

Marx's engagement with the Russians revolves around the interpretation to be given to accumulation. In the letter Marx wrote to the *Otechestvennye Zapiski* editorial board at the end of 1877, he stressed that the purpose of the chapter on primitive accumulation was only 'to trace the road followed in Western Europe', presenting 'the historical movement that, by divorcing the producers from their means of production, transforms them into wage-workers (proletarians in the modern sense of the word) and the owners of the means of production into capitalists'.[61] The basis of the entire process, he immediately added, is the 'expropriation of the agricultural producers'. Capitalism is not the arithmetic sum of 'separation' and 'expropriation'. Rather, it is the event produced by a particular combination of these two histories: the secant that crosses times of separation and expropriation along a new temporal line, that of the Western-capitalist mode of production. The historical outline of the genesis of capitalism in Western Europe thus cannot be interpreted as an 'historico-philosophical theory of general development, imposed by fate on all peoples'; during Roman history, the expropriation of free peasants and their separation from the means of production did not, in fact, change Roman proletarians into waged workers, but in a 'slacking mob'; it did not give rise to a capitalist mode of production, but to a slave-mode of production.[62]

The capitalist mode of production is the result of a combination of different circumstances with their own historical temporality. Separation does not automatically give rise to capitalism: it can give rise to it, but it can also give rise to slavery; or it can be combined with the expropriation of agricultural producers, opening up the possibility for capitalist development. The accumulation of capital is combined with the agrarian question, with the expropriation of small owners and the privatisation of common lands that pushed masses of

---

59. On the centre-periphery issue, Dussel states that Marx overcame his own Eurocentrism at the end of the 1860s, opening up to the idea of a 'peripheral' Russia. See Dussel 1990a.

60. See Smith 2002, p. 79. According to Smith, the study of non-capitalist societies by ethnologists helped Marx to clarify the historical contingency of the capitalist mode of production.

61. Marx 1989d, p. 199.

62. Ibid.

peasants into swelling the ranks of the proletariat. This creates a reserve-pool of labour-power, and then capitalist exploitation can be introduced into agriculture. It was, in fact, the need to graft the socialist revolution on a development of agriculture that generated a vision of a need to accelerate capitalist progress. The Stalinist conceptions of a cement-and-steel socialism and the hyper-technological visions of postmodern Marxism are both complicit in the productivist and mechanical myth that is the fruit of a proto-capitalist conception of history. Much of twentieth-century Marxist thought believed that the task of the labour-movement, when not the completion of the bourgeois revolution, was to push capitalism towards its intensive phase. In the belief that it was building the most powerful ideological weapon, Marxism took from Marx a determinist philosophy of history and called it 'dialectical materialism', a conception of the world that shared the same philosophy of history as that of the winners. The proletariat was encouraged to board the train of progress towards accumulation. In Russia, Plekhanov believed that backward countries would progress by repeating the same stages experienced by developed countries; hence, Russia necessarily had to pass through all the phases of capitalist development.[63]

Vera Zasulich posed Marx an important question on 16 February 1881:

> Honoured Citizen, you are not unaware that your *Capital* enjoys great popularity in Russia.... Nowadays, we often hear it said that the rural commune is an archaic form condemned to perish by history, scientific socialism and, in short, everything above debate. Those who preach such a view call themselves your disciples par excellence: 'Marksists'...So you will understand, Citizen, how interested we are in Your opinion. You would be doing us a very great favour if you were to set forth your ideas on the possible fate of our rural commune, and on the theory that it is historically necessary for every country in the world to pass through all the phases of capitalist production.[64]

In the early, 1880s Marx's knowledge of Russia was already extensive. He had decided to study Russian in 1869, when Daniel'son asked him permission to translate *Capital* and sent him a copy of V.V. Bervi's ('Flerovsky's') book on the situation of the working class in Russia,[65] telling him about Chernyshevsky's writings on village-communes.[66]

---

63. Walicki 1979a, p. 361; Walicki 1979b.
64. Cited in Shanin (ed.) 1983, pp. 98–9.
65. See Flerovsky 1869; Wada 1983. Burgio writes: 'In Marx's intellectual biography the reading of *Flerovsky* is an event, the start of a rich season of studies that would leave behind two cubical squared meters of official statistics, more than three thousand pages of notes, new political and theoretical hypothesis': Burgio 2002, p. 204.
66. Chernyshevsky 1983; Eaton 1980, p. 101.

Studying the Russian populists,[67] Marx grasped the inadequacy of the stageist hypothesis, and began to think about the *obshchina* as a cell of new possibilities for social relations. The question raised by Chernyshevsky concerned the possibility of skipping the historical stages undergone by Western Europe, saving the *obshchina* as a form of communal ownership. We cannot find in Chernyshevsky any trace of the Slavophilic romanticists or of the conservative positions of papers like *Žurnal zemlevladel'cev* [*Farmers' Magazine*] or the *Russkaja beseda* [*Russian Conversation*],[68] which sought to save the communal property of land in order to ensure farmers' payments through collective responsibility and to prevent possible uprisings. For Slavophiles like Kireevski,[69] it was a question of conserving the ethical principle of the agricultural community against the abstract individuality of Western property-relations. Chernyshevsky took his distance both from the positions of the conservatives who were 'proud of the survival of such vestiges of primitive antiquity', but also from those of the progressives who considered private ownership of land the most modern and evolved form of property, which 'has supplanted apparently communal ownership'; furthermore, they also declared that if the Russians wanted to 'go forward along the path of development', they had to abandon that primitive form of land-ownership.[70]

As against these promoters of progress, who declared themselves to be 'followers of the new German philosophy', Chernyshevsky, after underlining that he was not a disciple either of Hegel or of Schelling, rhetorically used the dialectic of history to overturn their idea of progress and to demonstrate how 'the higher stage of development resembles the source from which it proceeds',[71] but in a richer and more elevated form. Chernyshevsky thus enunciated the two main principles of populism:

1. the higher stage of development coincides in form with its source;
2. under the influence of the high development which a certain phenomenon of social life has attained among the most advanced peoples, this phenomenon can develop very swiftly among other peoples, and rise

---

67. See Wada 1983, p. 45. On the influence of Russian populism on Marx's opinions about primitive communities, see also Walicki 1979a, pp. 385–7.

68. See Natalizi 2001, p. 70. Chernyshevsky wrote: 'We are far from praising the current social situation in Europe, but we believe that it has nothing to learn from us. If there has been preserved in Russia, from the patriarchal (savage) times, a principle that in some way corresponds to one of the situations towards which the advanced peoples tend, it is still true that Western Europe is moving towards the realisation of this principle completely independently from us'. Cited in Venturi 1972, p. 270. See Natalizi 2006, pp. 52–75.

69. Kireevski 1966; also Natalizi 2001, p. 9.

70. Chernyshevsky 1983, p. 183.

71. Chernyshevsky 1983, p. 184.

from a lower level straight to a higher one, passing over the intermediate logical moments.[72]

What is important is the transition of information, science and technologies from one degree of development to the other, such that intermediate moments of development can be passed over in the course of the real process of a determined event. The intermediate steps of knowledge and technology can be skipped through the direct appropriation of the knowledge objectified in the most recent result of technological development. Communication between different levels of development allows leaps, benefiting from the experience and the science of advanced peoples, thus enabling an accelerated process of development.[73] The European experience was not to be rejected, as the Slavophiles tended to do; rather, it had to be 'used' to ensure that Russia could 'leap over all the intermediate moments of development, or at least shorten considerably their duration, depriving them of intensity'.[74] Chernyshevsky's programme was to avoid going through the stages of capitalist production and use the Russian communal property of the village as an anticipated form of socialism. However, if Chernyshevsky's problem was the acceleration of the process and the skipping of historical stages, Marx's problem was the co-presence and the friction between historical-political layers that could produce a path alternative to that of Western-capitalist modernisation.

These Marxian reflections occurred in a conjuncture marked by the defeat of the Paris Commune and the expectation of an imminent Russian revolution. Until 1871, the core of the European political problem was the support that the proletariat had to give to the liberal-national revolutions, seeking to transform them into proletarian revolutions once the bourgeoisie became counter-revolutionary. The experience of the Paris Commune, however, showed that European armies were already united against the proletariat. Alliance with the liberal-national revolution was no longer on the agenda. The revolutionary model built following the 1789–93 sequence of events in France had to be rethought.[75] The imminence of revolution in Russia opened up new issues. Russia

72. Chernyshevsky 1983, p. 188.
73. In an article about the Slavophiles published in 1857 in *Sovremennik* [The Contemporary], Chernyshevsky wrote: 'The West teaches us a lesson that we can use. Now, while we are just starting to foresee these transformations, it is necessary to get ready in order to deal with future events and to manage their course'. Quoted in Natalizi 2001, p. 11.
74. Chernyshevsky quoted in Venturi 1972, p. 256.
75. At the beginning of the 1860s, Marx conceived the Russian revolution according to the example of the French Revolution; this tendency was a constant in Engels and

has long been on the verge of an upheaval.... All strata of Russian society are economically, morally and intellectually in a state of complete disintegration. This time the revolution will begin in the East.[76]

This revolution would not be a single revolution, but probably a combination of different revolutions, even more articulated than the ones that occurred during the course of the French Revolution. This was because Russia had an extremely diversified social and economic reality, which witnessed the coexistence of agricultural communities, serfdom and urban proletariat. Russia was not only facing a double revolution: on one hand, the bourgeoisie against feudalism; on the other hand, the proletarian's insertion in this first revolution beside and against the bourgeoisie. In Russia, rather, these revolutionary temporalities could encounter the historical temporality of primitive communism and the peasants' revolt against the tsarist state and the *boyar*-aristocracy, leaping directly to socialism on the basis of a communal property that already existed.

This possibility is expressed in the preface to the 1882 second Russian edition of the *Communist Manifesto*:

> can the Russian obshchina, a form of primeval common ownership of land, even if greatly undermined, pass directly to the higher form of communist common ownership? Or must it, conversely, first pass through the same process of dissolution as constitutes the historical development of the West? The only answer possible today is this: If the Russian Revolution becomes the signal for a proletarian revolution in the West, so that the two complement each other, the present Russian common ownership of land may serve as the starting point for communist development.[77]

A mutual completion of the two revolutions, the Russian and the Western ones, would have allowed the development, in the communist sense, of the communal ownership of the land that existed in Russia.[78]

Ever since his response to the editorial board of *Otechestvennye Zapiski*, Marx had looked at Russia from the perspective of its relationship with Western Europe. The problem was to identify a model alternative to the capitalist path

influenced Russian Marxism to a great extent in the years to come. See Poggio 1978, p. 51, and Engels's letter to Bignami of 12 January 1878.
76. Marx 1991b, p. 278. On the imminence of the Russian revolution, see also Engels 1998; 1991.
77. Marx and Engels 1989, p. 426.
78. The unfortunate path of the Stalinist construction of socialism in only one country began from a feudal state, and developed into an industrial state-capitalism and a capitalist and precapitalist form of rural economy, within a national mercantile context, with a growing tendency towards internationalisation. See Bordiga 1975, p. 131.

of Western Europe. This is the question that led Marx to read and take notes on L.H. Morgan's 1877 work *Ancient Society*. In Marx's annotations, there are frequent references to Slavs in relation to the communist organisation of the original families.[79] Showing the persistence of some forms of community that existed at the same time as capitalist production, Marx delineates the possibility of a new régime of combination of historical times. There is something of the future encapsulated in the past that can be freed from the contemporaneity of the archaic: 'The history of the decline of primitive communities (it would be a mistake to place them all on the same level; as in geological formations, these historical forms contain a whole series of primary, secondary, tertiary types, etc.) has still to be written'.[80]

Investigating the origin of the German 'agricultural commune' as the '*most recent type* of the archaic form of societies',[81] Marx reinterpreted the historical development of Western Europe as a period of transition from communal property to private property, from a primary to a secondary formation, to use a geological metaphor.[82] In Marx's historiographical outline, there are two indispensable acquisitions: on the one hand, this passage concerns only the history of Western Europe, and is not intended in any way as an historical law of the dissolution of common property;[83] on the other hand, the geological metaphor expresses a stratification of geological layers, and not a succession of stages. The secondary is superimposed on the primary without deleting it. The historical materialist, dealing with periods of history as if they were geological epochs, simultaneously ensures the visibility of the different layers. The historical forms do not follow a linear model of past and present, but they become 'geological formations' in which the already-been coexists with the now, allowing us to think the co-presence of temporalities on a surface and not according to a linear vector.

---

79. Between 1880 and 1881, Marx read and took notes from Lewis Morgan's *Ancient Society*. These notes are published in Marx 1972. A complete edition of Marx's historical and anthropological notes of those years is about to be published in Volume IV/27 of *MEGA*. On Marx's reading of Morgan, see Shaw 1984.

80. Marx 1989e, p. 358.

81. Marx 1989e, p. 352.

82. On the spatial connotation of history, Koselleck observes that the 'spatialising metaphor, which allows the concept of time to be pluralised, has an advantage. "Temporal layers" [*Zeitschichten*] refer, as in the geological model, to many levels of time [*Zeitebenen*] of different durations and provenances, but which nonetheless are contemporarily present and active'. Koselleck 2000, p. 9. Anderson writes that the theoretical core of Marx's ethnological notebooks is constituted by a 'multilinear model of historical development' opposed to a unilinear one: Anderson 2002, p. 90. See also Krader 1972.

83. 'But does this mean that in all circumstances the development of the "agricultural commune" must follow this path? Not at all': Marx 1989e, p. 352.

The dissolution of common property and the assertion of private property are not the necessary outcome of some preordained historical development:[84] different configurations of the secondary could and can arise from the primary. Different geological formations, although belonging to different historical periods, coexist at the same time. Traces of the Archeozoic era coexist alongside with those of the Cenozoic and Neozoic. Just as a pickaxe-blow can, even today, reveal a fossil dating back to the Archeozoic era, so political historiography can show the not-yet that has remained encapsulated in the already-been.

Russia was not obliged to pass through the 'fatal dissolution of the Russian peasants' commune',[85] which can, instead, become 'an element of collective production on a nationwide scale'.[86] In the drafts of Marx's letter to Zasulich,[87] the layers of different histories are put into friction, one on top of the other. On one side, there is the 'contemporaneity' of capitalist production; on the other side, the current Western-European social system that is in a state of crisis.[88] Once the paradigm of collapse is abandoned, the crisis poses 'a social system ... in battle both with the working-class masses, with science, and with the very productive forces which it engenders'.[89] What is interesting is the point of observation. The capitalist mode of production is condemned for its failure to develop technology and the combination of the social process of production without undermining the sources of wealth, namely, the land and the worker. From the perspective of the Russian commune, it is possible to put an end to the crisis through the elimination of capitalist production and through 'the return of modern societies to an "archaic [archaïque]" type of communal property'.[90] The encounter between different historical temporalities, the Russian agricultural commune and the crisis of capitalism, ignites new possibilities of liberation. Marx, quoting Morgan, wrote that modern societies tend towards 'a revival in a superior form of an archaic social type'. He then notes that 'we must not let ourselves to be alarmed at the word "archaic"'.[91]

Marx overturned Vera Zasulich's problem and concerns. The 'Marksists', Zasulich wrote to Marx, argue that the rural commune 'is an archaic form condemned to perish by history, scientific socialism'.[92] 'Marksist' histori-

---

84. Federici 2004.
85. Marx 1989e, p. 349.
86. Ibid.
87. Marx wrote four drafts of this letter. The different versions were published in 1924 by David Ryazanov in the first volume of the *Marx-Engels Archives*; Shanin 1983, p. 18.
88. Marx 1989e, p. 349.
89. Marx 1989e, p. 350.
90. Ibid.
91. Ibid.
92. Shanin (ed.) 1983, pp. 98–9.

cism would repeat this *geschichtsphilosophisch* form countless times. Marx overthrows all of this. History, and specifically English primitive accumulation, does not follow any preordained course. The European episodes are not universally valid; the archaic, being contemporary, is not condemned to die, but can be combined with the temporality of capitalist modernity, thus giving rise to a new social formation. The real issue is to think of the alternative not on the path of the historical rhythms of capitalist modernity, in order to put a brake on its destructive outcomes or to accelerate its tendencies, but in order to think the deviations from the line. The romantic return to the archaic is still anchored to a unilinear representation of time; but if history is represented by means of geological layers, then the archaic, as our contemporary, is one of the frictional surfaces that can give rise to a new beginning. Marx thus addressed once again the problem of defining the communist-social formation. He did not do this, however, in the way he had in the 1840s, by following dialectical models applied to history. Rather, he now looked for an alternative to the course of capitalist modernisation.

In *Ancient Society*, Morgan noted that property had become an 'uncontrollable power'; the 'human mind stands bewildered in the presence of its own creation', and calls for a time when 'human intelligence will rise to the mastery over property'.[93] Morgan concluded that 'It will be a revival, in a higher form, of the liberty, equality and fraternity of the ancient gentes'. Marx noted that this revival will consist in 'a higher plan of society':[94] 'plan', and not 'plane [*Stufe*]', as it was erroneously translated in the German edition.[95] Marx conceives of a society that organises work deliberately, with the aim of satisfying the needs of the human community. In a non-capitalist mode of production, the 'socialised human being [*der vergesellschaftete Mensch*], the associated producers, rationally regulat[e] their interchange with Nature, bringing it under their common control [*gemeinschaftliche Kontrolle*], instead of being ruled by it as by the blind forces of Nature'.[96] The possibility of a non-capitalist mode of production is indicated by the presence of past and present historical forms, as in the case of the Indian community, in which the 'there is social division of labour, without production of commodities'.[97] The capitalist mode of production is thus confined to an infinitesimal segment of human history.

History should be read with a new criteria: 'The time which has passed away since civilization began', Marx copied from Morgan, 'is but a fragment ['and a very small one', Marx adds in German] of the past duration of

---

93. Morgan 1877, p. 552. Marx copied these paragraphs in Marx 1972, p. 139.
94. Marx 1972, p. 139.
95. Marx 1976e, p. 190.
96. Marx 1998, p. 807; translation modified.
97. Marx 1996, p. 52.

man's existence, and but a fragment of the ages yet to come'.[98] Calculated in terms of successive generations, capitalist modernity amounts to approximately twenty generations. It is a small episode in the history of humankind, which was, however, able to produce a new type of individualistic and selfish human being. The coexistence and the clash between different temporalities show that historical possibilities do not collapse in the one-way temporality of capitalist civilisation. Instead, we see that alternative routes are constantly being reopened. It is a matter of reading the convergence of historical times that are able to make the present explode.

The ancient-Indian community is not the model to replicate. There is no nostalgia or romanticism in Marx's notes on primitive communities. No return is possible, or even desirable. In such communities, the common possession of land is combined with a fixed and rigid division of labour, which is unacceptable once the principle of equality has become a popular assumption. Rather, the issue is, on the one hand, the plan as a political limit applied to production and consumption; and, on the other hand, the abolition of private property as *jus utendi et abutendi*. Marx underlines how, 'from the standpoint of a higher economic form of society', property does not pass into the hands of the entire society or the state, or into the hands of entire societies of the same era taken contemporaneously. They are not proprietors [*Eigentümer*] but only possessors [*Besitzer*] of the land, and its 'usufructuaries [*Nutznießer*], like *boni patres familias*, must hand it down to succeeding generations in an improved condition'.[99] Communism is counterposed, point-by-point, to the capitalist mode of production. The latter loots and recklessly destroys, without any regard for future generations; the former merely uses the land and limits production by aiming only to satisfy needs, reducing labour-time to a minimum. The plan indicates, in Marx, a third option between fusional regression and antithetical self-destructiveness: the political control over production, and over the quality and quantity of work needed to satisfy social needs: production that aims at use-values and human communities. The 'plan' does not produce a pacific society transparent to itself, but gives rise to new modalities of conflict over the forms of being together, of command, and of distribution of communal work. Starting from the *1844 Manuscripts*, passing through the *Grundrisse* up to his final writings on the peasant-commune, Marx expressed great interest in the anthropological changes produced by capitalist modernity. The elements of possessive individualism are represented as characters of a phenotype, that of the modern individual, which is to be overcome.

---

98. Marx 1972, p. 139.
99. Marx 1998, p. 763

Crossroads

The crisis discloses possibilities that critique can decline in different and opposite directions. Pessimistic and decadent conceptions of history arise, which, in Russia, are crossed with Herzen's socialism.[100] Herzen's vision was characterized by a kind of *Finis Europae*[101] that brought him close to the positions of Haxthausen, whose positive evaluation of the village-community, Marx observed, 'merely served as an argument to show that old, rotten Europe must be regenerated victory of pan-Slavism'.[102] Decadent conceptions of history and analysis of peasant-communities are thus combined. For Haxthausen, Russian agricultural communes offered a model of social cohesion alternative to the individualism that threatened to disrupt the organisational texture of European societies:

> The constitution of the Russian commune, described above in its principal features, is politically of the greatest value for Russia, especially today. All western states suffer from the same illness, which threatens them with death and which they do not yet know how to cure: pauperism and proletarianism. Russia, being saved from it by the communal constitution, does not have this illness. Every Russian has a home and a communal share of the land.[103]

A new form of conservative thought was arising, one that sought to halt European decline, by inserting in its dying body the principle of the Russian commune, as Haxthausen and Bruno Bauer later would, or revitalising the old structure of estates, anchoring it in natural differences, as Riehl tried to do.[104] Marx opposed these decadent philosophies of history. Chernyshevsky was trying to do the same thing in Russia.[105]

The crisis is neither a sign of decadence nor a sign of progress. It is not the low or the high point of a *sine*-curve. The historical materialist does not follow the tendency of the *sine*-curve of capitalist development, but cuts it, vertically, in a precise moment corresponding to a political situation able to show not the tangent of a tendency, but the cusp, where there is either no tangent or

---

100. Walicki 1989, pp. 580 et sq.
101. Groh 1959.
102. Marx 1983j, p. 134.
103. Haxthausen 1852.
104. Riehl 1861; Chignola 2004, pp. 257–61.
105. In the article 'On the Causes of the Fall of Rome', Chernyshevsky aimed to dismantle the hypotheses about the equivalence between the European decadence and that of the Roman Empire. He argued that at the time of the barbarian invasions, the Roman Empire showed many signs of cultural, economic and administrative progress. Rather, it was the fall of the Roman Empire that precipitated a regressive development: Chernyshevsky 2001, pp. 227–58.

there are infinite tangents. It is a new beginning. The possibilities are given by the encounter between different temporalities, in their new combination. It was a mistake to superimpose the time of revolutionary politics onto the tendency of capitalist development.[106] The dominant capitalist temporality does not coincide with that of the highest technological development; the temporality of revolutionary politics can also pass through seemingly archaic layers of time.

The historical existence of social forms based on the production of use-objects, in order to satisfy the needs of the community, shows, on the one hand, the historical-epochal character of the capitalist mode of production and of its constitutive inversion; and on the other hand, it shows the political direction towards emancipation. Marx did not indulge in a romantic recovery of archaic communities. Marx replied to the populists, who sought to save the Russian commune, that it could only be saved by a Russian revolution, but not through suicidal isolation from the rest of the capitalist world: 'It is precisely thanks to its contemporaneity with capitalist production that it may appropriate the latter's *positive acquisitions* without experiencing all its frightful misfortunes'.[107] In Marx's analysis, there is never a single revolution, but a meeting of different revolutionary temporalities and the different interests of different classes and strata of the population.

The conditions existing in Russia made a different history possible. While Europe had passed from a form of private property to a specifically capitalist form of property, in Russia the existence of common property allowed for the possibility of a development alternative to that known by capitalist modernity. This is a departure from the negative judgement regarding the communal institutions of the Slavic people which Marx had expressed at the time of the *Grundrisse*.[108] His Prometheanism gave rise to ambiguities with respect

---

106. From this perspective, today as well as yesterday, 'nine-tenths of the world have become "questions", "anomalies", "survivals" – objectively progressive for a while perhaps, but destined to disappear, sociologically, analytically, politically': Wallerstein 2001, p. 160. According to Wallerstein, in the 'wilderness through which we are wondering, there are two possible paths we can take. We can decide that it is only in the most "advanced" country that the transition to socialism can occur (or can first occur)....We can decide that the situation is so special in the country which dominates the world market that it tells us nothing of real politics elsewhere'. Marx, states Wallerstein, advocates the thesis of a 'revolutionary zigzag': Wallerstein 2001, p. 157.

107. Marx 1989e, p. 349.

108. Poggio 1978, p. 141. Recently, Anderson noted that the Marxian conception of history was Eurocentric and unilinear up to the end of the 1850s, and that only the in-depth study of non-capitalistic societies made Marx abandon the unilinear pattern in favour of 'multilinear pathways of development': Anderson 2002 pp. 85–6; Anderson 2010, pp. 228–9.

to colonialism, which, in the early 1850s, had been justified as the bearer of that profound revolution in Asiatic social relations that would have heralded social revolution.[109] From this perspective, Marx spoke of a 'double mission' that England had to pursue in India, 'one destructive, the other regenerating – the annihilation of old Asiatic society, and the laying of the material foundations of Western society in Asia'.[110]

Marx was not indifferent to the devastating effects of the British colonialism on the Indian population, but he read destruction and regeneration as the two sides of the same coin. The 1857 Sepoy Mutiny and the brutal British retaliation, which Indians called 'the wind of the devil', had not yet taken place. Some harsh paragraphs that Marx wrote were due to the polemic that he, together with Engels, conducted against the positions of Henry Carey and the *New York Daily Tribune*, who believed that the cause of all evil was to be found both in the centralising action of large-scale industry and in the panacea of protectionism. According to Marx, the whole question consisted in an artificial increase of the same development that had been placed in doubt.[111] In the late 1860s, Marx wrote to Engels that he had changed his mind regarding what the *New York Tribune* claimed; the 'driver' of change was now sited within the colonies: 'The English working class *will never accomplish* anything before it has got rid of Ireland. The lever must be applied in Ireland'.[112]

The change of judgement on India was also clear by 1881: 'as for the East Indies, for example, everyone except Sir Henry Maine and others of his ilk realises that the suppression of communal landownership out there was nothing but an act of English vandalism, pushing the native people not forwards but backwards'.[113] The activity of British colonialism and the destruction of the common property of land were now seen as regressive phenomena.[114] Since the 1860s, Marx had also clarified for himself the colonial relation of the world-market: colonialism in industrialised countries does not push the

109. Marx 1979c.
110. Marx 1979d, pp. 217–18.
111. Marx 1983h.
112. Marx 1988c, p. 398. Jaffe, commenting on the letters concerning this context, states that Marx's position, according to which the English working class was partly an accomplice of British colonialism, is sometimes presented as that of a 'Third Worldist': Jaffe 1976, pp. 106–9.
113. Marx 1989h, p. 365.
114. Mohri observes, in relation to this change in perspective, that the 'double mission' of British free trade should be interpreted not in the sense of a combination of 'the destruction of the old society' and 'the regeneration of a new society', as Marx thought up to the late 1850s, but rather in the sense of a double mission of destruction, meaning both 'the destruction of the old society' and the destruction of some of the essential conditions for 'regeneration of a new society': Mohri 1979, p. 41.

colonised countries forward, but turns them into 'settlements for growing the raw material of the mother country', creating a new international division of labour, and transforming 'part of the globe into a chiefly agricultural field of production, for supplying the other part which remains a chiefly industrial field'.[115] The attention given to the world-market is also necessarily directed towards the integration of different social groups. These integrations cause frictions between different temporal layers, and this friction is manifested in many forms of anti-colonial, nationalistic, and rural insurgencies. The political question, posed in the dialogue with the populists, concerned the transfer of Western-capitalist know-how and workers' knowledge to those social formations through the contemporaneity of apparently backward insurgencies. In other words, it was a matter of the counterposition of the revolutionary temporality of insurgencies reciprocally contemporary to the synchronisation operated by the market on the basis of the rhythm of socially-necessary labour.

The question of communism, especially after the failure of the Paris Commune, had to be configured not according to the development of productive forces, but in a new emancipatory nexus. An alternative path was needed, one different from the path that had produced both the capitalist mode of production and individuals who were hostile to each other. Marx's historical point of view, especially after the Commune, was that of the possibilities that, beginning with Thomas Müntzer onward, could have led to another modernity. If history [Geschichte], as a singular collective, linear process, is characteristic of the point of view of the winners, the losers write different plural histories [Historie].[116] The unwritten history of the oppressed cannot be grasped with the tools of historicist historiography, but only with a sensitivity towards the different temporal rhythms of histories that are simultaneously present. From this perspective, non-capitalist forms should not be regarded as stages towards the capitalist mode of production and as the individual's liberation from the communal bonds, but as contemporary alternatives.

When a scenario changes, it is not enough to fix the single pieces of the theoretical construction. It is necessary to work on the foundations. The Russians, who asked Marx to give a historical account of accumulation, posed both a theoretical and a political issue. The supposed historical inevitability of the capitalist phase in Russia affected what revolutionary politics could be undertaken. It was necessary to disrupt the stagist sequence of forms of production: historical phenomena, Marx wrote in his letter of 1877, cannot be

---

115. Marx 1996, p. 454, where Marx gives the example of the relation between Great Britain and the East Indies.
116. Koselleck 2000, p. 67.

understood with 'the *passe-partout* of an historical-philosophical theory whose great virtue is to stand above history'.[117] In his answer to Vera Zasulich on the 'genesis of capitalist production', dated 8 March 1881, Marx declared that the historical destiny of this process, in terms of the separation of producers from the means of production and the expropriation of peasants, is limited to Western-European countries.[118] Within this development, an English revolution is not a necessity, but a possibility.[119]

Marx's answer to the question posed by Vera Zasulich was transformed through these successive drafts. The changes in the categorial framework were so important that when the publisher, in 1881, wanted to print the third edition of the *Capital* in 3,000 copies, Marx suggested printing only 1,000, with very few changes, so as to have enough time to rework the text for a subsequent edition.[120] However, the third edition appeared in 1883, after Marx's death. In his later works, his historical and ethnological studies were mixed up with reflections stimulated by his engagement with the Russian populists.[121] Marx was interested in extending the historical field of forms that were not subjected to the domination of exchange-value and that were still oriented towards the production of use-values, thus, conversely, restricting the historical period of the existence of specifically capitalist social forms.

If capitalist modernity had dissolved communal forms, producing individuals subjected to the domination of value, Marx was interested in investigating the genesis of the 'individuality of the person' from the dissolution of the *gens*:[122] the relation between the dissolution of the community and the birth of modern egoistical individuals. Marx was against any metahistorical assumption; thus, he was interested in understanding the configuration in which, along with the capitalist mode of production, the modern concept of the individual arises. The issue on which these latter Marxian reflections focus is how to find a path that is alternative to capitalist civilisation and to the dissolution of the community into mutually hostile individuals. The *obshchina*, rejected by Bakunin because it did not allow the development of the individual and the separation of classes,[123] was understood by Marx, following

---

117. Marx 1989d, p. 201.
118. Marx 1992a, p. 71.
119. 'If you say that you do not share the views of my party for England I can only reply that that party considers an English revolution not necessary, but – according to historic precedents – possible': Marx 1992a, p. 49.
120. Marx 1992c, p. 60.
121. See Walicki 1979a, p. 386.
122. Marx 1972, p. 119.
123. Poggio 1978, p. 190.

Chernyshevsky, Kovalevsky and others, as a new possibility for the emancipation of humanity on a communitarian basis.[124]

To find 'what is newest in what is oldest'',[125] does not mean to close history up in a circle, bringing it back to its starting point. Rather, it means to grasp in the oldest hints of the future that may lead to a path different to that undertaken by capitalist modernity. What is oldest carries traces of a different mode of production, one that regulates the quality and the extent of labour according to the use-values that are necessary to satisfy human needs. It is a rationality that differs from the calculated rationality that developed in capitalist modernity and that is exalted in the irrationality of the *homo economicus*. Capitalist modernity, which has invaded the globe, is only one of the possible paths of modernisation. It is the path that was undertaken in Europe, but it was not the only possibility. Other modernities were and are possible. However, these may spring only from the origin of modernity, not by going backwards, but through a different combination of the diverse historical temporalities that modernity tries constantly to synchronise through the imposition of the law of value; not by changing the organisation of the elements, but by breaking the rules of their possible combinations.

The capitalist mode of production tends to become more natural the more it develops, as the trinitarian formula outlined in the third volume of *Capital* shows. In the 'enchanted and perverted world'[126] of capital, its constitutive categories are personified and naturalised. Therefore, beginning from the implicit coincidence of labour with wage-labour, it follows that 'capital and monopolised land must also appear as the natural form of the conditions of labour in relation to labour in general'.[127] Hence, the eternalisation of these categories becomes possible; if they can be found in every historical context and formation, they can also legitimise the image of an ahistorical and eternal present. These categories become autonomous subjects and are exemplified by 'Madame la Terre' and 'Monsieur le Capital', who appear to have rent and profit as their offspring. Marx reveals the 'mystifying character that transforms the social relations' due to the commodity, showing how the triad capital-profit, land-rent, and labour-wages is nothing more than a mirror that conceals the *pumping of surplus-labour*, and therefore surplus-value, which then is divided into capital, rent and profit. Directing his perspective

---

124. On September 1879, Kovalevsky sent his book on *Communal Land Tenure, Causes, Course and Consequences of Its Expansion* to Marx. The book was important for Marx in order to rethink the concept of Asian property and the *obshchina*: see Eaton 1980, p. 103.

125. Marx 1987d, p. 557.

126. Marx 1998, p. 814.

127. Marx 1998, p. 812.

to relations of production allows him to show the phantasmagorical nature of those personifications, which, however, operate in a real sense, constituting the self-representation of capitalist modernity.

These phantoms animate the 'enchanted and perverted world' of individuals who, having assumed the historical categories of that mode of production, perform the daily functions of this 'religion'.[128] In this phantasmagorical representation, the circulation-process is no longer only about the realisation of surplus-values that capital has pumped out in the production-process; rather, value seems to flow forth directly from it. In this way, the labour carried out during the productive process is concealed because it is unimportant, secondary, and residual, while the notion of productivity is extended to every human activity.

With the absolutisation of circulation and the naturalisation of capital there 'develops a working class, which by education, tradition, habit, looks upon the conditions of that mode of production as self-evident laws of Nature'.[129] The naturalisation of the capitalist mode of production creates individuals that accept its laws as natural. Marx argues:

> The organisation of the capitalist process of production, once fully developed, breaks down all resistance. The constant generation of a relative surplus population keeps the law of supply and demand of labour, and therefore keeps wages, in a rut that corresponds with the wants of capital. The dull compulsion [*der stumme Zwang*] of economic relations completes the subjection of the labourer to the capitalist.[130]

The coercion of capital becomes silent in the same way that the laws of nature are. Marx continues:

> Direct force, immediate extra-economic violence [*Außerökonomische, unmittelbare Gewalt*], is of course still used, but only exceptionally. According to the natural flows of the events [*den gewöhnlichen Gang der Dinge*] the worker is left with 'the natural laws of production', that is to say, his own dependence from the capital, that derives from the same productive relations that perpetuate and allow it.[131]

Extra-economic violence continues to be used, but only in 'exceptional circumstances'. Extra-economic violence does not disappear, but in the ordinary course of events, that is to say as long as living labour remains within the

---

128. Marx 1998, p. 814.
129. Marx 1996, p. 726.
130. Ibid.
131. Ibid.

tracks of valorisation, the silent coercion of economic relations is sufficient. 'Education, tradition and habit' ensure the incorporation and naturalisation of those relationships. Direct violence intervenes whenever living labour derails from the tracks of valorisation – or when new masses of workers have to be sent along those tracks and synchronised.

The capitalist mode of production and the modern political form, eternalising themselves through the image of an ahistorical present, also produce a concept of time that is adequate to this image. This is what Walter Benjamin called 'homogeneous and empty time'. If Marx gave up the idea of a static Asiatic stage – and the corresponding concept of the emancipatory and civilising force of capital – that can still be found in his writings up to the 1850s,[132] this change of perspective was also due to a vision free from the idea of progress and which was able to comprehend the destructive – both of men and nature – side of the process of valorisation, a process that can also become entirely self-destructive. Marx saw progress to be not a potential path of liberation, but as exploitation of labour-power. Finally, on an analytical level, he now had a clear vision of the global combination among the different modalities of extortion of surplus-value. The world-market is a field where different temporalities are continuously synchronised. The long war of modern capitalism against common property and common rights is fought through the instruments of accumulation and extra-economic violence that, with the coming of the world-market, have given rise to the international civil war. Communism is neither a degree of further escalation of this war, nor its goal. Rather, it is the name of its end.

---

132. Mohri 1979. Jaffe attributes pro-colonialist positions to Engels alone: see Jaffe 2007.

References

Adamson, Walter L. 1981, 'Marx's Four Histories: An Approach to His Intellectual Development', *History and Theory*, 20, 4: 379–402.

Adorno, Theodor 1973, *Negative Dialectics*, New York: Continuum.

—— 1991, 'On the Fetish-Character in Music and the Regression of Listening', in *The Culture Industry: Selected Essays on Mass Culture*, London: Routledge.

Althusser, Louis 2006, *Philosophy of the Encounter, Later Writings, 1978–1987*, edited by François Matheron and Oliver Corpet, translation and introduction by G.M. Goshgarian, London: Verso.

Anderson, Kevin B. 2002, 'Marx's Late Writings on Non-Western and Precapitalist Societies and Gender', *Rethinking Marxism*, 14, 4: 84–96.

—— 2010, *Marx at the Margins. On Nationalism, Ethnicity, and Non-Western Societies*, Chicago: University of Chicago Press.

Arendt, Hannah 1963, *On Revolution*, New York: Viking Press.

Arthur, Chris 2004, *The New Dialectic and Marx's 'Capital'*, Leiden: Brill.

Assoun, Paul-Laurent 1978, *Marx et la répétition historique*, Paris: PUF.

Attali, Jacques 2005, *Karl Marx, ou, l'esprit du monde*, Paris: Fayard.

Aveling, Edward and Eleanor Marx Aveling 1891, *The Factory Hell*, Aberdeen: James Leatham.

Backhaus, Hans-Georg 1970, 'Zur Dialektik der Wertform', in *Beiträge zur marxistischen Erkenntnistheorie*, edited by Alfred Schmidt, Frankfurt: Suhrkamp.

—— 1974, 'Materialen zur Rekonstruktion der Marxschen Werttheorie', in Backhaus et al., *Gesellschaft. Beiträge zur Marxschen Theorie*, Vol. 1, Frankfurt: Suhrkamp.

Bagù, Sergio 1949, *Economía de la Sociedad Colonial*, Buenos Aires: Ateneo.

Bahr, Hans-Dieter 1970, *Kritik der 'Politischen Technologie'*, Frankfurt: Europäische Verlagsanstalt.

Balibar, Étienne 1970, 'The Basic Concepts of Historical Materialism', in Louis Althusser and Étienne Balibar, *Reading 'Capital'*, London: Verso.

Barot, Emmanuel 2007, 'D'un Napoléon à l'autre: l'intelligibilité d'un étrange présent', in Karl Marx, *Le 18 Brumaire de Louis Bonaparte*, Paris: Le livre de poche.

Bartolovich, Crystal and Neil Lazarus (eds.) 2002, *Marxism, Modernity and Postcolonial Studies*, Cambridge: Cambridge University Press.

Basso, Luca 2008, *Socialità e isolamento: la singolarità in Marx*, Rome: Carocci.

Bauer, Bruno 1843a, 'Neueste Schriften über die Judenfrage', *Allgemeine Literatur-Zeitung*, 1.

—— 1843b, *Die Judenfrage*, Braunschweig: Druck und Verlag von Friedrich Otto.

—— 1844a, 'Was ist jetzt der Gegenstand der Kritik?', *Allgemeine Literatur-Zeitung*, 8.

—— 1844b, 'Correspondenz aus der Provinz', *Allgemeine Literatur Zeitung*, 6.

—— 1844c, 'Die Gattung und die Masse', *Allgemeine Literatur-Zeitung*, 10.

—— 1845, 'Charakteristik Ludwig Feuerbachs', *Wigand's Vierteljahrsschrift*, 3.

—— 1882, 'Vorwort', *Schmeitzner's Internationale Monatsschrift. Zeitschrift für allgemeine und nationale Kultur und deren Litteratur*, 1.

188 • References

— 1965 [1845], *Geschichte der Politik, Cultur und Aufklärung des achtzehnten Jahrhunderts. Fortsetzung. Deutschland und die französische Revolution. Dritte Abtheilung: Die Politik der Revolution vom Baseler Frieden bis zum Rastadter Congress*, Aalen: Scientia Verlag.

— 1972a [1846], *Geschichte Deutschlands und der französischen Revolution unter der Herrschaft Napoleons*, Vol. 2, Aalen: Scientia Verlag.

— 1972b [1842], *Die gute Sache der Freiheit und meine eigene Angelegenheit*, Aalen: Scientia Verlag.

— 1972c [1853], *Russland und das Germanentum*, Aalen: Scientia Verlag.

— 1979 [1882], *Disraelis romantischer und Bismarcks sozialistischer Imperialismus*, Aalen: Scientia Verlag.

— 1989 [1843], 'Das entdeckte Christentum. Eine Erinnerung an das achtzehnte Jahrhundert und ein Beitrag zur Krisis des neunzehnten', in *Das entdeckte Christentum im Vormärz. Bruno Bauers Kampf gegen Religion und Christentum und Erstausgabe seiner Kampfschrift*, edited by Ernst Barnikol, Aalen: Scientia Verlag.

Bauer, Bruno, Edgar Bauer, et al. 1846, *Beiträge zum Feldzuge der Kritik. Norddeutsche Blätter für 1844 und 1845*, Berlin: Adolph Rieß.

Bauer, Edgar 1843, *Bailly und die ersten Tage der Französischen Revolution*, Charlottenburg: E. Bauer Verlag.

Bauman, Zygmunt 1982, *Memories of Class: The Pre-History and After-Life of Class*, London: Routledge and Kegan Paul.

Bellofiore, Riccardo 1996, 'Marx rivisitato: capitale, lavoro e sfruttamento', *Trimestre*, XXIX, 1–2: 29–86.

— 1998, 'Teoria del valore e processo capitalistico. Note di teoria marxiana', *Vis-à-Vis*, 6, available at: <http://web.tiscalinet.it/visavis/6zc.pdf>.

— 2004, 'As if Its Body Were by Love Possessed. Abstract Labour and the Monetary Circuit: A Macro-Social Reading of Marx's Labour Theory of Value', in *Money, Credit, and the Role of the State. Essays in Honour of Augusto Graziani*, edited by Richard Arena and Neri Salvadori, Aldershot: Ashgate.

— 2005, 'La teoria marxiana del valore come teoria macromonetaria dello sfruttamento', in *Karl Marx. Rivisitazioni e prospettive*, edited by Roberto Fineschi, Milan: Mimesis.

— 2007, 'Quelli del lavoro vivo', in *Da Marx a Marx?*, edited by Riccardo Bellofiore, Rome: manifestolibri.

— 2008a, 'Dai *Manoscritti del 1844* al *Capitale*, e ritorno. Storia e natura, universalità e lavoro, crisi e lotta di classe nei *Grundrisse*', in *La lunga accumulazione originaria*, edited by Devi Sacchetto and Massimiliano Tomba, Verona: Ombre corte.

— 2008b, 'Centralizzazione senza concentrazione?', in *Pensare con Marx*, edited by Cinzia Arruzza, Rome: Alegre.

Bellofiore, Riccardo and Massimiliano Tomba 2009, 'Lesearten des Maschinenfragments. Perspektiven und Grenzen des operaistischen Ansatzes und der operaistischen Auseinandersetzung mit Marx', in *Über Marx hinaus*, edited by Marcel van der Linden and Karl-Heinz Roth, Berlin: Assoziation A.

Bellofiore, Riccardo and Roberto Finelli 1998, 'Capital, Labour and Time. The Marxian Monetary Labour Theory of Value as a Theory of Exploitation', in *Marxian Economics: A Reappraisal. Vol. I: Method, Value and Money*, edited by Riccardo Bellofiore, London: Macmillan.

Benjamin, Walter 2002, *The Arcades Project*, translated by Howard Eiland and Kevin MacLaughlin, Cambridge, MA.: Harvard University Press.

— 2003, 'On the Concept of History', in *Selected Writings*, Vol. 4, Cambridge, MA.: Harvard University Press.

Benot, Yves 2003, *La modernité de l'esclavage. Essai sur la servitude au coeur du capitalisme*, Paris: La Découverte.

— 2004, *La Révolution française et la fin des colonies 1789–1794*, Paris: La Découverte.

Bensaïd, Daniel 1995, *La Discordance des temps. Essai sur les crises, les classes, l'histoire*, Paris: Les Éditions de la Passion.

— 2002, *Marx for Our Times. Adventures and Misadventures of a Critique*, London: Verso.

—— 2007, *Les Dépossédés. Karl Marx: Les voleurs de bois et le droit des pauvres*, Paris: La Fabrique.

Blackburn, Robin 1997, *The Making of New World Slavery. From Baroque to the Modern 1492–1800*, London: Verso.

Bloch, Ernst 1969, 'Thomas Müntzer als Theologe der Revolution', in *Werkausgabe*, Vol. 2, Frankfurt: Suhrkamp.

—— 1975, *Experimentum Mundi*, Frankfurt: Suhrkamp.

—— 1985, *Erbschaft dieser Zeit*, Frankfurt: Suhrkamp.

—— 1986, *The Principle of Hope*, Vol. 1, translated by Neville Plaice, Stephen Plaice and Paul Knight, Oxford: Blackwell.

—— 1987, *Natural Law and Human Dignity*, translated by Dennis J. Schmidt, Cambridge, MA.: MIT Press.

—— 1990, 'Non-Contemporaneity and Obligation to Its Dialectic', in *Heritage of Our Times*, Berkeley, CA: University of California Press.

Bloch, Marc 1930, 'La lutte pour l'individualisme agraire dans la France du XVIII siècle', *Annales d'histoire économique et sociale*, 2, 7: 329–83.

Bodei, Remo 1979, *Multiversum. Tempo e storia in Ernst Bloch*, Naples: Bibliopolis.

Bonefeld, Werner 2001, 'The Permanence of Primitive Accumulation: Commodity Fetishism and Social Constitution', *The Commoner*, 2, available at: <http://www.commoner.org.uk/02bonefeld.pdf>.

—— 2008, *Subverting the Present. Imagining the Future*, New York: Autonomedia.

Bordiga, Amadeo 1975 [1954], *Russia e rivoluzione nella teoria marxista*, Milan: Edizioni il Formichiere.

—— 1979 *Mai la merce sfamerà l'uomo*, Milan: Iskra.

Boutang, Yann Moulier 1998, *De l'esclavage au salariat. Economie historique du salariat bridé*, Paris: PUF.

Brenner, Neil 2004, *New State Spaces. Urban Governance and the Rescaling of Statehood*, Oxford: Oxford University Press.

Brunner, Otto 1956, 'Das "Ganze Haus" und die alteuropäische "Ökonomik"', in *Neue Wege der Verfassungs- und Sozialgeschichte*, Göttingen: Vandenhoeck and Ruprecht.

Burgio, Alberto 2000, *Strutture e catastrofi*, Rome: Editori Riuniti.

Caffentzis, George 2003, 'The End of Work or the Renaissance of Slavery?', in *Revolutionary Writings*, edited by Werner Bonefeld, New York: Autonomedia; available at: <http://info.interactivist.net/node/1287>.

Cairnes, John Elliott 1862, *The Slave Power: Its Character, Career and Probable Designs*, London: Macmillan.

Callinicos, Alex 2004, *Making History. Agency, Structure, and Change in Social Theory*, Leiden: Brill.

Camatte, Jacques 1975, *Comunità e comunismo in Russia*, Milan: Jaca.

—— 2002, *Forme et histoire*, Turin: Cooperativa Colibri.

Carlyle, Thomas 1840, *On Chartism*, London: J. Fraser.

Carver, Terrell 2002, 'Imagery/Writing, Imagination/Politics: Reading Marx through the *Eighteenth Brumaire*', in *Marx's Eighteenth Brumaire: (Post)modern Interpretations*, edited by Mark Cowling and James Martin, London: Pluto Press.

Cassina, Cristina 2001, *Il bonapartismo o la falsa eccezione. Napoleone III, i francesi e la tradizione illiberale*, Rome: Carocci.

Castle, Terry 1988, 'Phantasmagoria: Spectral Technology and the Metaphorics of Modern Reverie', *Critical Inquiry*, 15, 1: 26–61.

Chakrabarty, Dipesh 2007 [2000] *Provincializing Europe, Postcolonial Thought and Historical Difference*, Princeton: Princeton University Press.

Chan, Anita and Zhu Xiaoyang 2003, 'Disciplinary Labor Regimes in Chinese Factories', *Critical Asian Studies*, 35, 4: 559–84.

Chernyshevsky, Nikolai Gavrilovich 1983, 'A Critique of Philosophical Prejudices against Communal Ownership', in Shanin (ed.) 1983.

—— 2001 *Scritti politico-filosofici*, Lucca: Maria Pacini Fazzi.

Chignola, Sandro 2004, *Fragile cristallo. Per la storia del concetto di società*, Naples: Editoriale scientifica.

Chitty, Andrew 2006, 'The Basis of the State in the Marx of 1842', in *The New Hegelians*, edited by Douglas Moggach, Cambridge: Cambridge University Press.

Cieszkowski, August von 1919 [1848], *The Desire of all Nations. Our Father (Oicze Nasz)*, London: Student Christian Movement.

Cohen, Margaret 1989, 'Walter Benjamin's Phantasmagoria', *New German Critique*, 48: 87–107.

Coldagelli, Umberto 2005, *Vita di Tocqueville (1805–1859). La democrazia tra storia e politica*, Rome: Donzelli.

Colletti, Lucio 1970, *Ideologia e società*, Bari: Laterza.

Conze, Werner 1992, 'Vom "Pöbel" zum "Proletariat". Sozialgeschichtliche Voraussetzungen für den Sozialismus in Deutschland', in *Gesellschaft–Staat–Nation. Gesammelte Aufsätze*, edited by Ulrich Engelhardt, Reinhart Koselleck, and Wolfgang Schieder, Stuttgart: Klett-Cotta.

Davis, Mike 2002, *Late Victorian Holocausts*, London: Verso.

De Angelis, Massimo 2001, 'Marx and Primitive Accumulation: The Continuous Character of Capital's Enclosures', *The Commoner*, 2, available at: <http://www.commoner.org.uk/02deangelis.pdf>.

—— 2007, *The Beginning of History. Value Struggles and Global Capital*, London, Pluto Press.

De Certeau, Michel 1997a, *The Capture of Speech and Other Political Writings*, Minneapolis: University of Minnesota Press.

—— 1997b, 'Individual Rights and Collective Rights', in *The Capture of Speech and Other Political Writings*, Minneapolis: University of Minnesota Press.

De Certeau, Michel 1988, *The Writing of History*, New York: Columbia University Press.

Descartes, René 2008 [1641], *Meditations on First Philosophy: With Selections from the Objections and Replies*, Oxford: Oxford University Press.

Di Marco, Giuseppe A. 2005, *Dalla soggezione all'emancipazione umana. Proletariato, individuo sociale, libera individualità in Karl Marx*, Soveria Mannelli: Rubbettino.

Didi-Huberman, Georges 2000, *Devant le temps. Histoire de l'art et anachronisme des images*, Paris: Minuit.

Dimoulis, Dimitri and John Milios 2004, 'Commodity Fetishism vs. Capital Fetishism. Marxist Interpretation vis-à-vis Marx's Analyses in Capital', *Historical Materialism*, 12, 3: 3–42.

Donoso Cortés, Juan 2000, 'Speech on Dictatorship', in *Selected Works of Juan Donoso Cortés*, translated, edited, and introduced by Jeffrey P. Johnson, Westport: Greenwood Press.

Dussel, Enrique 1990a, *El último Marx (1863–1882) y la liberación latinoamericana. Un comentario a la tercera y cuarta redacción de "El Capital"*, Mexico City: Siglo XXI.

—— 1990b, 'Marx's Economic Manuscripts of 1861–63 and the "Concept" of Dependency', *Latin American Perspectives*, 17: 62–101.

—— 1993, *Las metáforas teológicas de Marx*, Estella: Editorial Verbo Divino.

—— 1998, *Hacia un Marx desconocido. Un comentario de los Manuscritos del 61–63*, Mexico City: Siglo XXI.

Eaton, Henry 1980, 'Marx and the Russians', *Journal of the History of Ideas*, 41, 1: 89–112.

Ehrenreich, Barbara and Arlie Russell Hochschild (eds.) 2004, *Global Woman: Nannies, Maids, and Sex Workers in the New Economy*, New York: Owl Books.

Elster, Jon 1991, *Making Sense of Marx*, Cambridge: Cambridge University Press.

Engels, Friedrich 1960 [1850], *Die Zehnstundefrage*, in *Marx-Engels Werke*, Vol. 7, Berlin: Dietz.

—— 1975 [1844], *The Condition of the Working Class in England*, in *Marx and Engels Collected Works*, Vol. 4, London: Lawrence & Wishart.

—— 1976a [1846], 'The Festival of Nations in London', in *Marx and Engels Collected Works*, Vol. 6, London: Lawrence & Wishart.

—— 1976b [1847], 'The Chartist Banquet in Connection with the Elections of 1847', in *Marx and Engels Collected*

Works, Vol. 6, London: Lawrence & Wishart.

—— 1978 [1850] 'The Ten Hours' Question', in *Marx and Engels Collected Works*, Vol. 10, London: Lawrence & Wishart.

—— 1982a [1844], 'Engels to Marx. 19 November', in *Marx and Engels Collected Works*, Vol. 38, London: Lawrence & Wishart.

—— 1982b [1845], 'Engels to Marx. 22 February–7 March', in *Marx and Engels Collected Works*, Vol. 38, London: Lawrence & Wishart.

—— 1982c [1851], 'Engels to Marx. 3 December', in *Marx and Engels Collected Works*, Vol. 38, London: Lawrence & Wishart.

—— 1988 [1871], 'Engels to Enrico Bignami, editor of La Plebe', in *Marx and Engels Collected Works*, Vol. 23, London: Lawrence & Wishart.

—— 1991 [1879], 'Engels to Thomas Allsop. 14 December', in *Marx and Engels Collected Works*, Vol. 45, London: Lawrence & Wishart.

Fanon, Frantz 2005 [1961], *The Wretched of the Earth*, New York: Grove Press.

Faraguna, Michele 2003, ' "Nomisma" e "polis". Aspetti della riflessione greca antica sul ruolo della moneta nella società', in *Moneta, mercanti, banchieri. I precedenti greci e romani dell'Euro*, edited by Gianpaolo Urso, Pisa: ETS.

Farnesi Camellone, Matteo 2007, *Giustizia e storia. Saggio su Strauss*, Milan: Franco Angeli.

—— 2009, *La politica e l'immagine. Saggio su Ernst Bloch*, Macerata: Quodlibet.

Federici, Silvia 2004, *Caliban and the Witch: Women, the Body and Primitive Accumulation*, New York: Autonomedia.

Fietkau, Wolfgang 1978, *Schwanengesang auf 1848. Ein Rendezvous am Louvre: Baudelaire, Marx, Proudhon und Victor Hugo*, Reibeck bei Hamburg: Rowohlt.

Finelli, Roberto 1987, *Astrazione e dialettica dal romanticismo al capitalismo*, Rome: Bulzoni.

—— 2004, *Un parricidio mancato: Hegel e il giovane Marx*, Turin: Bollati Boringhieri.

—— 2005, 'La scienza del *Capitale* come "circolo del presupposto-posto" ', in *Sulle tracce di un fantasma. L'opera di Karl Marx tra filologia e filosofia*, edited by Marcello Musto, Rome: manifestolibri.

Fineschi, Roberto 2001, *Ripartire da Marx. Processo storico ed economia politica nella teoria del 'capitale'*, Naples: La Città del Sole.

—— 2002, 'MEGA²: dalla filologia alla interpretazione critica', in *MEGA²: Marx ritrovato*, edited by Alessandro Mazzone, Rome: Mediaprint.

—— 2003, 'Marx dopo la nuova edizione storico-critica (MEGA²): le edizioni del primo libro del *Capitale*', *Quaderni materialisti*, 2: 165–83.

Fischer, Emil 1932, 'Bruno Bauer, der Einsiedler von Rixdorf. Zu seinem 50 jährigen Todestage', *Berlin-Neuköllner Heimat-Blätter*.

Flerovsky, N. 1869, *The Condition of the Working Class in Russia*, St. Petersburg: N.P. Polyakov.

Fogel, Robert W. 1989, *Without Consent or Contract. The Rise and Fall of American Slavery*, New York: W.W. Norton & Co.

Foster, John Bellamy 2002, 'Marx's Ecology in Historical Perspective', *International Socialism Journal*, 96: 71–86.

Fraas, Karl Nikolaus 1847, *Klima und Pflanzenwelt in der Zeit: ein Beitrag zur Geschichte beider*, Landshut: Krüll.

Frank, Andre Gunder 1978, *World Accumulation, 1492–1789*, New York: Monthly Review Press.

—— 1998, *ReORIENT. Global Economy in the Asian Age*, Berkeley: University of California Press.

—— 2004, *Per una storia orizzontale della globalizzazione*, edited by Annamaria Vitale, Soveria Mannelli: Rubbettino.

Freud, Sigmund 2000, *Three Essays on the Theory of Sexuality*, New York: Basic Books.

Furet, François and Denis Richet 1986, *La Révolution française*, Paris: Hachette.

Gambino, Ferruccio 2003, *Migranti nella tempesta. Avvistamenti per l'inizio del nuovo millennio*, Verona: Ombre Corte.

Gambino, Ferruccio and Devi Sacchetto 2009, 'Die Formen des Mahlstroms. Von den Plantagen zu den Fließbändern', in *Über Marx Hinaus*, edited by Marcel van der Linden and Karl-Heinz Roth, Berlin: Assoziation A.

Gauthier, Florence 1989, 'Le droit naturel en révolution', in Étienne Balibar et al., *Permanences de la Révolution*, Paris: La Brèche.

—— 1992, *Triomphe et mort du droit naturel en Révolution. 1789–1795–1802*, Paris: PUF.

Gidwani, Vinay 2008 'Capitalism's Anxious Whole: Fear, Capture and Escape in the *Grundrisse*', *Antipode*, 40, 5.

Glassman, Jim 2006, 'Primitive Accumulation, Accumulation by Dispossession, Accumulation by "Extra-Economic" Means', *Progress in Human Geography*, 30, 5: 608–25

Goethe, Johann Wolfgang 2001 [1808], *Faust. A Tragedy*, New York: W.W. Norton & Company.

Goody, Jack 2006, *The Theft of History*, Cambridge: Cambridge University Press.

Gould, Stephen Jay 1990, *Wonderful Life: The Burgess Shale and the Nature of History*, New York: W.W. Norton & Company.

—— 1992, *Ever Since Darwin: Reflections in Natural History*, New York: W.W. Norton & Company.

Groh, Dieter 1959, *Russland und der Selbstverständnis Europas. Ein Beitrag zur europäischen Geistesgeschichte*, Darmstadt: Wissenschaftliche Buchgesellschaft.

Hardt, Michael and Antonio Negri, 2004, *Multitude*, London: Penguin.

Hartog, François 2003, *Régimes d'historicité: présentisme et expériences du temps*, Paris: Éditions du Seuil.

Harvey, David 2002, *Spaces of Capital: Towards a Critical Geography*, London: Routledge.

—— 2003, *The New Imperialism*, Oxford: Oxford University Press.

—— 2006, *Spaces of Global Capitalism: A Theory of Uneven Geographical Development*, London: Verso.

—— 2010 [1982], *Limits to Capital*, London: Verso.

Hatem, Jad 2006, *Marx, philosophe du mal*, Paris: L'Harmattan.

Haxthausen, August von 1852, 'Baron von Haxthausen on Russia in 1843–1844', available at: <https://tspace.library.utoronto.ca/citd/RussianHeritage/4.PEAS/4.L/XIV.26.html>.

Hayes, Peter 1993, 'Marx's Analysis of the French Class Structure', *Theory and Society*, 22, 1: 99–123.

Hecker, Rolf 1987 'Zur Entwicklung der Werttheorie von der 1. zur 3. Auflage des ersten Bandes des "Kapitals" von Karl Marx (1867–1883)', *Marx-Engels-Jahrbuch*, 10: 147–96.

Hegel, Georg Wilhelm Friedrich 1971 [1837], *Vorlesungen über die Philosophie der Geschichte*, 'Rom vom zweiten punischen Kriege bis zum Kaiserthum', in *Sämtliche Werke*, Vol. 11, Stuttgart: Friedrich Frommann Verlag.

—— 1986, [1812–31], *Wissenschaft der Logik*, in *Werke in zwanzig Bänden*, Vol. 5, edited by Eva Moldenhauer and Karl Markus Michel, Frankfurt: Suhrkamp.

—— 1991 [1837], *The Philosophy of History*, New York: Prometheus Books.

—— 2001 [1820], *Philosophy of Right*, translated by Samuel Waters Dyde, Kitchener: Batoche Books.

—— 2010 [1812–31], *The Science of Logic* [1812–31], edited and translated by George di Giovanni, Cambridge: Cambridge University Press.

Heinrich, Michael 1999, *Die Wissenschaft vom Wert*, Münster: Westfälische Dampfboot.

—— 2002, 'Der 6-Bücher-Plan und der Aufbau des Kapital', in *Berliner Verein zur Förderung der MEGA-Edition e.V., Wissenschaftliche Mitteilungen*, Vol. 1, *In Memoriam Wolfgang Jahn*, Hamburg: Argument; also available at: <http://www.oekonomiekritik.de/3061%20Aufbauplan.rtf>.

—— 2005 *Kritik der politischen Ökonomie*, Stuttgart: Schmetterling Verlag.

—— 2008, *Wie das Marxsche Kapital lesen? Hinweise zu Lektüre und Kommentar zum Anfang von 'Das Kapital'*, Stuttgart: Schmetterling Verlag.

—— 2009, 'Reconstruction or Deconstruction? Methodological Controversies about Value and Capital, and New Insights from the Critical Edition', in *Re-Reading Marx. New Perspectives after the Critical Edition*, edited by Riccardo Bellofiore and Roberto Fineschi, New York: Palgrave.

Hindess, Barry and Paul Q. Hirst 1975, *Pre-Capitalist Modes of Production*, London: Routledge.

Hobsbawm, Eric J. 1971 [1964], 'Introduction' in Karl Marx, *Pre-Capitalist Economic Formations*, translated by Jack Cohen, New York: International Publishers.

—— 1990, 'The Making of a "Bourgeois Revolution"', in *The French Revolution and the Birth of Modernity*, edited by Ferenc Fehér, Berkeley: University of California Press.

Howgego, Christopher 1995, *Ancient History from Coins*, London: Routledge.

Howitt, William 1838, *Colonization and Christianity. A Popular History of the Treatment of the Natives by the Europeans in all their Colonies*, London: Longman, Orme, Brown, Green, & Longmans.

Iacono, Alfonso 1985, *Teorie del feticismo. Il problema filosofico di un 'immenso malinteso'*, Milan: Giuffré.

—— 2001a, 'L'ambiguo oggetto sostituito. Il feticismo prima di Marx e Freud', in *Figure del feticismo*, edited by Stefano Mistura, Turin: Einaudi.

—— 2001b, 'Feticismo', in *Lessico postfordista. Dizionario di idee della mutazione*, edited by Adelino Zanini and Ubaldo Fadini, Milan: Feltrinelli.

Jaeck, Hans-Peter 1979, *Die französische bürgerliche Revolution von 1789 im Frühwerk von Karl Marx (1843–1846)*, Vaduz: Topos Verlag.

Jaffe, Hosea 1976, *Marx e il colonialismo*, Milan: Jaca.

—— 2007, *Davanti al colonialismo: Engels, Marx e il marxismo*, Milan: Jaca.

Jahn, Wolfgang 1968, *Die Marxsche Wert- und Mehrwertlehre*, Berlin: Dietz.

—— 1978, *Die Entwicklung der Ausgangstheorie der politischen Ökonomie des Kapitalismus in den Vorarbeiten zu Marx' 'Kapital'*, in *'...unserer Partei einen Sieg erringen'. Entstehung- und Wirkungsgeschichte des "Kapitals" von Karl Marx*, Berlin: Dietz.

James, Cyril Lionel Robert 1963, *The Black Jacobins: Toussaint L'Ouverture and the San Domingo Revolution*, New York: Random House.

—— 2009, 'Marx's *The Eighteenth Brumaire of Louis Bonaparte* and the Caribbean', in *You Don't Play with Revolution*, edited by David Austin, Oakland: AK Press.

Jessop, Bob 2002 'The Political Scene and the Politics of Representation: Periodising Class Struggle and the State in the *Eighteenth Brumaire*', in *Marx's Eighteenth Brumaire: (Post)modern Interpretations*, edited by Mark Cowling and James Martin, London: Pluto Press.

Julius, Gustav 1845, 'Der Streit der sichtbaren mit unsichtbaren Menschenkirche oder Kritik der Kritik der kritischen Kritik', *Wigands Vierteljahresschrift*, 2.

Jung, Georg 1975a [1844], 'Jung to Marx. 26 June 1844' in *Marx-Engels-Gesamtausgabe*, III/1, Berlin: Dietz.

—— 1975b [1844], 'Jung to Marx. 31 July 1844'; in *Marx-Engels-Gesamtausgabe*, III/1, Berlin: Dietz.

Karatani, Kojin 2003, *Transcritique: On Kant and Marx*, Cambridge, MA.: MIT.

Kemple, Thomas M. 1995, *Reading Marx Writing. Melodrama, the Market, and the 'Grundrisse'*, Stanford: Stanford University Press.

Kempski, Jürgen von 1992, 'Über Bruno Bauer. Eine Studie zum Ausgang des Hegelianismus', in *Brechungen. Kritische Versuche zur Philosophie der Gegenwart. Schriften 1*, Frankfurt: Suhrkamp.

Kim, Henry S. 2001, 'Archaic Coinage as Evidence for the Use of Money', in *Money and Its Uses in the Ancient Greek World*, edited by Andrew Meadows and Kirsty Shipton, Oxford: Oxford University Press.

Kireevski, Ivan V. 1966 [1852], 'On the Nature of European Culture and its Relations to the Culture of Russia', in *Russian Intellectual History: An Anthology*, edited by Marc Raeff, New York: Harcourt, Brace & World.

Korsch, Karl 1963 [1938], *Karl Marx*, New York: Russell & Russell.

Koselleck, Reinhardt 2000, *Zeitschichten: Studien zur Historik*, Frankfurt: Suhrkamp.

Koselleck, Reinhart et al 1975, 'Geschichte, Historie', in *Geschichtliche Grundbegriffe. Historiches Lexikon zur politisch-sozialen Sprache in Deutschland*, Vol. 2, Stuttgart: Klett Cotta.

Kouvelakis, Stathis 2003, *Philosophy and Revolution: from Kant to Marx*, London: Verso.

—— 2007, 'Marx's Critique of the Political', *Situations*, 2: 81–93.

Krader, Lawrence 1972, 'Introduction', in *Ethnological Notebooks of Karl Marx*, edited by Lawrence Krader, Assen: Van Gorcum.

Krahl, Hans-Jürgen 1971, *Konstitution und Klassenkampf. Zur historischen Dialektik von bürgerlicher Emanzipation und proletarischer Revolution*, Frankfurt: Verlag Neue Kritik.

—— 1984, *Vom Ende der abstrakten Arbeit*, Frankfurt: Materialis Verlag.

L'Ouverture, Toussaint, 2008, *The Haitian Revolution*, London: Verso.

Lambrecht, Lars 1989, 'Zum historischen Einsatz der wissenschaftlichen und politischen Studien Bruno Bauers zur Französischen Revolution', *Deutsche Zeitschrift für Philosophie*, 37, 8: 741–52.

Laska, Bernd A. 1996, 'Katechon contro Eigner? La reazione di Carl Schmitt nei confronti di Max Stirner', *De Cive*, 1, 1: 43–54.

Le Goff, Jacques 1980, *Time, Work & Culture in the Middle Ages*, Chicago: University of Chicago Press.

Lefort, Claude 1986 [1965], 'Marx: From One Vision of History to Another', in *The Political Forms of Modern Society*, Cambridge, MA.: MIT Press.

Levi, Primo 1989, *The Drowned and the Saved*, New York: Vintage.

Lipovetsky, Gilles 2006, *Le bonheur paradoxal, Essai sur la société d'hyperconsommation*, Paris: Gallimard.

Löwy, Michael 1989, 'La «poésie du passé»: Marx et la Révolution française', in Étienne Balibar et al., *Permanences de la Révolution*, Paris: La Brèche.

—— 2002, *The Theory of Revolution in the Young Marx*, Leiden: Brill.

Lüning, Otto 1845, 'Die heilige Familie oder Kritik der kritischen Kritik. Gegen Br. Bauer und Consorten von F. Engels und K. Marx, Frankfurt 1845', *Das Westphälische Dampfboot*, 1: 206–14.

Luxemburg, Rosa 1951, *The Accumulation of Capital*, edited by Dr. W. Stark, London: Routledge.

Maffi, A. 1979, 'Circolazione monetaria e modelli di scambio da Esiodo ad Aristotele', *Annali dell'Istituto Italiano di Numismatica*, 26: 161–84.

Marini, Ruy Mauro 1991, *Dialéctica de la dependencia*, Mexico City: Ediciones Era.

Markus, Gyorgy 2001, 'Walter Benjamin or: The Commodity as Phantasmagoria', *New German Critique*, 83: 3–42.

Martin, James 2002, 'Performing Politics: Class, Ideology and Discourse in Marx's *Eighteenth Brumaire*', in *Marx's Eighteenth Brumaire: (Post)modern Interpretations*, edited by Mark Cowling and James Martin, London: Pluto Press.

Marx, Karl 1956a [1843] 'Briefe aus den Deutsch-Französischen Jahrbüchern', in *Marx-Engels Werke*, Vol. 1, Berlin: Dietz.

—— 1956b [1844], 'Zur Kritik der Hegelschen Rechtsphilosophie. Einleitung', in *Marx-Engels Werke*, Vol. 1, Berlin: Dietz.

—— 1959a [1847], *Das Elend der Philosophie*, in *Marx-Engels Werke*, Vol. 4, Berlin: Dietz.

—— 1959b [1849], *Lohnarbeit und Kapital*, in *Marx-Engels Werke*, Vol. 6, Berlin: Dietz.

—— 1959c [1847], *Arbeitslohn*, in *Marx-Engels Werke*, Vol. 6, Berlin: Dietz.

—— 1959d [1848], 'Die Krisis und die Kontrerevolution', in *Marx-Engels Werke*, Vol. 5, Berlin: Dietz.

—— 1960a [1852], *Der achtzehnte Brumaire des Louis Bonaparte*, in *Marx-Engels Werke*, Vol. 8, Berlin: Dietz.

—— 1960b [1850], *Die Klassenkämpfe in Frankreich 1848–1850*, in *Marx-Engels Werke*, Vol. 7, Berlin: Dietz.

—— 1961a [1857], 'Einleitung zur Kritik der Politischen Ökonomie', in *Marx-Engels Werke*, Vol. 13, Berlin: Dietz

—— 1961b [1859], *Zur Kritik der politischen Ökonomie*, in *Marx-Engels Werke*, Vol. 13, Berlin: Dietz

—— 1962a [1867], *Das Kapital. Band I*, in *Marx-Engels Werke*, Vol. 23, Berlin: Dietz.

—— 1962b [1881], 'Randglossen zu Adolph Wagners "Lehrbuch der politischen Ökonomie"', in *Marx-Engels Werke*, Vol. 19, Berlin: Dietz.

—— 1963 *Das Kapital. Band II*, in *Marx-Engels Werke*, Vol. 24, Berlin: Dietz.

—— 1964 *Das Kapital. Band III*, in *Marx-Engels Werke*, Vol. 25, Berlin: Dietz.

—— 1965 [1861–3], *Theorien über den Mehrwert*, in *Marx-Engels Werke*, Vol. 26.1, Berlin: Dietz.

Marx, *Cont.*

—— 1967 [1861–3], *Theorien über den Mehrwert*, in *Marx-Engels Werke*, Vol. 26.2, Berlin: Dietz

—— 1968 [1861–3], *Theorien über den Mehrwert*, in *Marx-Engels Werke*, Vol. 26.3, Berlin: Dietz.

—— 1972, *Ethnological Notebooks of Karl Marx*, edited by Lawrence Krader, Assen: Van Gorcum.

—— 1973 [1844], *Ökonomisch-philosophische Manuskripte*, in *Marx-Engels Werke*, Vol. 40, Berlin: Dietz

—— 1975a [1844], 'Marx to Feuerbach. 11 August', in *Marx-Engels-Gesamtausgabe*, III/1, Berlin: Dietz.

—— 1975b [1844], 'Marx to Feuerbach. 11 August', in *Marx and Engels Collected Works*, Vol. 3, London: Lawrence & Wishart.

—— 1975c [1843], 'A Contribution to the Critique of Hegel's Philosophy of Right. Introduction', in *Marx and Engels Collected Works*, Vol. 3, London: Lawrence & Wishart.

—— 1975d [1845], 'Theses on Feuerbach', in *Marx and Engels Collected Works*, Vol. 5, London: Lawrence & Wishart.

—— 1975e [1844], 'Critical Marginal Notes on the Article "The King of Prussia and Social Reform. By a Prussian"', in *Marx and Engels Collected Works*, Vol. 3, London: Lawrence & Wishart.

—— 1975f [1844], *Economic and Philosophic Manuscripts of 1844*, in *Marx and Engels Collected Works*, Vol. 3, London: Lawrence & Wishart.

—— 1976a [1847], 'Moralising Criticism and Critical Morality', in *Marx and Engels Collected Works*, Vol. 6, London: Lawrence & Wishart.

—— 1976b [1847], *The Poverty of Philosophy*, in *Marx and Engels Collected Works*, Vol. 6, London: Lawrence & Wishart.

—— 1976c [1847], *Wages*, in *Marx and Engels Collected Works*, Vol. 6, London: Lawrence & Wishart.

—— 1976d, *Exzerpte und Notizen. Bis 1842*, in *Marx-Engels-Gesamtausgabe*, IV/I, Berlin: Dietz.

—— 1976e, *Die ethnologischen Exzerpthefte*, edited by Lawrence Krader, translated into German by Angelika Schweikhart, Frankfurt: Suhrkamp.

—— 1977a [1848], 'The Bourgeoisie and the Counter-Revolution', in *Marx and Engels Collected Works*, Vol. 8, London: Lawrence & Wishart.

—— 1977b [1849] *Wage Labour and Capital*, in *Marx and Engels Collected Works*, Vol. 9, London: Lawrence & Wishart.

—— 1977c [1848], 'The Crisis and the Counter-Revolution', in *Marx and Engels Collected Works*, Vol. 7, London: Lawrence & Wishart.

—— 1978a [1867], 'The Value Form', *Capital and Class*, 4: 130–50.

—— 1978b, [1861–3] *Zur Kritik der politischen Ökonomie (Manuskript 1861–1863)*, in *Marx-Engels-Gesamtausgabe*, II/3.3, Berlin: Dietz.

—— 1979a [1852], *The Eighteenth Brumaire of Louis Bonaparte*, in *Marx and Engels Collected Works*, Vol. 11, London: Lawrence & Wishart.

—— 1979b [1850], *The Class Struggles in France*, in *Marx and Engels Collected Works*, Vol. 11, London: Lawrence & Wishart.

—— 1979c [1853], 'The British Rule in India', in *Marx and Engels Collected Works*, Vol. 12, London: Lawrence & Wishart.

—— 1979d [1853], 'The Future Results of British Rule in India', in *Marx and Engels Collected Works*, Vol. 12, London: Lawrence & Wishart.

—— 1980 [1858], *Zur Kritik der politischen Ökonomie. Urtext*, in *Marx-Engels-Gesamtausgabe*, II/2, Berlin: Dietz.

—— 1983a [1855], 'Marx to Engels. 14 December', in *Marx and Engels Collected Works*, Vol. 39, London: Lawrence & Wishart.

—— 1983b [1857–8], *Ökonomische Manuskripte*, in *Marx-Engels Werke*, Vol. 42, Berlin: Dietz.

—— 1983c [1857], 'Marx to Engels. 20 October', in *Marx and Engels Collected Works*, Vol. 40, London: Lawrence & Wishart.

—— 1983d [1856], 'Marx to Engels. 26 September', in *Marx and Engels Collected Works*, Vol. 40, London: Lawrence & Wishart.

—— 1983e [1857], 'Marx to Engels. 8 December 1857', in *Marx and Engels Collected Works*, Vol. 40, London: Lawrence & Wishart.

Marx, *Cont.*
—— 1983f [1858], 'Marx to Engels, 8 October', in *Marx and Engels Collected Works*, Vol. 40, London: Lawrence & Wishart.
—— 1983g [1858], Marx to Engels. 14 January', in *Marx and Engels Collected Works*, Vol. 40, London: Lawrence & Wishart.
—— 1983h [1853], Marx to Engels. 14 June, in *Marx and Engels Collected Works*, Vol. 39, London: Lawrence & Wishart.
—— 1983i, *Das Kapital. Erster Band*, in *Marx-Engels-Gesamtausgabe*, II/5, Berlin: Dietz.
—— 1983j [1877], 'A Letter to the Editorial Board of *Otecestvenniye Zapisky*', in Shanin (ed.) 1983.
—— 1985a [1862], 'Marx to Engels. 29 October 1862', in *Marx and Engels Collected Works*, Vol. 41, London: Lawrence & Wishart.
—— 1985b [1865], *Value, Price and Profit*, in *Marx and Engels Collected Works*, Vol. 20, London: Lawrence & Wishart.
—— 1985c [1864] 'The Inaugural Address of Karl Marx', in *Marx and Engels Collected Works*, Vol. 21, London: Lawrence & Wishart.
—— 1985d [1852], *Der achtzehnte Brumaire des Louis Bonaparte*, in *Marx-Engels-Gesamtausgabe*, I/11, Berlin: Dietz.
—— 1985e [1869] 'Preface to the Second Edition of *The Eighteenth Brumaire of Louis Bonaparte*', in *Marx and Engels Collected Works*, Vol. 21, London: Lawrence & Wishart.
—— 1986 [1857–8], 'Outlines of the Critique of Political Economy', in *Marx and Engels Collected Works*, Vol. 28, London: Lawrence & Wishart.
—— 1987a [1859], 'Contribution to the Critique of Political Economy, in *Marx and Engels Collected Works*, Vol. 29, London: Lawrence & Wishart.
—— 1987b [1858], 'Second Draft of the Critique of Political Economy', in *Marx and Engels Collected Works*, Vol. 29, London: Lawrence & Wishart.
—— 1987c [1857–8], 'Outlines of the Critique of Political Economy', in *Marx and Engels Collected Works*, Vol. 29, London: Lawrence & Wishart.

—— 1987d [1868], 'Marx to Engels. 25 March', in *Marx and Engels Collected Works*, Vol. 42, London: Lawrence & Wishart.
—— 1987e [1872], *Ergänzungen und Veränderungen zum ersten Band des «Kapitals» (Dezember 1871–Januar 1872)*, in *Marx-Engels-Gesamtausgabe*, II/6, Berlin: Dietz.
—— 1987f [1865], 'Marx to Engels. 20 May 1865' in *Marx and Engels Collected Works*, Vol. 42, London: Lawrence & Wishart.
—— 1987g [1866], 'Marx to F. Lafargue, 12 November', in *Marx and Engels Collected Works*, Vol. 42, London: Lawrence & Wishart.
—— 1988a [1861–3] *Economic Manuscripts of 1861–63*, in *Marx and Engels Collected Works*, Vol. 30, London: Lawrence & Wishart.
—— 1988b [1868], 'Marx to Kugelmann. 11 July', in *Marx and Engels Collected Works*, Vol. 43, London: Lawrence & Wishart.
—— 1988c [1869], 'Marx to Engels. 10 December', in *Marx and Engels Collected Works*, Vol. 30, London: Lawrence & Wishart.
—— 1989a [1863], *Theories of Surplus Value*, in *Marx and Engels Collected Works*, Vol. 31, London: Lawrence & Wishart.
—— 1989b [1881], 'Marginal Notes on Adolph Wagner's *Lehrbuch der politischer Oekonomie*', in *Marx and Engels Collected Works*, Vol. 24, London: Lawrence & Wishart.
—— 1989c [1861–3], *Theories of Surplus Value*, in *Marx and Engels Collected Works*, Vol. 32, London: Lawrence & Wishart.
—— 1989d [1877] 'Letter from Marx to Editor of the *Otechestvennye Zapiski*', in *Marx and Engels Collected Works*, Vol. 24, London: Lawrence & Wishart.
—— 1989e [1881], 'First Draft of Letter to Vera Zasulich', in *Marx and Engels Collected Works*, Vol. 24, London: Lawrence & Wishart.
—— 1989f [1872–5], *Le Capital*, in *Marx-Engels-Gesamtausgabe*, II/7, Berlin: Dietz.

Marx, *Cont.*
—— 1989g [1883] *Das Kapital. Erster Band*, in *Marx-Engels-Gesamtausgabe*, II/8, Berlin: Dietz.
—— 1989h [1881] 'Third Draft of Letter to Vera Zasulich', in *Marx and Engels Collected Works*, Vol. 24, London: Lawrence & Wishart.
—— 1990 [1861–3], *Ökonomisches Manuskript 1861–1863*, in *Marx-Engels Werke*, Vol. 43, Berlin: Dietz.
—— 1991a [1877], 'Marx to Mrs. Wollmann. 19 March' in *Marx and Engels Collected Works*, Vol. 45, London: Lawrence & Wishart.
—— 1991b [1877], 'Marx to Friedrich Adolf Sorge. 27 September' in *Marx and Engels Collected Works*, Vol. 45, London: Lawrence & Wishart.
—— 1992a [1881], 'Marx to Vera Zasulich. 8 March', in *Marx and Engels Collected Works*, Vol. 46, London: Lawrence & Wishart.
—— 1992b [1880], 'Marx to Henry Mayern Hyndman, 8 December,' in *Marx and Engels Collected Works*, Vol. 46, London: Lawrence & Wishart.
—— 1992c [1881], 'Marx to Carl Pearson. 15 February', in *Marx and Engels Collected Works*, Vol. 46, London: Lawrence & Wishart.
—— 1992d, *Ökonomische Manuskripte 1863–1867*, in *Marx-Engels-Gesamtausgabe*, II/4.2, Berlin: Dietz.
—— 1992e [1865], *Value, Price and Profit*, in *Marx-Engels-Gesamtausgabe*, I/20, Berlin: Dietz.
—— 1992f [1865], 'Inaugural Address of the International Workingmen's Association', in *Marx-Engels-Gesamtausgabe*, I/20, Berlin: Dietz.
—— 1996 [1867], *Capital. Volume I*, in *Marx and Engels Collected Works*, Vol. 35, London: Lawrence & Wishart.
—— 1997 [1885], *Capital. Volume II*, in *Marx and Engels Collected Works*, Vol. 36, London: Lawrence & Wishart.
—— 1998 *Capital. Volume III*, in *Marx and Engels Collected Works*, Vol. 37, London: Lawrence & Wishart.
Marx, Karl and Friedrich Engels 1959, *Manifest der Kommunistischen Partei*, in *Marx-Engels Werke*, Vol. 4, Berlin: Dietz.
—— 1960a [1850], *Ansprache der Zentralbehörde an den Bund vom März 1850*, in *Marx-Engels Werke*, Vol. 7, Berlin: Dietz.
—— 1960b [1850], *Ansprache der Zentralbehörde an den Bund vom Juni 1850*, in in *Marx-Engels Werke*, Vol. 7, Berlin: Dietz.
—— 1975 [1845], *The German Ideology*, in *Marx and Engels Collected Works*, Vol. 5, London: Lawrence & Wishart.
—— 1976 [1848], *Manifesto of the Communist Party*, in *Marx and Engels Collected Works*, Vol. 6, London: Lawrence & Wishart.
—— 1978a [1850] 'Address of the Central Committee to the Communist League, March 1850', in *Marx and Engels Collected Works*, Vol. 10, London: Lawrence & Wishart.
—— 1978b [1850] 'Address of the Central Committee to the Communist League, June 1850', in *Marx and Engels Collected Works*, Vol. 10, London: Lawrence & Wishart.
—— 1989 [1882], 'Preface to the Second Russian Edition of the *Manifesto of the Communist Party*', in *Marx and Engels Collected Works*, Vol. 24, London: Lawrence & Wishart.
—— 2004 [1845], *Marx-Engels-Jahrbuch 2003. Die Deutsche Ideologie*, Berlin: Akademie Verlag.
Mehlman, Jeffrey 1977, *Revolution and Repetition. Marx/Hugo/Balzac*, Berkeley: University of California Press.
Mill, John Stuart 1989, *On Liberty and Other Writings*, Cambridge: Cambridge University Press.
Mirami, Rafael 1582 *Compendiosa introduttione alla prima parte della specularia, cioè della scienza de gli specchi, opera nova, nella quale breuemente, e con facil modo si discorre intorno a gli specchi e si rende la cagione, di tutti i loro miracolosi effetti*, Ferrara: Rossi & Tortorino 1582.
Moggach, Douglas 2003, *The Philosophy and Politics of Bruno Bauer*, Cambridge: Cambridge University Press.
Mohri, Kenzo 1970, 'Marx and "Underdevelopment"', *Monthly Review*, 30, 11: 32–42.
Morgan, Lewis H. 1877, *Ancient Society, Or Researches in the Lines of Human Progress*

from Savagery through Barbarism to Civilization, London: Macmillan.

Moss, Bernard H. 1985, 'Marx and Engels on French Social Democracy: Historians or Revolutionaries?', *Journal of the History of Ideas*, 46, 4: 539–57.

Murray, Patrick 2000, 'Marx's "Truly Social" Labor Theory of Value: Part II, How Is Labour that Is Under the Sway of Capital Actually Abstract?', *Historical Materialism*, 7: 99–136.

—— 2004, 'The Social and Material Transformation of Production by Capital: Formal and Real Subsumption in Capital, Volume 1', in *The Constitution of Capital: Essays on Volume I of Marx's 'Capital'*, edited by Nicola Taylor and Riccardo Bellofiore, Basingstoke: Palgrave Macmillan.

Natalizi, Marco 2001, 'Introduzione', in Nikolai Gavrilovich Chernyevksy, *Scritti politico-filosofici*, Lucca: Maria Pacini Fazzi.

—— 2006, *Il caso Černyševskij*, Milan: Mondadori.

Negri, Antonio 1998, 'Prefazione', in *Marx oltre Marx*, Roma: manifestolibri.

—— 2007, *Goodbye Mr. Socialism*, New York: Seven Stories Press.

Neocleous, Mark 2005, *The Monstrous and the Dead: Burke, Marx, Fascism*, Cardiff: University of Wales Press.

Ngai, Pun 2005, *Made in China: Women Factory Workers in a Global Workplace*, Durham, NC.: Duke University Press.

Ngai, Pun and Li Wanwei 2008, *Dagongmei. Arbeiterinnen aus Chinas Weltmarktfabriken erzählen*, Hamburg: Assoziation A.

Osborne, Peter 1998, 'Remember the Future? *The Communist Manifesto* as Historical and Cultural Form', in *The Socialist Register*, edited by Colin Leys and Leo Panitch, London: Merlin.

Padover, Saul K. 1979, *The Letters of Karl Marx*, Englewood Cliffs: Prentice-Hall.

Pennavaja, Cristina 1975, 'Introduzione', in Karl Marx, *L'analisi della forma di valore*, Bari: Laterza.

Pétré-Grenouilleau, Olivier 2004 *Les traites négrières. Essai d'histoire globale*, Paris: Gallimard.

Petry, Sandy 1988, 'The Reality of Representation: Between Marx and Balzac', *Critical Inquiry*, 14, 3: 448–68.

Poggio, Pier Paolo 1978, *Comune contadina e rivoluzione in Russia. L'obščina*, Milan: Jaca.

Proudhon, Pierre-Joseph 1852, *La Révolution sociale démontrée par le coup d'État du 2 décembre 1851*, Paris: Garnier Frères.

Raffles, Thomas Stamford Bingley 1817, *History of Java and Its Dependencies*, London: Black, Parbury, and Allen, and John Murray.

Rampini, Federico 2005, 'I lager cinesi che fabbricano il sogno occidentale', *La Repubblica*, 19 May, available at: <www.repubblica.it/2005/e/sezioni/economia/nostrolusso/nostrolusso/nostrolusso.html>.

Rawls, John 1971, *A Theory of Justice*, Cambridge: Harvard University Press.

—— 1993, *Political Liberalism*, New York: Columbia University Press.

Reuten, Geert 2004, 'Productive Force and the Degree of Intensity of Labour', in *The Constitution of Capital. Essays on Volume I of Marx's 'Capital'*, edited by Nicola Taylor and Ricardo Bellofiore, Basingstoke: Palgrave Macmillan.

Reuten, Geert and Peter Thomas 2011, 'From the "Fall of the Rate of Profit" in the *Grundrisse* to the Cyclical Development of the Profit Rate in *Capital*', *Science and Society*, 75, 1: 74–90.

Ridder, Widukind de 2008, 'Max Stirner, Hegel and the Young Hegelians: A Reassessment', *History of European Ideas*, 34: 285–97

Riehl, Wilheim Heinrich 1861, *Die bürgerliche Gesellschaft*, Stuttgart: Verlag der J.G. Cotta'schen Buchhandlung.

Rieser, Vittorio 2004, 'La qualità alienata', *La Rivista del manifesto*, 50: 5–15.

Riquelme, John Paul 1980, 'The *Eighteenth Brumaire* of Karl Marx as Symbolic Action', *History and Theory*, 19, 1: 58–72.

Roberts, William Clare 2005, 'Marx in Hell: The Critique of Political Economy as Katabasis', *Critical Sociology*, 31: 39–55.

Robertson, Étienne-Gaspard 1985, *Mémoires récréatifs, scientifiques et anecdotiques d'un physicien-aéronaute*, Langres: Clima.

Rosdolsky, Roman [1968] 1977. *The Making of Marx's 'Capital'*, London: Pluto Press.

Rubin, Isaak Ilich 1972 [1928] *Essays on Marx's Theory of Value*, Detroit: Black and Red.

Sacchetto, Devi 2007, 'Offshore Outsourcing and Migrations: the South-Eastern and Central Eastern European Case', *The Commoner*, 12, available at: <www.commoner.org.uk/12sacchetto.pdf>.

Sacchetto, Devi and Massimiliano Tomba (eds.) 2008, *La lunga accumulazione originaria. Politica e lavoro nel mercato mondiale*, Verona: Ombre Corte.

Sanyal, Kalyan 2007, *Rethinking Capitalist Development. Primitive Accumulation, Governmentality and Post-Colonial Capitalism*, London: Routledge

Sauvage, Emmanuelle 2004, 'Les fantasmagories de Robertson: entre "spectacle instructif" et mystification", in *Conférences en ligne du Centre canadien d'études allemandes et européennes*, 1, 2, available at: <http://www.cceae.umontreal.ca/IMG/pdf/CEL_0102.pdf>.

Schofield, Malcolm 1993 *Plato on the Economy*, in *The Ancient Greek City-State*, edited by Mogens Herman Hansen, Copenhagen: Royal Danish Academy of Sciences and Letters.

Seliger, Walter 1995, *Das einzige Metaphysische. Vom Ich als Prinzip und Dementi der Philosophie*, Bergisch Gladbach: E. Fergan Verlag.

Sewell, William H. 2008, 'The Temporalities of Capitalism', *Socio-Economic Review*, 6: 517–37.

Sereni, Paul 2007, *Marx: la personne et la chose*, Paris: Harmattan.

Shanin, Teodor 1983, 'Late Marx: Gods and Craftsmen', in Shanin (ed.) 1983.

—— (ed.) 1983a, *Late Marxism and the Russian Road: Marx and 'the Peripheries of Capitalism'*, New York: Monthly Review Press.

Shaw, William H. 1984, 'Marx and Morgan', *History and Theory*, 23, 2: 215–28.

Silver, Beverly J. and Eric Slater 1999, 'The Social Origins of World Hegemonies', in *Chaos and Governance in the Modern World System*, edited by Giovanni Arrighi and Beverly J. Silver, Minneapolis: University of Minnesota Press.

Simmel, Georg 1957 [1903], *Die Großstädte und das Geistesleben* in *Brücke und Tür*, Stuttgart: K.F. Koehler Verlag.

Smith, David N. 2002, 'Accumulation and the Clash of Cultures: Marx's Ethnology in Context', *Rethinking Marxism*, 14, 4: 73–83.

Smith, Neil 1990, *Uneven Development: Nature, Capital and the Production of Space*, Oxford: Blackwell.

Sombart, Werner 1967, *Luxury and Capitalism*, Ann Arbor: University of Michigan Press.

Spivak, Gayatri 1999, *A Critique of Post-Colonial Reason. Toward a History of the Vanishing Present*, Cambridge, MA.: Harvard University Press.

Stedman Jones, Gareth 2006, 'Engels and the Industrial Revolution', in *The New Hegelians*, edited by Douglas Moggach, Cambridge: Cambridge University Press.

Stirner, Max 1848a, 'Das widerrufliche Mandat', *Journal des Österreichischen Lloyd*, 15 August.

—— 1848b, 'Die Deutschen im Osten Deutschlands', *Journal des Österreichischen Lloyd*, 24 July.

—— 1848c, 'Reich und Staat', *Journal des Österreichischen Lloyd*, 12 September.

—— 1907 [1845] *The Ego and his Own*, translated by Steven T. Byington, with an introduction by J.L. Walker, New York: B.R. Tucker.

Texier, Jacques 1992 'Les formes historiques du lieu social dans les *Grundrisse* de Karl Marx', *Actuel Marx*, 11: 137–70.

Thompson, Edward Palmer 1967, 'Time, Work-Discipline and Industrial Capitalism', *Past and Present*, 38, 1: 56–97.

Thomson, Ernie 2004, *The Discovery of the Materialist Conception of History in the Writings of the Young Karl Marx*, Lewiston: The Edwin Mellen Press.

Tocqueville, Alexis de 2011 [1856], *The Ancien Régime and the French Revolution*, Cambridge: Cambridge University Press.

Tomba, Massimiliano 1997, 'Politica e storia nel Vormärz: August von Cieszkowski', in August von Cieszkowski, *Prolegomeni alla storiosofia*, translated and edited by Massimiliano Tomba, Milan: Guerini e Associati.

—— 2002a, 'Filosofia della crisi. La riflessione post-hegeliana', *Filosofia politica*, 2: 193–222

Tomba, *Cont.*
—— 2002b, *Crisi e critica in Bruno Bauer*, Naples: Bibliopolis.
—— 2005 'Bruno Bauer und Max Stirner vor der Krise und dem Europäertum', *Der Einzige. Vierteljahresschrift des Max-Stirner-Archiv-Leipzig*, 1/2: 3–19.
—— 2006a, 'A. von Cieszkowski: Philosophie der Praxis und Theorie der Geschichte', in *Philosophie, Literatur und Politik vor den Revolution von 1848*, Vol. 2, edited by Lars Lambrecht, Frankfurt: Peter Lang.
—— 2006b, 'Exclusiveness and Political Universalism in Bruno Bauer', in, *The New Hegelians: Politics and Philosophy in the Hegelian School*, edited by Douglas Moggach, Cambridge: Cambridge University Press.
—— 2009a, 'Von der Geschichtsphilosophie zur Politik. Strömungen des Radikalismus im Vormärz: Bruno Bauer, Max Stirner und Karl Marx', in *Freiheit, Gleichheit, Solidarität. Beiträge zur Dialektik der Demokratie*, edited by Werner Goldschmidt, Bettina Lösch and Jörg Reitzig, Frankfurt: Peter Lang.
—— 2009b, 'Historical Temporalities of Capital. An Anti-Historicist Perspective', *Historical Materialism*, 17, 4: 44–65.
—— 2009c, 'Another kind of Gewalt: Beyond Law. Re-Reading Walter Benjamin', *Historical Materialism*, 17, 1: 126–44.
—— 2011, 'Hans-Jürgen Krahl: contestazione e rivoluzione', in *Il sistema e i movimenti. Europa 1945–1989*, edited by Pier Paolo Poggio, Milan: Jaca.
Tombazos, Stavros 1994, *Le temps dans l'analyse économique. Les catégories du temps dans le Capital*, Paris: Cahiers des saisons.
Tomich, Dale W. 2003, *Through the Prism of Slavery. Labor, Capital, and World Economy*, Lanham: Rowman & Littlefield.
Tuchscherer, Walter 1968, *Bevor "Das Kapital" entstand. Die Herausbildung und Entwicklung der ökonomiscen Theorie von Karl Marx in der Zeit von 1843 bis 1858*, Berlin: Akademie Verlag.
Vadée, Michel 1998, *Marx penseur du possible*, Paris: L'Harmattan.
Van der Linden, Marcel 2005, 'Plädoyer für eine historische Neubestimmung

der Welt-Arebeiterklasse', *Social Geschichte*, 20: 7–28.
—— 2007, 'Warum gab [und gibt] es Sklaverei im Kapitalismus? Eine einfache und dennoch schwer zu beantwortende Frage', in *Unfreie Arbeit. Ökonomische und kulturgeschichtliche Perspektiven*, edited by M. Erdem Kabadayi and Tobias Reichardt, Hilesheim: Georg Olms Verlag.
Venturi, Franco 1972, *Il populismo russo*, Turin: Einaudi.
Vygodsky, Vitaly 1974, *Introduzione ai 'Grundrisse' di Marx*, edited by Cristina Pennavaja, Florence: La Nuova Italia.
Wada, Haruki 1983, 'Marx and Revolutionary Russia', in Shanin (ed.) 1983.
Wainwright, Joel 2008, 'Uneven Developments: From *Grundrisse* to *Capital*' *Antipode*, 40, 5.
Walicki, Andrzej 1979a, 'Socialismo russo e populismo', in *Storia del marxismo*, Vol. 2: *Il marxismo nell'età della seconda Internazionale*, Turin: Einaudi.
—— 1979b, *A History of Russian Thought from the Enlightenment to Marxism*, Stanford: Stanford University Press.
—— 1989, *The Slavophile Controversy: History of a Conservative Utopia in Nineteenth-Century Russian Thought*, Notre Dame, IN.: University of Notre Dame Press.
Walker, Richard A. 2004, *The Conquest of Bread: 150 Years of Agribusiness in California*, New York: The New Press.
Wallerstein, Immanuel 2001, *Unthinking Social Science*, Philadelphia: Temple University Press.
Weckwerth, Christine 2009, 'Kritik an Feuerbach und Kritik der Feuerbach-Kritiker', in *Karl Marx und Friedrich Engels: Die deutsche Ideologie*, edited by Harald Bluhm, Berlin: Akademie Verlag.
Wendling, Amy E. 2003, 'Are All Revolutions Bourgeois? Revolutionary Temporality in Karl Marx's *Eighteenth Brumaire of Louis Bonaparte*', *Strategies*, 16, 1: 39–49.
—— 2009, *Karl Marx on Technology and Alienation*, New York: Palgrave Macmillan.
Weston, George M. 1857, *The Progress of Slavery in the United States*, Washington, DC.: The Author.

Wheeler, John Archibald 1983, 'Law Without Law', in *Quantum Theory and Measurement*, edited by John Archibald Wheeler and Wojciech Hubert Zurek, Princeton: Princeton University Press.

Wheen, Francis 2006, *Marx's 'Das Kapital'. A Biography*, New York: Grove Press.

White, Hayden 1973, *Metahistory. The Historical Imagination in Nineteenth-Century Europe*, Baltimore: Johns Hopkins University Press.

Wiedenhofer, Siegfried 2004, 'Tradition, Traditionalismus', in *Geschichtliche Grundbegriffe*, Vol. 6, edited by Otto Brunner, Werner Conze and Reinhart Koselleck, Stuttgart: Klett-Cotta.

Wilson, Dominic and Roopa Purushothaman 2003. 'Dreaming With BRICs: The Path to 2050', *Global Economics Paper*, 99, available at: <http://www2.goldmansachs.com/ideas/brics/book/99-dreaming.pdf>.

Wilson, Edmund 2003 [1940], *To the Finland Station*, New York: NYRB Classics.

Wolff, Robert Paul 1988, *Moneybags Must be So Lucky: On the Literary Structure of 'Capital'*, Amherst: University of Massachusetts Press.

Zanin, Valter 2002, *Studi sul lavoro coatto contemporaneo*, Padua: CLEUP.

Index

CPSIA information can be obtained
at www.ICGtesting.com
Printed in the USA
JSHW020938080919
1383JS00003B/8

9 781608 463398